First published in 2010 by Blue*imprint*
Copyright © 2010 by the Contributors

Library and Archives Canada Cataloguing in Publication

    Body heat : the story of the Woodward's redevelopment / edited by Robert Enright ;
    architecture by Henriquez Partners.

Includes bibliographical references.
ISBN 978-1-897476-01-7

    1. Woodward's Limited--History. 2. Downtown-Eastside (Vancouver, B.C.).
    3. Urban renewal--British Columbia--Vancouver. I. Enright, Robert

HT178.C22V2923 2009   307.3'4160971133   C2009-904061-1

We gratefully acknowledge for their financial support of our publishing program the
Canada Council for the Arts, the BC Arts Council, and the Government of Canada
through the Book Publishing Industry Development Program (BPIDP).

 Canada Council   **Conseil des Arts**
      for the Arts   **du Canada**

Book design by Pablo Mandel / CircularStudio.com

10 9 8 7 6 5 4 3 2 1

Printed in China

UNDER CONSTRUCTION

BODY HEAT
THE STORY OF THE *Woodward's* REDEVELOPMENT

Architecture by Henriquez Partners
Edited by Robert Enright

CONTENTS

INTRODUCTION
STORIES AND MORE STOREYS: HOW WOODWARD'S GOT REBUILT
Robert Enright

Robert Enright
Journalist/Art Critic

Robert Enright is the University Research Professor in Art Theory and Criticism at the School of Fine Art and Music at the University of Guelph, where he teaches in the Graduate Programme. He is also the Senior Contributing Editor and film critic for *Border Crossings* magazine. He has received 14 nominations at the National and Western Magazine Awards for his writing in its pages, winning four gold and two silver medals. He is a frequent contributor to the arts section of *The Globe and Mail*, and has written articles and conducted reviews for *frieze, Modern Painters, ArtReview* and *ARTnews*. Professor Enright has also written introductions, essays and published interviews in over 40 books and exhibition catalogues. He has published a monograph on the American painter, Eric Fischl with the Monacelli Press in New York and a collection of interviews with contemporary artists called, *Peregrinations*. In 2005 he was made a Member of the Order of Canada.

ANYONE WITH AN INTEREST IN FILM over the last 25 years will recognize two things about the title of this book. *Body Heat* is the name of the 1981 film starring William Hurt and Kathleen Turner, a noirish story about a *femme fatale* and the less-than-sharp lawyer she variously engages as her toy and her dupe. Written and directed by Lawrence Kasdan, it is memorable principally because of Ms. Turner's breakthrough performance (who can forget her initial appearance as she leaves an outdoor concert, dressed primarily in white and completely in attitude), and for the heat of what we might discreetly call its amorous incidents. In the film, there were two bodies and together they generated some high temperatures.

In this book version of *Body Heat,* which documents one of the most ambitious urban redevelopment projects in Canadian history, there are many more bodies and the commingling of their ideas and actions have produced a considerable degree of city heat. Because of its scale and complexity, the Woodward's project is the most written about and the most anticipated architectural development in the country. Once completed, it will occupy one million square feet, and will facilitate a myriad of organizations, institutions and individuals. Occupants of single non-market housing units will mingle with art and theatre students from Simon Fraser University (SFU); city and federal government employees and bank clerks will share the atrium with shoppers and condo owners and street people. The Woodward's site will inevitably reflect the complexity of the Downtown Eastside neighbourhood. What you will see is what you have always seen, but with additions, and in a new configuration.

While it is true that there have already been many people involved, they represent only the beginning of the social and economic partnerships the Woodward's project will encourage. There will be more—many more—in the future. If Woodward's functions as its supporters are convinced it will, the project is destined to fundamentally change the most infamous area in one of Canada's best-known cities. The Downtown Eastside is the country's poorest postal code; it is a location in which the deficits of urban life are most conspicuously visible. Drug use, prostitution, HIV infection and abject poverty are as familiar as the ocean air that drifts through the neighbourhood. The stakeholders in the project, those who have built it and those who will live and work in it, are none of them innocent utopians. But as humans we live pragmatically and we live imaginatively; we live in real cities and in imagined ones. The Woodward's redevelopment, against some formidable odds, is practically imagining a better city than the one that currently exists. It is a kind of social incubator, birthing new states of being out of urban conditions that won't go away. A number of individuals who have contributed to this book talk about the need to maintain the "gritty factor" in the area. Grit is an acceptable four-letter word. Something else is needed, too. In Yaletown they would politely call it intestinal fortitude. In the Downtown Eastside, it's just guts.

I mentioned two things that are noticeable about *Body Heat;* both film and book are a narrative. It is no accident that the book's subtitle is *The Story of the Woodward's Redevelopment*. Woodward's is an extraordinary project, and it encompasses the range of will, hope and chance that makes a story worth telling in the first place and worth paying attention to once realized. It is a story about convincing urban planners that population density and the models necessary to accommodate that density are paramount considerations; they override a simple adherence to formal and historical agendas that no longer address the reality of neighbourhoods like the Downtown Eastside.

Woodward's is a tale told by savants who recognize that the body heat necessary to make the project succeed can only come about through the invention of a new model of inclusivity, one that acknowledges the past but is not enslaved by it. 'Body heat', a phrase that Gregory Henriquez has used from the beginning of the Woodward's project, means 5,000 people a day doing any number of unexceptional things: attending classes, watching a film, going to the bank or drugstore, shopping, hanging out. Body heat is a narrative of conventional urban life; it is a story of living and working in a neighbourhood.

The Woodward's department store was itself an important story. It is difficult to find a family with any history in Vancouver that doesn't have some connection with Woodward's and a story to tell about it. It seems to be a defining characteristic for being a Vancouverite. What became apparent in conducting the 23 interviews that make up the core of this book is that many of the participants were persuaded by the symbolic significance of redeveloping Woodward's. The original Woodward's was a symbol of a certain kind of social and economic dynamic, an innovative department store that served a broad community. Its demise came about through a predictable combination of circumstances—too much expansion, too much borrowed money, and a rapidly changing consumer base that wanted different things in different ways. The world changed and Woodward's remained the same.

When Woodward's closed in 1993, it left a huge hole in the heart of the Downtown Eastside and the neighbourhood has not been the same since. Which is why the redevelopment of the site is so important to Vancouver and why it carries such symbolic weight. What else explains the number of times in the past 12 years that various combinations of government, business, social service agencies, and the development community have attempted to find ways to bring Woodward's back to life? What else explains the time and expense the Henriquez/Westbank/Peterson partnership spent trying to save the iconic 'W' sign and the small-scale replica of the Eiffel Tower on which it sat? What else explains remaking the letter and reconstructing a new tower (this time with better and more durable materials), so that the proud 'W' can again announce the presence of a vital neighbourhood? And what else, other than a commitment to the symbolic, explains placing what remains of the old 'W' in a glass case in the atrium so that people can see the past in the reflecting glow of the present?

Memory is always the engine that drives story. Remembering where we've been is the only responsible way to understand where we might go. In this sense, the Woodward's Redevelopment Project is memory being activated in a contemporary urban environment. Perhaps the most compelling example of how memory can be instrumental in changing how we look at the urban space we live in and the history we inherit, is the massive, two-sided photograph made by Stan Douglas, called *Abbott & Cordova, August 7, 1971*. The photograph, a restaging of the Gastown Riot that took place in Vancouver that summer, occupies a dominant space in the public atrium. Douglas' practice as an artist has been to concentrate on pivotal moments in history when things could have changed and gone one way or another. *Abbott & Cordova, August 7, 1971* commemorates a moment in Vancouver's history that was to have a devastating effect on the Downtown Eastside. But his restaging also re-imagines what it could have meant; it revisits the past to catalyze a new present. For Douglas, the riot was a pivotal event and in reconfiguring it, he obliges us to consider how we interpret history. His photograph perfectly reflects the larger urban project of which it is a part. The completion of the Woodward's redevelopment is also a pivotal moment for the Downtown Eastside; the art project is a metonymic model for the architectural project. It is the part that stands in for the whole.

The project is also an honest reflection of the process that got it made. Through the ideas and words of a number of individuals who have been instrumental in the Woodward's project, this book documents a complicated process that moves towards a complex product. The intriguing thing about the Woodward's redevelopment is that the process following from the physical completion of the project is going to be as critical, and probably more so, than the labyrinthine one that resulted in its being built in the first place. The pattern from process to product and back to process again represents the open-ended future Woodward's faces as its range of stakeholders not only learn to use the space, but get to see whether it will work at all. Flux is another applicable four-letter word.

A final thing about *Body Heat.* In the film, Matty Walker issues a warning to Ned Racine about the plot they have hatched to kill her wealthy husband. "Don't talk about it. Talk is dangerous," she says. "It makes things happen." Like everything else, she's right about language and what it can accomplish. Matty has figured out the power of words. They most assuredly make things happen. This version of *Body Heat* is the record of a miscellany of conversations that have taken place and will continue to be held, as the changing story of the Woodward's project tells itself into the future.

FOREWORD: A PERFECT STORM
Chris Macdonald

Chris Macdonald
Director
UBC School of Architecture (1998-2006)

Chris Macdonald is a professor at the School of Architecture and Landscape Architecture at the University of British Columbia (UBC). He was educated at the University of Manitoba and the London-based Architectural Association School. During the 1980s, his partnership, Macdonald and Salter, produced a number of significant design projects while he taught in various capacities at the Architectural Association School. Prior to joining UBC, Mr. Macdonald taught at the University of Texas in Austin.

In 2005, Mr. Macdonald was involved in *Cabin, Cottage and Camp: New Design on the Canadian Landscape,* an exhibition and symposium on contemporary house design in the Canadian landscape, and edited the accompanying book. He was co-curator of *Sweaterlodge,* Canada's contribution to the 2006 Venice Biennale in Architecture. *West Coast Residential: The Modern and the Contemporary,* a definitive historical survey of early modern houses in the Vancouver region co-authored by Mr. Macdonald, was published in 2007. His current research activities include preparing for the publication of *Unreconstructed Modern: Three Houses by Judith Chaffee* and conducting a study of contemporary urban housing practices across Canada.

OBSERVING THE WOODWARD'S PROJECT from its formation through to its realization, important issues are raised regarding architecture's sense of purpose and its manner of execution. The historic modern alliance between architectural practice and social change re-emerges in the service of an extraordinary collection of disparate interests, while the role of the architect within that constellation presents a new and challenging trajectory. Although the full consequences of the project remain untested, consideration here would hope to frame the significance of the work outside the scope of its eventual material and social conclusion, in the very specific conditions of its genesis.

The Woodward's project is—arguably above all else—profound in the manner in which it represents a coalition of interests unprecedented in their variety and aggregate size. The project includes 200 units of low-cost rental housing, the creative arts program of a major public university, a new civic plaza, and a variety of other community-based tenants—already the constituents of a significant public works project. Simultaneously, 536 units of market housing, a food store and a regional chain drugstore provide the accumulation of an equally significant market-driven commercial development. While the story of how this unique coalition was assembled is elaborated elsewhere, the unlikelihood of its assembly is particularly vivid in the context of prevailing conventions of urban, architectural and development practice.

The initial conception of the modern project in architecture contained an embedded concern for progressive social ideals. In the Canadian context—and certainly in Vancouver—this inclination was largely embraced, with a robust and local modernist idiom being the result. In the context of post-war economic expansion, this practice was exercised in the representation of the liberal state as well as in the depiction of private sector capital expansion. In due course, this initial pairing of social aspiration and expression within the commercial realm became disentangled, with modernism assuming the position of one rather specific choice among an array of contemporary and historicist styles. In contrast, public and institutional works continued to observe this alliance between political aims and modernist rhetoric, as is evidenced in an evolving "modern" manner even today.

This schism in expressive intent between public and private works occurs across much of Canadian architectural practice, and results in hard distinctions drawn between practice profiles. The result is that practices are seldom able to balance a commitment to public and institutional work with expressly commercial projects. It is interesting to consider this dichotomy as an issue of temperament above all, especially as it relates to the nature of client-architect communication and attendant decision-making. This is an especially important point with respect to the role of the architect when mediating between disparate communities with often conflicting values and aspirations.

In this respect, Henriquez Partners Architects presents a distinct practice profile, having for some years engaged public and private, institutional and commercial clientele. Borne initially out of a pragmatic response to fluctuating economic cycles and the necessities of a small practice, this balance has offered the practice access to a broad spectrum of projects in which their design and management expertise has been exercised. Henriquez Partners had also early on understood the value of establishing project-specific team building, facilitating their participation in projects much larger than they might claim individually. Significantly, this mode of operation built a practice culture in which complex associations of client groups, consultants and public interests would need to be absorbed and reconciled. Not incidentally, this promotes a strong, central role for the partners in responding to client needs and maintaining design authority over the duration of any given project.

The ability of Henriquez Partners to provide leadership to a project in which mercantile interest and public policy intersect came to be effectively unique among practices in Vancouver. While establishing a broad level of professional confidence, this ability also permits the role of the architect to expand into the very formulation of the project and the delineation of program in the first place. This special combination of the capacity to execute and the appetite to engage in such a manner is expressly evident when comparing the three competitive finalists seeking to secure crucial city support for the Woodward's project.

The radically distinct social and commercial interests represented by each of the three projects speak directly to the extraordinary degree of discretionary power that the Vancouver Charter grants to the city in effecting planning decisions. While in this case the city also serves as an implicit and critical development partner—holding ownership of the land—even in entirely private projects, the city has a history of seeking deemed public benefit through the course of negotiating planning constraints. This tactic has evolved into normative practice in much of the downtown peninsula of the city, and reaches its most vivid expression to date with the Woodward's project.

Historically, the capacity to negotiate restrictions and allowances on a case-by-case basis with an intent to contribute directly to the public realm was instituted in the late 1970s under the guidance of Ray Spaxman, the director of planning between 1973 and 1989. While the many amenity spaces created through this process vary in design quality and in their true contribution to fully accessible public participation, there is no question that collectively these amenity spaces dramatically expand the visual domain of the urban landscape. In doing so, they relieve the ubiquity of the gridiron urban plan, adding spatial complexity and strongly contributing to the unique character of Vancouver's city centre.

During the 1990s and beyond—encouraged by an unusually robust development economy—negotiations became more proactive and included the allowance of increased volumes of building in return for the constitution of specifically targeted public facilities. In the case of major redevelopments such as northeast False Creek and Coal Harbour, public parks, schools and community centres were brought into being in part through negotiated planning agreements. As well, in an era when the largesse of the state—especially for capital projects—had been generally curtailed, this mechanism allowed for the renewal and upgrading of local cultural institutions such as the Contemporary Art Gallery and the Vancouver Film Institute. In both instances, the mere representation of an expanded public realm was superseded by direct 'bricks-and-mortar' legacies effecting progressive and significant change. With the election of the Council of 2002, including Mayor Larry Campbell and long-time community activist Jim Green, it seemed possible to turn this anomalous planning tool to the task of leveraging construction of new social housing in the city.

That the city of Vancouver should be actively engaged in pursuing social housing policy is in itself quite remarkable. While the formation of housing policy and the funding of public housing construction are located in the domains of provincial and national governments, in recent practice both levels of government have reduced their commitment to this portfolio. Since 1993, virtually all federal support for social housing programs has ceased, while since 2001 the provincial policy shifted—quite dramatically—to provide specific support for populations of seniors and those with disabilities. The city of Vancouver, however, holds the capacity to intervene with respect to social housing provision through the agency of its Property Endowment Fund, making it virtually unique among municipalities in Canada. This holding of an inventory of city-owned properties—originating in land repossessed for tax arrears during the Depression—allows the city to support provincial or non-profit organizations in their efforts to provide social housing by leasing land at nominal cost and forgiving property taxes. Most recently fourteen new sites were made available using this mechanism, leading to the creation of 1,100 new housing units over the next four years.

Removing property costs relieves a formidable pressure on these projects, and one result has been the establishment of a tradition of remarkable design ambition and accomplishment within the challenges of providing affordable housing. Distinguished local architects such as Arthur Erickson, Nigel Baldwin and Henriquez Partners have contributed to the success of such work at both building and urban scales. Significantly, they have done so almost exclusively using the expressive motifs of a developed modern palette. It is in this local cultural landscape that the Woodward's redevelopment project occurs, a landscape that provides one specific lens through which its singular complexion may be observed.

In terms of professional practice norms, the Woodward's project prompted Henriquez Partners to act proactively on a number of fronts, most especially during the formation of the project. They identified the significance of the project in its immediate social context, established alliances with local community activists in parallel with the earliest design formulations, and prompted the engagement of specific and sympathetic private sector investment. Initially undertaken at considerable financial risk to the practice, their engagement with the Woodward's project speaks to a committed position of social advocacy. Such a position is implicit in various earlier commissions, but is declared here with vigour and—as noted—lodged within a culture of practice virtually unique in its breadth of experience and capability.

If the role of the architect was amplified by the special circumstances of the project, conventional planning procedures were also extended and re-shaped—in particular with respect to the exercise of community consultation in 2003 and 2004. Jim Green, then a Vancouver city council member, was instrumental in identifying the crucial role this consultation would play in the overall success of the project. He recognized that the several months of extended workshops and invitations for community comment held the capacity to engender a meaningful degree of community ownership of the project, and that whatever the ultimate configuration of program and its design might bring, this ownership could effectively deflect the project from the conventional charges of aggressive gentrification.

The outpouring of sentiment prompted by this process was compelling, although at the time appeared to set up a potential shortfall between the expressed desire to

Both the VanCity Place for Youth (1999) project designed by Nigel Baldwin Architect (above) and the Lore Krill Co-op (2002) by Henriquez Partners (left and below) offer evidence of the strong design traditions accompanying the provision of social housing in Vancouver. Coincidentally, both projects' capital funding was the result of previous, failed efforts to rehabilitate the Woodward's site.

conserve the building fabric as a repository of meaning, and the degree to which new construction would be necessary in order to render the project financially viable. The ultimate strength of the reflective nostalgia evident in the consultation process was most vividly tested as the project moved into the first phases of demolition and excavation. While highly specific memories of Christmas display windows and individual light fittings characterized the expressed memory of Woodward's articulated in the community consultations, evidence of the full scope of demolition in 2006 was met without a single expression of outrage or criticism of the consultative process itself. Even more significant than the successful sales of market housing units or the eventual casting of provincial support for the SFU facility, this litmus test of public opinion gave clear evidence that the project had been successfully founded on a powerful measure of public trust.

In its alliance of social and commercial motives and in its configuration of both design and regulatory practices, the Woodward's project challenges convention. Beyond its resolution as a singular redevelopment project, however, remains a question of how such a project contributes to broader urban concerns. A key issue in discussions of urban design is that of the development increment. In its constitution as three quarters of a city block and its programmatic ambition to proportionately mirror the diversity of the city's demographic, the Woodward's project aspires to be a distillation of all of its varied constituencies. As such, the project invites consideration as a model of urban practice.

Beyond the project's deft fulfillment of the needs of its varied communities, there remains the essential question of the capacity to construct a vital public domain. The city's insistence that the central courtyard spaces be expressly assigned as public space bodes well, yet the final adjudication of open access to these territories remains in flux. The extent to which the conclusion of these deliberations results in a new and potentially vital public space is compelling to observe—especially so in the context of a city in which spatially distinct common ground is so unusual. The conclusion in a merely symbolic expression of public space would ultimately render the project as yet another instance—however nuanced—of the inclination for large-scale urban developments to erode the inheritance of a public landscape capable of active inhabitation beyond the habits of consumption.

The perfect storm of architectural capacity, political will, community support, client commitment and—unquestionably—historical moment have provided a unique occasion on which to imagine the contrary.

Concert Properties Ltd. / The Holborn Group

Concert Properties Ltd. is a diversified real-estate enterprise that develops and acquires industrial and commercial properties, rental housing, multi-family condominium housing, resort developments and seniors living communities in British Columbia, Alberta and Ontario. Exclusively owned by Canadian union and management pension plans, Concert's completed developments total in excess of $1.9 billion and it holds assets of more than $1.3 billion. It brought over two decades of local development experience on projects such as condominiums near the Vancouver General Hospital and at Arbutus Walk to its partnership with architecture firm Musson Cattell Mackey in the Woodward's competition.

The Holborn Group is a Malaysian-based development company with interests ranging from equity markets to hotels. Operating internationally in Asia, South Africa, Australia and Canada, Holborn has significant holdings in Vancouver and Whistler. It sought to gain more local development experience by entering the Woodward's competition and with projects such as the downtown Ritz-Carlton luxury hotel and condo project, which was suspended during the 2008 economic downturn. For the Woodward's competition, it partnered with DYSArchitecture, whose partner Ron Yuen was involved in many past attempts to redevelop Woodward's.

The Concert/Holborn competition scheme centred on a public plaza carved from the original building. Concert joined forces with Holborn when they saw the advantage of two lots owned by Holborn adjoining the Woodward's site for enlarging the plaza and creating a less imposing project. The original building contained loft-style market housing while a new tower accommodated the SFU School for the Contemporary Arts and non-market housing.

Millennium Properties Ltd.

Millennium Properties Ltd. is part of the real estate investment and development arm of Armeco Group of Companies, known for its commitment to high-quality architecture and luxurious design on projects such as Water's Edge in West Vancouver and the master-planned, seven-tower City in the Park community in Burnaby. The company is also the developer for the Olympic Village project for Vancouver 2010. Millennium has developed several hundred thousand square metres of high-quality residential, commercial and institutional space in Canada as well as projects in France and other parts of Europe.

For the Woodward's competition, Millennium partnered with architecture firm Gomberoff Bell Lyon and urban consultant Chuck Brook on a proposal for a 163-metre tower, which would have been the second highest tower in Vancouver if built, articulated in three offset components. The tower would act as a "vertical street" of market and non-market housing interspersed with "sky parks". Retail and commercial space was located on the ground floor with the SFU School for the Contemporary Arts in a cantilevered four-storey glass box. The 'W' sign was lowered from its original position on the roof to become the centrepiece of a commemorative street-level courtyard.

Westbank Projects / Peterson Investment Group

Established in 1992 by Ian Gillespie, Westbank is a Vancouver-based multi-disciplined developer of large-scale mixed-use projects, Class A office space, rental apartments, non-market housing, luxury condominiums, hotel properties and institutional facilities exceeding $3.8 billion. Westbank has evolved over the last few years from being the dominant neighbourhood shopping centre developer in North America to becoming one of the most active development companies on the West Coast. Westbank's portfolio of projects completed or underway consists of approximately 11 million square feet and includes developments such as Shaw Tower and Living Shangri-La in Vancouver, Century Park in Edmonton, Shangri-La in Toronto, Parc Residences, Shutters, and the Falls in Victoria and Azure in Dallas, Texas.

In 2006, Westbank commenced construction of the Fairmont Pacific Rim, an 800,000 square foot development featuring a world-class Fairmont Hotel and 175 exclusive residences located in Coal Harbour, adjacent to Shaw Tower. Known for their high quality, architectural distinction, and consideration for the environment, Westbank's developments have raised the standard for Vancouver's contemporary residential high-rise real estate market.

Peterson Investment Group is a progressive commercial real estate investor and developer with a broad portfolio that includes large mixed-use properties, major retail centres, office buildings, residential towers, and institutional assets. Established in 1989 by Ben Yeung, Peterson Investment Group is headquartered in Vancouver, Canada. With over 20 years of experience, the company is known in the commercial real estate community for its innovative and entrepreneurial approach in acquisitions and developments.

The Westbank Projects / Peterson Investment Group proposal centred on razing the site save the original Woodward's building at the corner of Hastings and Abbott streets. Four separate buildings accommodating the program surrounded a public space, allowing pedestrian access through the redevelopment. The project's aspiration to include the Downtown Eastside community was evident in the location of the family non-market housing units with market housing in the same building and the potential to accommodate up to 237 non-market units in the design when the RFP only required 100 units.

FOLIO I

WOODSQUAT 2002
Barry Calhoun

1

HISTORICAL CONTEXT
May So

May So
Architect/Author
Henriquez Partners Architects

May So worked for architecture firms in Calgary and Vancouver before joining Henriquez Partners in 2002. She has contributed to several of the firm's significant projects including the Woodward's redevelopment, for which she led detailing of the SFU and commercial building shells, the pedestrian bridge and exterior steelwork. Born in Hong Kong, she received a Bachelor of Fine Arts from the University of Calgary and a Masters of Architecture from UBC.

Her work has appeared in various publications. She co-authored *Towards an Ethical Architecture: Issues within the Work of Gregory Henriquez* (2006). Her paper "World Class Vancouver: A Terminal City Re-imagined," presented at the 7th Urban Planning and Environment Symposium in January 2007, was included in *World Cities and Urban Form: Fragmented, Polycentric, Sustainable?* (2008).

Her interest in addressing homelessness in Vancouver has led to her participation in several housing and community development initiatives and organizations.

VANCOUVER WAS A RAPIDLY EXPANDING CITY IN 1892 when Charles Woodward, a retailer from Ontario, opened the city's first department store on Main Street catering to working people. After incorporating in 1886 when the Canadian Pacific Railway announced the extension of its rail line there, Vancouver experienced large-scale immigration. The population swelled from 14,000 in 1891 to 60,000 in 1905, then to 100,000 in 1911. Demand for a greater variety of retail, manufacturing, and professional services increased. Transportation, wholesaling and resource management companies operating throughout the province began converging on Vancouver to make it one of Canada's largest metropolitan centres at the time. The establishment of an electric street-railway in 1890 facilitated interurban and, later, suburban growth. In the period leading up to World War I, the professional and entrepreneurial upper class moved their homes from the West End to Shaughnessy Heights and rural Point Grey, which afforded greater amenities and fewer threats of encroachment by business and the lower-classes. The working and middle industrial classes settled south and east of the downtown area, leaving a concentration of non-British foreigners, single transient men, seasonal labourers, the elderly and the poor living in cheap hotels, squatters' shacks and aging houses in the historic inner-city.

Buoyed by the successful launches of a drug department in 1895 and mail order service in 1897, Charles Woodward incorporated Woodward's Department Stores Limited and moved the store in 1903 to its final location at the corner of Hastings and Abbott streets in Gastown. The historic centre of Vancouver, Gastown had originated in 1867 as a cluster of saloons west of Hastings Mill serving mill workers and loggers and had grown to accommodate men employed in British Columbia's resource industries. While Hastings Street to the east of Woodward's was the main thoroughfare for the area's concentration of transient housing, brothels, employment agencies and cheap entertainment facilities, Hastings and Cordova streets to the west had emerged as Vancouver's premiere retail shopping district, making Woodward's accessible to the middle-class.

The pre-World War I period saw the construction of several landmark buildings in the downtown area, including the provincial courthouse, the 14-storey steel-framed Dominion Trust Building, the Vancouver Block topped by a large clock, the World Building on Pender Street, and a second CPR station. Downtown streets generally acted as public spaces for crowds of transient workers to do business, listen to labour speeches and music, and scan the boards of employment offices in search of work. As such, they were associated with the 'unorganized element' of society. Woodward's management complained in a 1904 letter to the mayor that the crowds in front of their premises hindered customers from being able to enter the store. In 1917, the killing of the chief of police on East Georgia Street by a morphine addict cemented the area's reputation as Vancouver's slum district.

The original Woodward's building took up almost a quarter of the city block and was four storeys tall, a significant size for a store at that time. Woodward's had separate departments, advertised with white signs painted on the brick exterior, that sold hardware, industrial products, pharmaceutical drugs, goods not available elsewhere, and groceries on a food floor, which at that time was North America's largest supermarket. The 25¢ Days promotion, introduced in 1910 and increased to 45¢, 95¢ and finally $1.49 over the next several decades, became a feature attraction in Vancouver, as evidenced by shoppers from across the city lining up on promotion days. In 1919, the food floor was transformed into a self-service groceteria where customers saved money by selecting groceries themselves. The Woodward's store grew rapidly in parallel with the growth of Gastown as the centre of the city's wholesale produce distribution. It opened the first out-of-province store in Edmonton in 1926 and built a 500-car parking garage, the largest in Canada at the time, across the street from its Vancouver store in 1927. Woodward's elaborately mechanized Christmas window displays were introduced in 1931 and drew a large number of viewers. The popularity of Woodward's and its centrality in the retail scene attracted many other businesses to the area. Three blocks west at Hastings and Richards, Spencer Department Store had been established in 1907, first as a dry goods shop, then expanding to become a department store occupying the entire city block. It rivaled Woodward's until 1948 when it was bought by the Eaton's store chain.

The Great Depression and the instigation of Prohibition ended Gastown's function as the centre of Vancouver's drinking life and triggered the neighbourhood's decline. In 1931, 500 men, who had no fixed addresses and therefore did not qualify for relief, camped in shacks and hovels on the recently filled False Creek Flats north of the CNR train station. Disease spread quickly with only one tap and no sanitation services. When a case of diptheria was discovered, the camp was dismantled and most of the men were sent to work camps in the interior, earning a dollar a day. In 1938, when the relief camps closed, 1,600 workers occupied the post office on Hastings Street, the art gallery and the Hotel Georgia, demanding better treatment and housing. Returning World War II veterans also could not find housing nor afford hotels, so 35 of them took over the old Hotel Vancouver at Granville and Georgia Streets that was slated for demolition and registered 700 men to live there with the support of local businesses and the public.

Following World War II, Gastown's central role in warehousing, transportation, and manufacturing operations based on resource extraction declined. Ownership consolidation of resource industries and the unionization of the workforce reduced the demand for migrant labourers. Waterfront industries like lumber mills and salmon canneries relocated to cheaper land outside of the downtown core. No longer defined by its work and industries, the neighbourhood became more associated with its dubious activities. A 1950 city plan to rebuild Strathcona, originally a collection of shacks and cottages south and east of the Hastings Mill popularly called the East End, made the distinction between the respectable, but poor immigrant family neighbourhood east of Main Street and the rowdy, disreputable zone to its west. This area west of Main Street began making headlines in the 1950s as skid row, a perilous territory of criminals, alcoholics, drug addicts and sex perverts.

Woodward's kept expanding and had come to define one-stop shopping in Vancouver by the mid-1950s, providing low- and modest-income shoppers with daily necessities, including a sizeable grocery floor that offered 200 types of cheeses, a pharmacy and a large selection of household items. Additionally, Woodward's provided men's and women's fashion, travel booking, cheque cashing, delivery and its own credit system. Its signature neon 'W' sign mounted on a 25-metre replica of the Eiffel Tower was highly visible across the city. Predicting that shopping malls

were the wave of the future, Woodward's opened its first mall location at Park Royal Shopping centre in 1950. It also opened two shopping centres and two freestanding stores. In 1954, BC Electric discontinued its interurban tram to Hastings and Carrall streets, which had made the Woodward's store regionally accessible. With the relocation of theatres and shops from Hastings west to Granville at this time, Hastings Street began to decline. By 1957, after nine principal phases of expansion, the downtown Woodward's store, occupied over three-quarters of the city block and reached 12 storeys.

Through progressive employee relations, Woodward's retained a high level of employee loyalty and nurtured close-knit family-style environments in each department. A staff advisory council with representatives from every department had been introduced in 1942 and met monthly to discuss ideas and concerns. Beginning in 1945, a bi-monthly staff newsletter called The Beacon kept staff informed of store developments and events. Employees received medical, holiday and insurance benefits, a staff pension plan, shopping discounts, scholarships for their children, a subsidized meal plan, profit sharing, and a savings plan. Staff enjoyed appreciation events such as picnics, boat rides and dances, and participated in themed sales promotional days involving costumes, music and song.

In 1960, the Downtown Business Association established a redevelopment advisory board to respond to pressures for large-scale redevelopment from a coalition of business elites, bankers, developers, city politicians and bureaucrats. In addition to the growth of white-collar jobs, the group was also concerned with the decline of inner-city districts, especially the Central Business District, threats to the downtown retail trade from suburbanization and the downtown's constricted street network limiting automobile access. In response, the city helped to assemble significant land holdings for commercial redevelopment. One of the largest redevelopments was Pacific Centre, comprising a two-block underground shopping mall,

Eaton's Department Store, a 30-storey Toronto Dominion Bank tower, a 19-storey IBM tower and a 20-storey hotel tower bounded by Howe, Georgia, Granville and Dunsmuir streets. In 1972, Eaton's transferred from Hastings and Richards streets to the Pacific Centre redevelopment, kitty-corner to the Bay department store. This represented a permanent shift of retail activity south and west towards the Central Business District and into suburban shopping centres.

In 1965, alarmed by the sharp decline in property values and rising vacancy rates, business and property owners around central Hastings street formed IDEAS, the Improvement of the Downtown East Area Society, to press the government to halt the decline. As part of the downtown modernization program, a 1967 transportation study recommended an east-west freeway originating from Highway 1 and passing through Chinatown on the southern edge of a proposed Strathcona urban renewal project. The freeway would connect to another freeway on Main Street that would run along the northern edge of downtown through Coal Harbour. The route would lead to a proposed Burrard Inlet tunnel connecting to the Upper Levels Highway that would improve truck access to the central port. The proposed freeway would demolish most of Chinatown and parts of Gastown while making feasible Project 200. Proposed as a large waterfront development between the Marine Building and the Woodward's department store, Project 200 would consist of 14 office towers, 1,000 apartments, a 600-room hotel and various retail sites.

Following the completion of an initial urban redevelopment in Strathcona, the city proposed a second scheme between Main and Richards streets that would turn the area into offices and parking lots serving the Central Business District. Public opposition was fierce, particularly when it became clear that the proposals were being steered by powerful landholders such as the National Harbours Board, Canadian Pacific, and BC Hydro to enhance their own development interests. Many argued that the developments would only displace rather than solve the area's problems. Neither the Downtown Business Association nor the Vancouver Board of Trade supported the proposals. The city was forced to relent its plans, and the incumbent Non-Partisan Association was defeated in the 1972 civic elections, ushering in a wave of urban planning reform.

Individual efforts and a city council beautification initiative in 1968 resulted in a certain amount of upgrading and restoration in Gastown. In 1971, a campaign led by businessmen, property owners and political protestors pressured the provincial government to declare Gastown an historic area. The same year, a riot erupted in Gastown when the Vancouver Police intervened in a marijuana "smoke-in". Like Gastown, Strathcona-Chinatown was declared a historic area in the early 1970s to the consternation of property owners who did not like the contrived character of beautification plans that called for traditional Chinese architectural features. In the central Hastings neighbourhood, campaigns for environmental, social and housing improvements became more organized through the formation of the Downtown Eastside Residents Association (DERA) in 1973. The association coordinated a small group of charismatic activists and community workers who campaigned for a wide range of social issues from closure of the local liquor store to the provision of a well-staffed community centre, with the issue of quality affordable housing becoming paramount. Its objective was to build a community that could empower itself despite poverty, addiction and other disadvantages. To this end, it named central Hastings as the Downtown Eastside to distinguish it from Gastown, Chinatown and Strathcona and dissociate it from previous derogatory references like skid row.

While the Woodward's company thrived as a major competitor on the Western Canadian retail scene during the 1970s with 18 stores opening throughout British Columbia and Alberta, often as anchors to major shopping centres, the Vancouver flagship store began to decline as business activity left West Hastings Street. Demise of the Woodward's retail empire began in the 1980s. The opening of four more Woodward's stores in 1981 during high interest rates, high inflation and large debt, combined with the recession, left the company financially fragile. To improve its situation, Woodward's began disposing its assets. In 1986, it sold the food floor, which represented 40 percent of its volume and cash source, to Safeway Canada. As Safeway had no interest in the location, the food floor operated as an IGA store until the building closed. The Woodward's family sold surplus land, shopping malls and other real estate holdings. Cost-saving measures were implemented, including relocating stores to cheaper locations. While downsizing and reorganizing parts of its business, Woodward's continued to pursue an aggressive retail expansion program, introducing exclusive Abercrombie & Fitch stores in Canada and opening two dozen bargain Woodwynn stores. Ultimately, these measures did not save the company and in 1989, management passed from members of the Woodward's family to professional managers.

As early as 1988, housing advocate and DERA member Jim Green saw the decline of Woodward's and proposed a plan to the provincial government to convert the Woodward's building into non-market housing. In 1992, Woodward's filed for bankruptcy and Hudson's Bay Company purchased most of its assets. As the Woodward's stores were generally well-located, most of them were converted to Zellers or Bay stores, but little interest was shown in the Vancouver flagship building on Hastings Street.

In 1993, shortly after its 100th anniversary, Woodward's closed its doors. Remaining retail stores on Hastings near Woodward's folded and in the retail vacuum that followed, an open drug economy seized the streets. While injection drug use had escalated in the 1980s with the increased popularity of cocaine, the introduction of crack cocaine in the 1990s offered an affordable and addictive alternative, sharpening the decline of the area. Pawnshops and 24-hour convenience stores thrived by fencing stolen goods or operating as drug fronts themselves. Other ventures like galleries, cultural institutions and restaurants left by the early 2000s.

With the withdrawal of legitimate businesses, property speculation increased in anticipation of redevelopment, leaving several blocks of Hastings largely vacant while owners waited for property values to rise. Having served as the shopping and social centre for the surrounding neighbourhoods and the city for almost a century, the closure of the Hastings Woodward's store ignited a long, simmering confrontation between an alliance of local business and residential property owners and non-profit community groups representing the area's majority population of low-income residents. The battle between these two groups was played out in the various development proposals for the Woodward's site presented over the next decade.

In 1995, Fama Holdings acquired the Woodward's site for $17 million and the city approved their application to develop a mixed-use project consisting of 400 market residential units, and commercial and retail space. Because the residential square footage exceeded what was permitted under the zoning, Fama agreed to designate Woodward's as a heritage "C" building on the Vancouver Heritage Registry in return for a relaxation of the residential floor space regulation. The proposed project generated much neighbourhood opposition due to its lack of social housing. In 1996, new discussions began with Fama for a mixed-market project negotiated through financing from the city of Vancouver and the New Democratic provincial government. The province would fund 200 cooperative housing units in the Woodward's building while the city would partner with VanCity to develop a 50-unit project in the Victory Square area for younger low-income singles not currently eligible for non-market housing because of age restrictions. Fama and the province were unable to come to an agreement on the viability of including non-market housing, so the province reallocated the Woodward's Co-op funding to the Lore Krill Co-op, which completed two buildings with a total of 200 units. VanCity Place for street youth was completed in 1998. After Fama announced its withdrawal from the Woodward's project, Downtown Eastside supporters held a sit-in protest at Fama's office. Having been granted a demolition permit, Fama begins removing non-structural components of the building. A third Fama scheme followed for five storeys of just over 400 market residential units above three lower storeys of small-unit commercial space grouped around a courtyard carved out of the existing building. Although this scheme again generated opposition from the public for excluding social housing, the city approved it as conforming to current zoning, supported by the Gastown Business Improvement Society and the Gastown Homeowners Association.

Momentum waned for several years while several developers attempted but were unable to develop a viable project. Jim Green, then community development coordinator in the Ministry of Employment and Investment of the New Democratic provincial government, negotiated the purchase of the Woodward's building from Fama Holdings in 2001 for $21.9 million with the intent of developing a 200-unit co-operative with 100 units allocated to deep-core need households, a home for

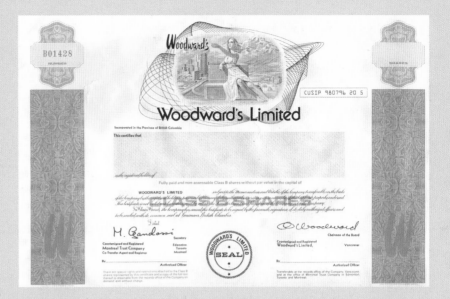

SFU's School for the Contemporary Arts and 18,600 square metres of commercial space. A month after the purchase, a new Liberal provincial government was elected and Jim Green was without a job. Unable to find a partner for the commercial component of the Woodward's project and canceling 1,000 planned non-market housing units, the province put Woodward's on hold in 2002. Madison Bellevue Apartments Corporation optioned the Woodward's building from the province for $18 million and proposed to develop the project under the approved 1997 development permit of just over 400 residential rental units and 17,700 square metres of commercial and retail space.

The Madison Bellevue proposal sparked many homeless people and community groups to express their demands for more social housing and to protest against gentrification in what became famously known as the Woodsquat, an occupation of the Woodward's building and surrounding streets. It began on September 14, 2002 when a group of activist organizers with the Anti-Poverty Committee opened the building and led a protest march there. Twenty-five people proceeded to occupy the building and immediately garnered widespread Downtown Eastside support, evidenced by the numerous donations of food, mattresses, and other life essentials. The squatters hung banners expressing demands for more social housing from the windows, the sides of the building, and the 'W' sign.

The organizers originally intended the squat to be a symbolic gesture in which the building would be occupied for a week and then vacated. Two days after the squat began, the provincial government obtained a court injunction to evict the squatters due to safety issues. Hundreds of supporters descended on the squat several days later to counter the injunction and many of them joined the squat, which grew to 100 people. As the police began negotiating with the pacifist organizers, a group of autonomist squatters, representing the sentiments of the majority, developed plans in case of a forced eviction. The group assembled barricades to slow down police attempts to storm the squat and built "lock-boxes" with which to secure themselves inside the building. Many planned to link arms in a circle to make their arrests more difficult. A week after the squat began, 100 riot police evicted the squatters and arrested 58 people. A defiant group of homeless squatters returned to the building the next night, but were arrested and their belongings thrown away. On September 23, public outcry culminated with 600 people rallying outside the Woodward's building and disrupting traffic in support of the squatters. More than 100 people resettled on the sidewalks around Woodward's, organized under the Woodward's Squatters Coalition. The squat, at its height, involved 280 people.

In October 2002, the city approved a heritage bonus of 9,200 square metres and a 10-year exemption for increases in property tax that would save Madison Bellevue $8.4 million. In return, Madison Bellevue would enter into a Heritage Revitalization Agreement to retain the building's heritage value and a housing agreement that required them to apply for 200 units of Residential Rehabilitation Assistance Program funding. It also required the residential units to be operated as rental for at least fifteen years with at least 100 units available for rent supplements to accommodate deep-core need households. Unable to make their proposal economically feasible and secure financing for the project, their option expired in November 2002.

On November 16, 2002, after a series of civic strikes and the ongoing Woodward's squat had left the ruling Non-Partisan Association unpopular, the Coalition of Progressive Electors won eight of the 10 city council seats in the civic election. By December, the squat still involved 100 people, many of whom were street homeless and without income assistance. The new city council moved quickly with a deal to house 54 homeless squatters in the Dominion Hotel under the management of PHS Community Services Society through municipal funding supplemented by a federal grant. On December 14, 2002, the Woodsquat ended and the squatters were settled into single rooms with rents set at the welfare housing allowance rate. The city provided funding to cover rents for people not on income assistance and support for those with mental illness and drug addictions. The squatters were later moved to more permanent rooms in the Stanley New Fountain Hotel, which was modestly refurbished and also managed by PHS.

Newly elected COPE councillor Jim Green and COPE mayor Larry Campbell, believing that the city was in the best position to find a workable solution for the Woodward's site, led negotiations for the city to purchase it from the province for $5.5 million in March 2003. The purchase was contingent on the left-leaning council's endorsement of the province's bid for Vancouver to host the 2010 Winter Olympic Games, which it would have otherwise opposed. Provincial funding was secured for 100 units of social housing for a redevelopment project on the Woodward's site. Two months later, the city relit the red neon 'W' sign on top of the Woodward's building, symbolizing a new beginning for the site, and launched an intensive public consultation process, the likes of which Vancouver had never before seen.

Welcome
to Vancouver
Canada

CANADA'S EVERGREEN GATEWAY TO THE PACIFIC AND HER THIRD LARGEST CITY WELCOMES YOUR VISIT

GREATER VANCOUVER

TOURIST GUIDE
& MAP
Published by
THE
ASSOCIATED AUTO
COURT OPERATORS
of
Vancouver and Vicinity
and
WOODWARD STORES
LIMITED

1960

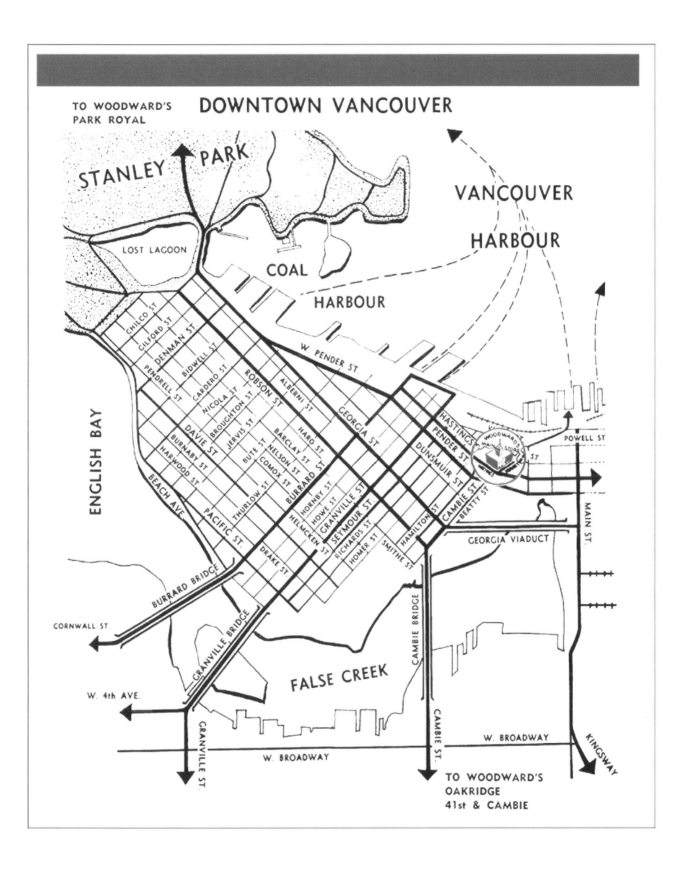

THE GREENING OF VANCOUVER
Jim Green

Jim Green
Councillor
City of Vancouver (2002-2005)

Jim Green, a native of Alabama, immigrated to Canada from America in the mid-1970s. He and many of his family live in the Strathcona area of Vancouver. He holds a Masters degree in Anthropology from UBC, and has studied at the Sorbonne, New York's Millennium Film Institute and the Universities of Carolina and Colorado.

Mr. Green is an adjunct professor of Anthropology at UBC, where he co-founded the university's Urban Field School. Green was chair of Four Corners Community Savings. He served on the board of the Federation of Canadian Municipalities.

In 2002, he was elected to Vancouver city council as a member of the Coalition of Progressive Electors, and subsequently, with mayor Larry Campbell and councillor Raymond Louie, left to form a new party, Vision Vancouver. Under the Vision Vancouver banner, he unsuccessfully ran for mayor in 2005.

Mr. Green is a well-known advocate for the city's Downtown Eastside and has led the development of many housing projects. He currently works as a development consultant for developers and non-profit community groups.

You've been directly involved in redeveloping Woodward's since around 1983. In the Woodward's documentary you said at one point that it was like a greased pig or slippery rugby ball, that on three earlier occasions you thought you had it, and each time it slipped away. What made this one stick after so many other attempts to try and do something?

In order to answer that I need to go back into a little bit of history. When I first started working to get Woodward's as a project it was what I would call one of my hobby studies. I watched what was going on inside; I watched Woodward's change retail philosophies almost daily. I saw staff no longer there and I watched Woodward's being sold off in different places. They closed down the food floor, which was extremely popular, and the decision caused mayhem in the community because the food floor delivered for free and that was really big for seniors. There were all these reasons why people were very attached to it. I did a study at one time and the Woodward's food floor was actually about 20 percent more expensive than anywhere else.

Yet it had a reputation for being the working-class department store?

Absolutely. When I realized this I started to interview all these seniors about why they went to Woodward's. First of all, it was a place where they could meet their friends and have a coffee. In those days—this was before ATMs—they cashed cheques. You could buy everything from pants to gardening supplies, but the main thing for the seniors was the free grocery delivery. They didn't have to get a taxi.

In 1983, when your active involvement began, what were you trying to do?

There was an architect from Victoria named John Nielsen, and he came to see me. I was a Downtown Eastside resident and the organizer of the Downtown Eastside Residents' Association. He had heard that I was playing around with Woodward's. Nielsen had a brother who was very active in the Canadian International Development Agency and he came up with a theory that we should try to get Woodward's as a CIDA project. This sounds crazy now but it didn't sound so crazy at the time: we could get the Downtown Eastside declared a third-world country. It wasn't that off at all. I mean we lead the nation in tuberculosis and poverty. So we worked on that for a while and then something went wrong. If I remember properly, his brother died. The next major event occurred when it became clear that Woodward's was going to close down. I made a lot of noise about the fact that it had to become an asset for the community. I convinced a guy named Randy Cook to put up enough money so that I could get together an actual proposal to give to the federal and provincial governments.

Was it going to be primarily social housing?

Social housing and retail. At that time we were looking at 400 housing units and, of course, that was controversial in itself. I can tell you that the first requirement when you're putting together a proposal for any level of government is that you have control over the land. Of course, I couldn't tie up the land because it was still an operating department store and they didn't care for the fact that I was running around talking about the store going under. It probably cost Randy $20,000, which in those days was a lot of money, to tie up the land in a returnable deposit, but that was the only way I could operate. I didn't have any access to funds at all. This was in 1986.

Going around talking about the inevitable demise of a department store that's operating wouldn't have made you the most popular guy I would imagine.

It didn't and I was often called a cockroach. A commie cockroach trying to destroy free enterprise, blah, blah, blah.

Free enterprise was doing a pretty good job of destroying itself at that point, wasn't it?

No kidding. The other thing is, in 1988 we had a conservative federal housing minister who came out here to do the ground-breaking for the Four Sisters Housing Co-op that I had developed. By the time people had moved in, Four Sisters was world famous. He utterly fell in love with it and wanted to have the grand opening. Well, we'd already had the fucking grand opening and he hadn't shown up, so I had to do it all again. The minister came and all the local media who had already covered it once, turned up again, and he was overjoyed. He sent me a bouquet of tulips. I went to Ottawa and met with him about Woodward's. He knew I could deliver, so he became our champion and he came out here again. I can't remember if he was leaving from here or not but he got on a plane very drunk and started making jokes about having a bomb and a gun. He was the federal housing minister and, of course, he lost his position. I'd been working with him for a year and was really getting somewhere.

I know you emigrated from the Southern US? Had you cut your teeth on social justice issues before you came to Canada?

I was born in Birmingham, Alabama. My dad was a sergeant in the army, my brother's a retired colonel in the Green Berets, and both of my uncles were killed in the wars. So we're completely Southern and completely military. My brother, who taught at West Point, went to Vietnam three times. He and I didn't speak for 20 years. It was awful. My mother and my brother turned me in to the FBI because they knew I was going to skip the country. I was about an hour across the border before they got there. It wasn't pleasant.

Why does this social justice thing matter so much to you? What keeps you at it?

I drink a lot of wine. I've been asked before but I have no answer for it. I don't really need to have a choice. I'm quite happy with the work I do. As I get older,

I realize some of the opportunities I may have passed up. But there's not a whole hell of a lot I would have changed.

But you knew from the start how important Woodward's was to that community. The fact that its closing was seen as a betrayal meant that it had to be re-imagined as a space that the community could take advantage of?

I think you're dead right. But let me add a couple of other things. The first thing is, what happens if you don't do what you need to do? If I didn't intervene in Woodward's there wasn't going to be anything for that community. It was going to be a symbol of gentrification. To have this symbol that we all loved—and Woodward's was a very egalitarian place to be—go down was something I don't think the neighbourhood would have easily recovered from. Here's another thing. DERA was a very democratic organization and I was always getting egged on to keep working and not give up on Woodward's. I got into doing housing because of a major battle. When I took over the organization they had just started to try to close down this liquor store at Main and Hastings. It was devastating to this community because, at that time, all the problems involved alcohol. Drunks from all over the Lower Mainland would come to that liquor store because they would sell to you. I actually had a picture of a guy crawling out of the store with a gallon of red wine. So we all got together and we were finally able to win the closure of that liquor store. At the next meeting someone got up and said, 'What are they going to do to pay us for the shit that we took all these years?' Someone said, 'They should pay us back in housing'. So a motion was put forward that I would go out and get housing and, believe it or not, I did within about two months. I started working on my first co-operative and built it. I think it opened around '84 or '85.

Is housing the key down there?

It is. I put together a little housing project for young people that I called Hip Hop. It stood for, 'Housing is priority in honing our potentials'. What I meant was you can put people in detox, or you can put them in university; they come home at night and home is an alley or a room in a single room occupancy hotel with no lock on the door. Or you're a woman trying to improve your life and you're on a floor with 25 guys sharing one toilet and your door doesn't lock. Things are not going to get better without proper housing. That's a very tricky thing too; what is the proper housing type? Sometimes you have to think not just of the needs of a particular person. For instance, the greatest need down here, everyone will tell you, is for single people. Almost half of the social housing units at Woodward's are for families. The reason for that is we have to think on the level of who's going to protect our community? If we're putting in older single guys or single people who have a lot of difficulties, they're not going to be able to advance the interests of that community. But I can guarantee you mothers are not going to let their children's lives be in danger. They're going to be the ones to make sure things are safe, that people live up to the deals that they've made. So we really want to have mothers in there, not just single guys. And the single guys behave much better if there are women and children around.

So what you want to establish is a sense of community that is also a functioning society?
Absolutely. And you know what also does that? When a guy who's been living in a 10 x 10 room for 15 years on welfare gets a self-contained unit that he can furnish, make his own and be proud of, in a brand new building, in a famous place like Woodward's, surrounded by women and children. He's going to invite his daughter over, who he hasn't seen in 25 years, because he couldn't bring her to the SRO. She'd probably get assaulted by 10 guys in the hallway. So there are all kinds of ramifications for good housing in the mix between families and singles.

Were you surprised at the extraordinary success the project has met with so far, especially the speed with which the units sold? On that site, there is an unusual social experiment going on.
Yes, but I know how popular Woodward's is for people, what it means and the depth of feeling they have toward it. But going in and spending 250,000 bucks to buy a little unit in there was a huge challenge. I think the design was excellent and I also think that Bob Rennie did an amazing job selling them. The Woodward's advertising campaign was one of the most brilliant campaigns I've ever seen. They came up with this slogan, 'Be Bold or Move to Suburbia.' What does this say to the cool dude? I've got to move to Surrey because I don't have the guts to buy into Woodward's? Fuck you, I've got the guts. It was a straight out challenge to people's coolness.

Elsewhere you've described the Woodward's project as 'a sonnet to inclusivity'. My sense is that you are optimistic that this fairly radical social experiment is going to work?
I'm pretty honest about how I present things. I went to Turino to represent Vancouver for the Olympics and the slideshow I brought had people shooting up and everything else. It showed the problems we're dealing with. So I wouldn't shy away from telling the truth about it. But I've already had the mixed-income co-op experiment with the Four Sisters and it's been there for 20 years. There are 19 different language groups in there and it works. You have a microcosm of the planet right here in the Downtown Eastside and we want it to be an example of how people can work together in peace and harmony.

What is the potential downside? There are those who would suggest that this is just the first—and pretty dramatic—foot in the door for gentrification. Even the height of the buildings changes the profile of Gastown as well. Are those legitimate complaints or fears?
They're legitimate fears but they're not based on knowledge. Here's the thing. I was speaking at city hall about this a couple of days ago and a woman who actually was at DERA before I was got up and said she opposes Woodward's; she opposes having a food floor there, she opposes employment for people, she opposes the university being there because it would bring students into the neighbourhood and she doesn't want any new businesses to start up because she thinks it will squeeze out the little businesses that are here now. But here's the flaw to all of that. Is the building too tall? Well, not for my taste but other people might not like it that much. But there's going to be 450 or so low-income people living in there and right now there's employment. We've got Blade Runners working on the site right now; I'm looking out the window at them. And we have agreements with the retail components that they will hire locally. We could

have had a building that was seven stories tall and it would have had 400 con-dominium units, period. That's initially what had been approved. So I would ask the people who oppose this, what have they done to advance social housing? Where is one unit that any of the critics have ever built? The answer is none.

Let's talk a bit about the politics of necessity. You were a pretty vociferous critic of the Olympics and by not speaking out against it, you made it clear that you decided it was more important to cut a deal that got you more social housing? Is that a fair way of seeing how it came down?

Yes, as a matter of fact, I did come out and support the Olympics during the referendum. I got 200 units at Woodward's out of it from a province that did not do any social housing at that time. We got those 200 units out of thin air. I got a promise, through the Olympics, of more social housing and of protecting people from being evicted because of the Olympics, as well as local hiring and local procurement. I have no ideological hatred of the Olympics, or anything else for that matter. I don't have an ideological hatred for rich people, you know? But because I've almost always worked with nothing, I've had to take what I can get, and Woodward's is better than anything I could have imagined. Anything. The fact that we're going to have a very tall building here is a symbol.

So Woodward's is an emblem again but for a different kind of social experiment.

That's right. And it's a great victory with the sign coming back and all that. There are hundreds of rank-and-file Downtown Eastsiders, who worked their asses off to get us to this point, who came up and spoke at the city and went to hundreds of meetings over the years. So it infuriates me when people who sat with their thumb up their butts come out and say, 'This is not right.' Where were they for the last 20 years?

THE WORLD ACCORDING TO WOODPENS
John Bishop and George Haywood

John Bishop
President, Woodpens' Club

John Bishop is a native of Vancouver, and graduated from UBC in 1958 with a Bachelors in Commerce. He joined Woodward Stores Ltd. in 1961 as Manager of the Oakridge Shopping Centre. Three years later, he opened the Kamloops Woodward's store before transferring back to Vancouver, where he remained, in various posts, until 1992. Mr. Bishop retired in 1994, and is the President of the Woodpens' Club, an association of former Woodward's employees and retirees. He is also involved in local sporting organizations and is a director with the North Shore Safety Council. Mr. Bishop also volunteers with the North Shore Disability Resource Centre.

George Haywood
Vice-President, Woodpens' Club

George Haywood was born and educated in Vancouver. After graduating from Sir Winston Churchill High School, he moved to Calgary in 1960 where he joined Woodward Stores Ltd. Mr. Haywood was a born merchant, perhaps influenced by his father who was co-founder of Vancouver's famous fishing and hunting specialty store, Harkley and Haywood, located for three decades across from Woodward's. Mr. Haywood's career with Woodward's was a perfect example of Woodward's policy of promotion from within. He soon worked his way up through the ranks in the hard goods division of the company. He was transferred to new stores as they opened in Edmonton and Calgary as manager of sporting goods, toys, housewares. In the late 1970s, Mr. Haywood was promoted to Toy Buyer—traveling the world in search of toys for "Woodward's Wonderful Toyland." In the early 1980s he became the Merchandise Manager of Woodward's Toy Division for BC and Alberta. Mr. Haywood helped to make Woodward's toy division the highest volume for department stores in the country.

JOHN *Woodpens stands for Woodward's Pensioners. They're actually just Woodward's retirees. It used to be for retirees and people with 20 years service or more. Because the company closed down in 1993, we weren't getting any new members. So we've opened it up to anybody who worked there—part-time, full-time, or whatever. The membership is about 640, but they're dying like flies right now. George is in charge of membership.*

GEORGE At one time we had 10,000 employees, including all the part-timers in 30 stores.

More than that. I think an awful lot of lawyers and doctors came to Woodward's as part-time employees while they were going to university. I'm still running into young people who used to work in my departments. You can't talk to any Vancouver family that hasn't had some connection with Woodward's. In their past, they've got an aunt or uncle, a niece or nephew, a son or a daughter, or a wife who worked for Woodward's when they went to school. My mom and dad were loyal shoppers. My mom and I would take the bus downtown, get off at Georgia and Granville and hit the Bay; go down to Spencer's, which is now Sears Tower and Simon Fraser; and then walk down the street to Woodward's. That would be our shopping trip. Then we'd jump on the streetcar and go home. Woodward's was the byword for most Vancouverites.

When I was a little kid we used to go to Spencer's downtown because they had the best Christmas windows. They were incredible. And then we went to Woodward's for the toy department.

The store started on Main Street, in 1892, then moved to Abbott and Hastings in 1903. It was truly a Western Canadian company. Mr. Woodward had a fire back in his original store in Ontario, so he came out here with his eight kids to try and figure out what he was going to do for the rest of his life.

One of the things that made the store special was that we probably had the best staff and the best service. Our policy was promotion from within; if you started out in the gas station you pretty much ended up there. So you knew everything there was to know about the gas station. The part-time staff was the same. We used to laugh at the Bay and Eaton's where you started out in sporting goods and they transferred you to ladies wear and then to housewares. Their staff knew a little bit about everything and nothing about anything. Our service was the best but our selection wasn't terribly high end. We catered to a mom and dad with two kids.

I think the people of Vancouver grew to love Woodward's because our target market was the average, middle-income, blue-collar family. That was the lion's share of the market. Eaton's was looking for a little bit higher niche.

They also didn't have the hard goods that we had. We were famous for our fishing ware and our plumbing and hardware. I don't think the Bay and Eaton's could say that. They were more fashion-oriented.

The middle-line department store is what they used to call it. Mr. Woodward opened the store in 1892 mainly with hard goods. He was an outfitter to the Klondike gold miners. Then there were the catalogues. The first ones came out in 1902, just before the new store opened in 1903 at Hastings and Abbott. The catalogue business continued until 1953 and when we had enough stores throughout the suburbs, the catalogue wasn't really needed. Today they'd probably have an internet department and online shopping.

But I started with the company in 1961 and retired in 1992. Then I went back under contract to manage a store while they were closing down. You felt you were part of the company. From day one, Charles Woodward, the founder, instilled a feeling that it was a family operation. The employees were very much a part of it. He used to acknowledge that the difference between Woodward's and other stores was that the staff were very much a part of the success of the company. We never had a union and there no attempts to form one. Why form a union if your staff are paid and get all the benefits that union employees were enjoying? I think we were also the first company to offer profit-sharing to the staff.

Then there was what we used to call "B Day." It started in the late '40s after the war. Mr. Woodward had made an offer for all the merchandise of a competitor that was going out of business. Some of our buyers said, "Sir, you're spending our budget and loading us up with a bunch of junk." So they started putting a lot of the stuff on sale for 95 cents and it become known as "95¢ Day." After the war with inflation it became $1.49 day. When we opened the doors you had to stand out of the way. The people would pour in from outside where they'd been standing in line well before the store opened. Our management was really service-oriented and visible all the time. They wanted to be seen and they had a hands-on approach. They'd be there on the floor and you would see the president just about run down by the mob. It was very, very busy. When we go into the Bay today and their staff says, "Boy, we're sure busy today," they don't know what busy is.

The windows at Christmas also brought a tremendous number of people into the store, or at least downtown. And it wasn't just the windows. Christmas was something you planned for eleven months ahead of time.

That's right. We'd be planning our buying programs and looking for the merchandise we wanted to have in the Christmas catalogue. We had Christmas boutiques throughout the store. We started trim-a-home shops and special shops, a store within a store. Shopping was an exciting experience. We felt that shoppers had to enjoy coming into our stores and seeing new merchandise presented in new ways. We were the only store to this day that ever had "Operation Wheelchair" at Christmas. We opened the store at night not to make money, but to invite people with disabilities to shop and experience something they normally wouldn't have the opportunity to do. We would have carolers strolling through the stores.

We'd be pushing people in hospital beds through the store.

Nobody there ever picked up on that. But the store was an exciting place during the Christmas season.

I also think we had the best toy department in the city.

He's not just being prejudiced. When George would go to a toy show he'd get the first appointments. Mattel would want to see him first and he would look at their packaging and their product. We had a buyer named Vern Tweed, who passed away from leukemia. He was legendary because he would tell them exactly what he thought. He never used any swear words. He'd just say, "You've got to do something with that crummy package," and they would actually stop production and make the corrections that Vern and George would suggest.

We certainly weren't the big guys but we were big enough to get respect. The Bay had four times the number of stores, so their volume was higher than ours. Sears would be the same because of the Sears Catalogue. Their volumes would be huge and, of course, they were right across Canada. We were only in two provinces but we owned the West. On a per store basis, we probably beat everybody in the country.

Woodward's and the West grew up together. When we opened the first couple of stores there were 14,000 people in Vancouver. Then the company expanded into Alberta. Vancouver was number one; Edmonton was two; and then we went to Port Alberni. That store was planned by Charles Woodward and H.R. MacMillan in the Malaspina Hotel over a bottle of scotch. MacMillan wanted him to come and open the store in Port Alberni where there was a lumber mill. Charles said, "If you close your commissary, I'll open a store." They agreed, shook on it, and that became store number three. Then Park Royal in West Vancouver—it was the first suburban shopping centre in the whole of Canada—was number four. The problems started when they decided to de-emphasize hard goods and go into more fashion merchandise. They were also dealing with the onslaught of the box stores, Canadian Tire, Toys 'R' Us, and all the competition that is so evident today. I don't think we responded fast enough. And what happened is we sold our assets.

The trouble began as soon as we did that. Then we sold the food floors and there went 40 percent of our volume, and the troubles continued.

I guess 40 percent of our business was in foods and 60 percent was in retail merchandising. The food operation was very strong. The nice thing about foods is that most people paid cash and we had the use of that cash for 30 or 60 days before we had to pay any bills. With retail merchandise a lot of people used credit. In those days, the charge account was very big compared to Visa, Mastercard or American Express. The demise of Woodward's started when we lost those assets. Company President Grant "Woodie" MacLaren, a cousin of Charles' grandson and CEO C.N. "Chunky" Woodward, was a chartered accountant and he read between the lines and could see what was happening. He warned us a few years in advance that we had to keep our inventories in line and expenses down. But we also expanded at the time when interest *rates went up to 18 percent or more. We built a $50 million warehouse and opened about four or five stores during the early '80s. Charles had died and he left the company to his two sons. One of them, William Culham Woodward, was a very colourful man who became Lieutenant Governor of British Columbia from 1941 to 1946. During the Second World War he was one of the dollar-a-year guys who donated his time to Ottawa. His brother, Percival Archibald Woodward, who was called "Puggy," ran the store.*

The problem wasn't that people weren't shopping at the store. They still came from everywhere.

It was a destination shopping trip. Woodward's had a lot of firsts. We were the first to ever have a parking lot; the first store to offer delivery; we had full-service food floors. All customers would walk out of the store with little packages neatly tied with a special handle. They packed these things for people to take home on the streetcar. We were the first ones to have a self-serve food floor. We were the first to start misting produce. We were the first store to make our own peanut butter. We owned the barbecue business. We had televisions made for Woodward's. We put the Woodward's brand on a lot of things, just as they do today on tires. We opened up extra checkouts. You didn't have to look for a sales clerk, and people were there to service you. It wasn't set up like a self-serve drug store. In the early days, when we were on Main Street, we had delivery boys with little carts who would deliver to your home. Then they went to horse-drawn wagons and eventually to the first motorized delivery truck.

I had a small replica made in China of that first delivery truck. It was dinky toy size and we sold thousands of them. But I didn't start in the toy department. I began pumping gas in 1960 and then in '65 I got transferred into sporting goods and toys. I probably hold the record for making the most mistakes in toys anybody could. I also did some good things. But the more you know, the less you know. It's hard to judge what a four-year-old is really going to be attracted to. The interesting part of the toy business is that it's always changing. There was certainly a lot of travel. I went to Hong Kong 28 times. My year started out about the 20th of January when I'd go to the toy show in Toronto. Then I'd go to Nuremburg and come back to New York. I was gone for three weeks and only home for about four days. I never saw my kids until the end of March. At one time I was responsible for about $75 million, but that was in sporting goods, toys and hardware. I think toys was about $22 million.

The downtown store was huge, somewhere between 10,000 to 15,000 square feet. One year the company sold a billion dollars worth of merchandise. I love merchandising. I love looking at the new Home Depots, Toys 'R' Us and Canadian Tire stores. It's a form of merchandising that certainly would have tested our abilities to compete. That's really the change I don't think we were ready for.

Everybody knew that we were…

…going downhill…

…heading for trouble. But it was still a surprise. I didn't think it was ever going to happen. The Woodward family was totally out of it at this point. It was the guys from the Bay who were running the place.

These people from the Bay came in to run the store. I often felt they speeded up the process by design. They didn't have the true interest of Woodward's at heart, and they certainly looked after themselves in the severance packages.

It's hard to imagine you can trash a company and be on the street with a huge severance. I'm not sure how that works, but it seems to. I read about it in the paper all the time. Still, I don't know of anybody who left Woodward's because they didn't like working there. You might have quit because you didn't like your job, or you didn't want to work nights, but not because Woodward's treated you badly. We treated staff very well with a profit-sharing plan and all that sort of stuff. We were so far ahead of the rest of them. It was a great place to work. I was there for 33 years, and I can proudly say that 31 of them were great years. The last 2 were ugly, but most people can't say they had 31 great years anywhere, so I feel fortunate. I can't remember too many days I didn't want to go to work. It was an awesome place to work.

They say only 5 percent of people who work for a living really enjoy what they do. I think many of us who worked at Woodward's were among that 5 percent. We loved getting up in the morning and going to work, to the point where we would skip holidays.

You know how good it was? I traveled with the guys from the Bay, Eaton's, Sears, and Toys 'R' Us. I had one of the few jobs in Canada where I could buy something without having to phone the boss and say, "I just found this doll and I could be going over budget a little but I think it's going to be really good, so can I do it, sir?" I didn't have to do that. If it worked out, I was in good shape; if it didn't work out so good, I was in trouble. But I didn't have to ask permission. The other guys had to do a lot of that. It was selection by committee. I was the envy of the industry in that they gave me a job to do, and they let me do it. They didn't tie my hands behind my back.

My best memory is the people. The people I worked with, the family feeling that you were part of an organization and they appreciated your contribution. Woodward's had a philosophy about customers: if you're not satisfied, bring it back. And they really meant it. I took back trailers that were bought for the purpose of going to Expo '67 in Montreal. We sold Triumph convertibles in May and they'd come back at the end of the summer. People would say, "It just isn't what I wanted," or "It didn't perform to our satisfaction," and we'd give them back their money back. Ladies would buy a dress for a special occasion and they'd come back and say, "Oh no, I never wore it," even though you could see sweat stains in the armpits. We took them back.

Ninety-nine percent of the customers thought they had a legitimate complaint. Even if the customer wasn't right, they thought they were. Our attitude was why antagonize somebody for a $20 refund and run the risk that they'll never come back? We were there to look after the customer.

FOLIO II

HISTORICAL PHOTOGRAPHS

2

GUIDING PRINCIPLES

IN MAY 2003, two months after purchasing the Woodward's site from the provincial government, the city of Vancouver began an extensive public consultation process of community visioning workshops, an ideas fair, open houses and meetings to understand the needs and desires of the communities directly affected by Woodward's. The city retained the Co-Design Group, an informal association of architect/artists based in Vancouver and Calgary, to conduct community events for the design of urban spaces and to engage the community and public in visualizing what could be achieved at the Woodward's site. Founded in 1979, the group has directed over 300 public design workshops for the revitalization of inner-city areas and small towns throughout British Columbia and Alberta, resulting in projects grounded in the context of local community life, economical, and humane in scale and detailing.

For the Woodward's redevelopment, the Co-Design process aimed to unite diverse communities in and around the Downtown Eastside under a common vision, provide a positive forum for dialogue to overcome the controversy and conflicts associated with redeveloping the site and ultimately raise the vitality of the affected communities.

To reach community members, brochures and posters about the Woodward's public consultation process were distributed to all the single-room occupancy hotels and to organizations operating in and around the Downtown Eastside. The Co-Design Group began the process with a series of short community visioning workshops lasting two to four hours at various locations around Woodward's, including the Carnegie Community Centre, the Chinese immigrant service agency S.U.C.C.E.S.S., Strathcona Community Centre, the Portland Hotel, and the Central Vancouver Public Library. The workshops required no preparation and the only confirmed programmatic element of the redevelopment was the 100 units of non-market housing. Participants were asked to visualize the daily activities and special events they wished to experience at the Woodward's project. Ideas for activities were listed along a time-line on a wide sheet of paper on the wall. When the list was complete, similar activities were grouped together.

A summary of activities and a count of their repetition in the community workshops and ideas fair were compiled on a chart called A Day in the Life of Woodward's. Using repetition to interpret community significance, the process found that participants overwhelmingly saw the Woodward's site as a place for living—a settled pedestrian community with supportive services nearby. After residential activity, strong desire was expressed for a vital community life underpinned by a public realm. Over 100 special events were suggested for the public realm. Incorporating economic, recreational, cultural and spiritual activities into the project was also seen as a priority.

The participants broke into groups and described a vision of what they would be doing at the redeveloped Woodward's. They imagined moving about the place, traced their preferred walking routes in the neighbourhood on a map, and considered details for people with disabilities. A Co-Design architect/artist first drew in the people conducting their activities, and then added furniture and the surrounding physical environment. As the drawings developed, participants saw the effects of their ideas and how the project could be related to their own lives, giving them meaningful access to the design process. The resulting scene drawn with coloured pens was annotated with words to describe the sounds, smells, lighting, timing, range of activities, and relationships between the activities. The participants listed the main features of their vision on a rating sheet beside the drawing. The completed drawings were placed on display tables around the room, and participants circulated and rated each vision's features, typically achieving consensus. Drawings from previous community visioning workshops were displayed to one side, but were not rated outside the session in which they were produced.

The workshops generated public interest and built momentum for the main event, a full-day ideas fair conducted at the Chinese Cultural Centre. As in the workshops, participants were invited to imagine a day at the redeveloped Woodward's site. They gathered in groups and, with their Co-Design architect/artist, and toured the site to look for qualities that would support their future activities. They imagined arriving, parking, walking to the activity, and doing the activity. They also considered their preferred directional orientation, views, colours, night-light, and sounds for the activities. Returning to the hall for lunch, the Co-Design architect/artist sketched the group's vision. Along with the drawings from the previous workshops, the new visions were displayed and rated by the ideas fair participants.

A broad consensus emerged from the workshops and ideas fair that the area would be made more vibrant by redeveloping Woodward's. The sessions generated a total of 50 drawings containing 461 features. Specific visions ranged from a rooftop sweat lodge to ground floor retail stores with a job-skills training centre. The participants expressly did not want drinking establishments nor a visible police presence at Woodward's.

Several key themes emerged for the future uses of Woodward's. The ratings demonstrated support for self-contained, flexible, and efficient residential units with a variety of unit types that could accommodate families, singles and the disabled. A mix of both market and non-market housing also received high ratings. Envisioning Woodward's as the hub and connector of local social services, participants wanted a childcare, a general resource centre with access to phones and computers, a health information centre, a library, a community kitchen, public meeting rooms, and space for non-profit offices. Participants desired employment services for local residents emphasizing skills retraining and upgrading and developing small businesses. The most popular commercial and retail use for the building was a grocery store or public food market, which was missing in the area. A grocery outlet in conjunction with mixed retail use would not only meet the needs of local residents, but attract shoppers and tourists and generate economic activity. Preferred health care activities emphasized complementary and alternative treatment and holistic services for both physical and spiritual well-being. SFU's School for the Contemporary Arts and the relocation of Vancouver city hall were desirable institutional components of a redeveloped Woodward's. Essential to the project would be recreational facilities available to both residents and the public, such as a gym, swimming pool, bowling alley and rooftop gardens, and a central public atrium or courtyard. Cultural uses, including art galleries, theatres, and artists' studios, were highly rated with preference expressed for multi-functional cultural performance spaces. There was strong desire to retain and promote the history of the building and the surrounding communities.

Able to quickly and effectively convey the ideas and visions of the involved communities, the drawings were displayed in a series of open houses to inform the public, solicit further feedback and unite the communities in a common vision. In November 2003, the city set up a Woodward's hotline and opened the 'W' Room Presentation Centre on the ground level of the existing building off Hastings Street. The room was used for community events and for providing updates on the Woodward's project. The Co-Design Group compiled a report of the visioning process with drawings and

a summary of the responses and ratings, which informed the city of community values and preferences and helped them produce design criteria for planners and architects. From this report, city planners derived guiding principles for the programming and design of the Woodward's project.

The city of Vancouver endorsed the following guiding principles in the Request for Proposals for the redevelopment of the Woodward's site. The Woodward's project must:

- Be financially viable and self-sustaining
- Be developed in a timely manner
- Include at least 100 units of non-market housing
- Be open and inclusive
- Be an urban revitalization catalyst
- Maintain and enhance the existing community
- Incorporate the talents, visions and desires of the
  downtown eastside community
- Incorporate the talents and ideas of people throughout the city
- Provide employment opportunities for local residents in the construction and
  operation of the new building
- Provide opportunities and create synergies for local owners and businesses
- Incorporate user group involvement in the design process
- Celebrate the symbolism of the historic building (eg. The lighted 'w', the façade,
  christmas displays, etc.)
- Be environmentally sustainable
- Create a lively street front (with animation at grade)
- Not be a 'black box' (eg. Accommodate and encourage pedestrian circulation, etc.)
- Provide appropriate parking
- Be accessible
- Take advantage of heritage opportunities
- Respond to the local, physical context

The city continued to consult the public after the community visioning workshops and ideas fair. After city council received a recommendation from the Woodward's Steering Committee on which developer to select in September 2004, a special council meeting was held to hear from members of the public. As the design of the selected project was further developed, a community advisory committee representing area residents, business stakeholders, and community advocates ensured ongoing public engagement. Council held another public hearing after the schematic design had been finalized and an application for development permit was made in November 2005. By March 2006, community consensus on the design of Woodward's had clearly been reached when no one from the public spoke at a hearing regarding two final project details. The last public open house for the Woodward's redevelopment in April 2006 unveiled the final scheme to the local communities.

QUALITY OF LIFER
Larry Beasley

Larry Beasley
Co-Director of Planning
City of Vancouver (1986-2006)

Larry Beasley is a former co-director of planning for the city of Vancouver. He is the Distinguished Practice Professor of Planning at UBC, School of Community and Regional Planning, and he is the founding principal of Beasley and Associates, an international planning consultant practice. He also chairs the National Advisory Committee on Planning, Design and Realty of Ottawa's National Capital Commission.

Over a span of 20 years, his key contributions in Vancouver included innovative land use and transportation plans followed by detailed design and careful development management that have dramatically reshaped the downtown core along New Urbanism lines.

Mr. Beasley is a Fellow of the Canadian Institute of Planners. In 1996, the United Nations recognized his work as one of the "world's 100 best planning practices"; the Royal Architectural Institute of Canada conferred on him its 2003 Medal of Excellence as "Advocate for Architecture." In 2004, he was made a Member of the Order of Canada for playing a leading roll in transforming Vancouver's downtown into a vibrant, livable urban community.

I was born in Georgia and raised in Las Vegas, Nevada. I went to school in Arizona until I was 17 and then came here to school.

What was it that made you choose Vancouver?

It was the Queen Elizabeth Theatre. I used to listen late at night to odd radio stations when I was in Arizona, and somehow I got the CBC. I'll never know to this day how I did it. But there would be these concerts from the Queen Elizabeth Theatre and I thought, "God, you mean on the North American continent there's a place named after the Queen of England? I've got to go see this place." I did and one thing led to another. I met my partner in life, and decided this is where we wanted to stay.

The CBC and the Queen Elizabeth are unusual reasons to relocate to the West Coast. The reasons people normally give is sex, drugs and rock-and-roll.

I was more of a conservative guy. I really wanted to see it. I came and stayed at the Hotel Vancouver and just fell in love with the city. With my background it seemed urban, although at the time it wasn't considered a very urban place. But it was a beautiful setting and I fell in love with Canadians. That's the other thing; I totally fell in love with the Canadian way of life and with the philosophy of Canadians.

As you moved up the urban planning ladder—which you did rather quickly—was there already a sense that Vancouver was a special place? It's an interesting city. It seems to have an effective and layered development sector. At the same time, you have this sensitive and ethical dimension operating on the social planning side of things.

It is relatively unusual in North American cities. To some degree, the civic agenda a little bit more like European cities. But the genesis of it really went back to that Reform Council that took power in 1972. It had a very modern, forward-looking agenda. I think they established the first social planning department in the nation, if not in North America. They were dedicated to public involvement. Before that you couldn't even get into city hall. They went in with a strong effort to stave off the decline of communities that we were starting to see throughout North America. There was a famous program at that time in Canada called the Neighbourhood Improvement Program. It invested a lot of money in inner-city neighbourhoods, which started initiatives here in Vancouver and Toronto. This national program probably had a lot to do with causing our cities to go a different way than American cities. Our cities kept building and building. The planning department established a very strong presence in city government, even to the point of building an accord with the engineering department, which is very unusual in cities. Those two interests are usually at odds with one another. The other thing you had was a long period of very consistent leadership on the planning side of things. We were also pretty lucky because Expo '86 created a lot of energy and a fair amount of wealth. We were getting in capital but we were never an industrial city, so the blight that comes with that in other other cities was never there. Vancouver was the founding place for Greenpeace. That's symbolic of the fact that there's always been a consciousness about the environment. I would even say we built a strong social movement here, favouring quality of life, neighbourliness and those aspects of urbanism which ended up being things that cities were later trying to do better all over North America. They became almost a foundation for our economic development, because we were what Sir Peter Hall calls one of those cities built on the service and tourism economy, and those cities have to have quality of life. That's how they sell themselves. So you had this economic drive that emerged when the natural resource sector was beginning to go down. You had a coming-together of this economic, cultural and social drive. I will say that in the last four or five elections there was no debate about the planning agenda. The first thing that every party did was to declare their support for the planning department and the agenda that we were pursuing. That was a strong enabling thing. If you're a planner and you don't have politicians working with you, you can only go so far.

Did you develop a vision fairly quickly? Because of the prominent role the city plays in policy development, did you see the potential for not only continuing that vision of the city, but also in augmenting and highlighting certain aspects of it?

Definitely. Part of it was the wonderful foundation through the time of Ray Spaxman. A lot of the right philosophy of urbanism was enshrined, not only in our regulatory regime and our policies, but also in the attitude of the whole organization. It was a time of big opportunity. Also everyone here is from somewhere else. It's a place of immigrants and people are very well-travelled. I think statistically, we're more widely travelled than in many other cities. People right across the spectrum of environmental professions were progressively creative in thinking about cities. Taking that kind of energy, and combining it with the fact that we've had a pretty wide conversation going on with our citizens, and the mutual learning that's occurring there, meant that we could do things that other cities are still struggling to do. Our 'Living First' strategy downtown is a vivid illustration of that. Remember, we generated that strategy in the late '80s, when in many parts of North America, living downtown was actually prohibited. There was a consciousness here that allowed us to restructure our entire downtown from a policy and a regulatory point of view, and at the same time open it up to opportunities which the development community jumped into. Another thing that's important to note is that what we are talking about here is a collaboration among people who don't normally collaborate.

You seem to have development high-rollers, the Bob Rennies and Ian Gillespies, working with a social service agency like the Portland Hotel Society. These communities are often at loggerheads.

I think that's part of it, but I'll tell you something else. I think there is an understanding of a formula here that is based on interest. It's in the way that the government has framed up what I call the privilege of development and not the opportunity of development. If you make a contribution to the commonwealth of the city, then a development opportunity opens up for you. Our job has been to understand economic development as well as the community has understood it. By the same token, the development community—through dialogue on hundreds of different projects—has to understand the needs of the public in the city. Then we discovered something that has proven to be very powerful for everyone; when we worked together to create the glue of the city through the public realm, we actually created products that were more attractive to consumers. Ironically, this is now proving to be a problem we'll have to solve because that attractiveness has also caused skyrocketing prices. We need to figure out another way to handle middle-income affordability in our city and develop what I'd like to call a third sector of housing.

In a way, the Woodward's project seems to be inevitable in this city because there's a pretty interesting social experiment going on there.

Yes, and it involves two things which are not related but parallel. On the one hand, you have this consciousness about the benefits of mixed-use and social use, not just among policy people and developers, but among the general public as consumers. That recognition has a long tradition here. The 20 percent social housing policy in our best neighbourhoods has been with us since the late '80s. That's vested deeply. But the other side of it is the magic of the personalities. In scale and complexity, this project did go beyond most of the hundreds of others that you might say were similar in their involvement with mixed-use. This was a complex project and it took everyone stretching their consciousness. What really allowed it to happen was the magic of the personalities who were prepared to come together. First of all, you had to have a developer who would undertake some pretty risky stuff. You had to have a sympathetic city council and we just elected a particularly progressive one, in a city where even the conservative city councillors were quite progressive. One of the strongest councillors happened to be a person who had been struggling with this very issue for 15 to 20 years. Jim Green provided extraordinary leadership as we went through. Then people within the bureaucracy had to step beyond policy in many cases and had to be with it spiritually, and they were. It wasn't a hard sell for people in the bureaucracy to see what was at stake here. In the wonderful story of Vancouver we had this crisis sitting in the Downtown Eastside, and we knew we had to be more clever. It was imperative for us as government, as private developers, and as community people to be more clever. All that was glued together by personalities who were prepared to do business in a way that perhaps they wouldn't normally.

And you had a gifted and sensitive architect in Gregory Henriquez. I think it was Ian Gillespie who said the Westbank/Henriquez partnership was the right mix of personalities to make it work.

Absolutely right. That's what I'm trying to say. People talk about the systems that create results, or about trends that create results. And a lot of that was at play here. But personalities also create results. Take Gregory, a young architect thrusting himself forward, and his father, one of the great architects of the country. Now Gregory is establishing a strong, independent identity and this project comes along and offers him a magic opportunity for that. You get Bob Rennie who is an absolute genius at the other end of the process. Our years of work could have fallen flat if the consumer didn't come. Rennie found a way not only to get the consumer to come, but to stand in line for two days.

Were you surprised by the response to the market housing side of it?

I wasn't, but that's only because this is my life and I've been watching the consumer changes here. I wasn't surprised mostly because of the relative affordability of these units compared to other products out there at the time. As I look back now, it was very, very reasonable. It may have been almost too reasonable. I know that Ian Gillespie has had to struggle with the numbers as construction prices have gone up. The system we have here, which you're starting to see elsewhere in the country but which was really pioneered here, allows people to buy off a plan, years before occupancy. It has had been wonderfully beneficial for the economy because those huge collapses in the market that you get from overbuilding in other cities haven't happened here. You just don't build a building unless consumers put their money down. The downside is that it can catch a developer.

Was the Downtown Eastside a special problem? You said that everybody had to raise the bar on their intelligence and social consciousness. Did all the stakeholders have to rise to the occasion because it was such a unique place?

Yes. But here's the surprising thing, and it will sound like an apology. When I compare the Downtown Eastside with similar areas in Regina, Toronto and Montreal, or in New York and San Diego, the comparisons are fairly similar. You'll hear that it's the poorest and worst postal code in the nation. But you can find these areas in every one of our cities, and it has to do with the fact that our senior governments have not really been responsible for 25 years. The economic shifts have been happening across the country. Our population has been aging and is leaving a lot of people behind. The thing that makes it so profoundly contradictory here is that right next door, literally sometimes across the street, you see this unbelievable prosperity.

So the optics are that much more dramatic?

Yes, I think the contrast hits us all very personally. I can tell you it has hit me that way. I feel one of the great failures of my time as a planner was not recognizing this whole alcohol and drug addiction problem. It snuck up on us. The tendency was for that to be focused and clustered in one area because of the prosperity in all the other areas. We had already decided as a city that we were in a crisis, and that crisis was more vivid here than other places. We felt so confident about our ability to manage the urban system in a positive way and then we have had this dramatic failure right under our noses. That's what created the dynamic atmosphere at city hall that allowed us to begin breaking a lot of rules and policies. Everyone realized this would be a catalyst to help change that. It would be a catalyst that would also be compatible with the sitting population.

It wasn't a question then of moving the resident population out. This is why housing was obviously critical because you had to get these people into places where they could develop some sense of self-respect.

That's why there had to be a significant component of non-market housing in the project. We had struggled—and I remember about three rounds through the years—with schemes where we didn't think we could get social housing into the equation. If it was in private ownership, no one was obliged to put in social housing. And every one of those faced a very hostile community. They just saw it as patent gentrification, and they were right. It was patent gentrification. So then the land found its way, through a series of dramas, into public ownership. I think Gordon Campbell realized that these were people from very different camps, but putting politics aside, something had to be done. So that created a possibility for the project to be catalytic. That's why the Portland Hotel Society came into it. These are not Casper Milquetoasts, as my grandmother used to say. These are aggressive advocates for housing, and advocates for a group of people that are totally disenfranchised.

They're pretty hard-nosed and they seem to wield an enormous amount of power?
Yes, and part of the magic of this project was that they were an integral part of it. In the generative time, they helped to set the nature of it. The other equally important part of the project was that it created a public place. If it was just housing, it wouldn't have a social development dimension. Creating what will ultimately be a very strong neighbourhood centre that invites in the existing community, as well as the new community, is very important.

Could it become just an experimental island where this extraordinary thing is going on? Does it have to leech into other parts of the Downtown Eastside? Has it got any spin-offs that aren't simply about gentrification, that rather are about the constant re-creation of the community?
I'm confident that will happen. The reason it will happen is that there are already landowners down there just waiting. You had this black hole across the street, so are you going to invest there? Of course you're not. Now you see this huge investment, public, private and philanthropic, all coming together, not just one with one government but with various governments. You see something that is really a commitment, so you think, 'this is the time to think about my site as well'. At the same time, you have a well-functioning mechanism within the city itself to ensure that there will be a mixture of both market and non-market activity going on. Just to step back a second, in the American literature, which is where we have learned most about this kind of planning, there are two models: one is gentrification, where basically a new development comes in, people are displaced, and there's a lot of speculative value created, and the other is ghettoization.

Which is what Pruitt-Igoe was, wasn't it?
Yes, and the banks draw a red line around it. They used to have maps and if you were on that map, you couldn't get a mortgage. They wouldn't invest. Unfortunately, because America been so huge in our consciousness, I think there have been a lot of assumptions that it's the model for these difficult inner-city situations. Maybe I can say this with the clarity of an immigrant, but this country can have a different model—a model of social integration. We've done it in other areas. We have very progressive policies not just here, but in other

cities in our country too. It means that we can have revitalization with a social integration approach. Ultimately there can be a mix and it can work.

Initially you didn't favour the Westbank/Henriquez proposal, or at least you were nervous about the scale?

I always look at projects in layers. In my initial reaction to the project, I was very confident in and supportive of the basic formula. I was also very comfortable with the formula of one of the other proponents. I was somewhat ambivalent about the scale, and the second part of it for me was the form. I had some difficulties with it. At one point, the towers were going to be up around 400 feet, which was not, in my opinion, an optimum urban form. But I had even more problems with the alternative scenario, and when I tested in my own way the potentiality to sculpt and shape that form, I found a design team that was totally open-minded. Gregory is a brilliant designer, but he was prepared to listen. Ian Gillespie was the same way. I said to them, "I think you need to bring the scale down and you need to have more individual building elements." They ultimately bought that approach. So I have to say, from nearly the beginning, I felt pretty confident in the way we were going. But there was one period in which we could have gone with either proposal and I felt that we could have made a project. Would we have made a project which is this profoundly good? Probably not, and it's because these other ingredients were brought into the mix. It might have been a nice supper but it wasn't going to be haute cuisine.

Are you unhappy that so little of the original buildings could be saved? I think everyone was surprised to find out how structurally unsound the buildings were?

I'll tell you honestly. I must say, as the director of planning, I often felt I was coping with the Woodward's building. During those early years, I had a pretty profound hope that we would find a solution that could be done within the envelope of that building. One time, we were decently close, but it turned out to be economically unfeasible. Skyrocketing prices made it less and less likely all the time. Secondly, I had hoped that there could be more retention of the existing fabric of the building as new things were added in simply because there's a strong emotional connection to that building that was felt by the community, by the heritage community and, frankly, by me. But I have to say it wasn't the justification of the fabric of the building that finally swayed me. It was the realization through the evolution of the project that, in order to achieve all the objectives we really had to achieve, it just couldn't fit in that envelope. It turns out the envelope wasn't sound. The diversity of things that needed to go in there—whether it was the special needs housing, or the market housing, or some of the SFU facilities—didn't comfortably fit the envelope. Then I thought, "Alright the symbolism here is to make sure that the original building was left." That happened. But the project was always fascinating at an intellectual level because it started as a simple heritage restoration project and it ended as a city building project.

This must be one of the largest redevelopment projects, at 1.2 million square feet, in the country?

I'm never good at saying what's the largest. What I can say is I suspect it's the most comprehensive project going on in the country. You'll see more complex projects being built because we learned how to do it. If you go to other cities, you'll find there are developers who do housing, developers who do offices, developers that do institutional, but no matter what they say, they're never going to mix. They're not good at putting partnerships together, and the result shows on the ground. You also have planners who are still into that old-fashioned idea of separating things out from one another so those kinds of projects just don't happen. Here they do happen.

Was there a point where you despaired that anything significant could be done on the Woodward's site?

My real despair was that something would be pushed forward that wasn't good enough.

I guess you wouldn't have wanted to be the person who said no to any project that was finally going to develop a site that seemed to be the ninth circle of hell?

Exactly. By the same token, there was more than one scenario of Woodward's when I was up at council. I was gritting my teeth because I wasn't happy with the shape of it, and I knew it wouldn't do what it needed to do. So you can imagine what it was like when this project started to take on life through the leadership of Larry Campbell and particularly Jim Green. Then we got this magic moment when the land shifted over to city ownership.

I guess you'll feel pretty good when that thing is finished and they hoist the 'W' back up on the building?

We've been lucky here in Vancouver. We've had a lot of defining projects, but this one is more symbolic than most because of the continuing struggle. We're not anywhere near the finish. The struggle remains to bring the same creative energy and prosperity from the rest of the core into that area without negatively impacting the existing community while simultaneously delivering a social infrastructure.

Jim Green talked about it being like a rugby ball that slipped out of his hands three times. It was the eel of projects, wasn't it?

It was just the complexity of it. You've got to realize that it sits within a set of political contradictions that are deep in the city. We've come to understand this area because it's an area where there are different classes fighting one another, an area where everyone feels terribly at risk. So how do you make anything happen in a city that's dedicated to pluralism and to public involvement? How do you make anything happen when you have that situation? What was so special about this project is the creativity that came from the architect, from the political people, from the people putting the formula of the building together, and from the city people to find a solution that actually responded sufficiently to all those interests that they would dare see themselves co-existing. That was very special. Going back to my previous point, in the final analysis, it's not trends that actually make change happen. It's the personalities. For the people who were involved, what they did was courageous and it continues to be courageous.

RULERS OF ENGAGEMENT
Michael Flanigan

Michael Flanigan
Director of Real Estate Services
City of Vancouver

Michael Flanigan is a graduate of UBC with a degree in Urban Land Economics and Finance. For the past 17 years, Mr. Flanigan has specialized in real estate development in the Lower Mainland and has been involved in over $2 billion of commercial and residential mixed-use projects.

After five years as Director of Leasing and Vice President for Hong Kong based Henderson Development, Mr. Flanigan joined the city of Vancouver as the Deputy Director of Real Estate Services. After six years with the city, Mr. Flanigan took over as Director of Real Estate Services in 2006 and is responsible for the strategic planning and financial management of the city's $2.6 billion Property Endowment Fund.

Mr. Flanigan currently oversees a number of the city's major real estate interests including the Woodward's project and is working closely VANOC on project oversight for the delivery of the 2010 Olympic Village Project. Mr. Flanigan is also extensively involved in Community Planning and Financing Vancouver's growth. Working closely with Vancouver's development community, Mr. Flanigan is committed to maximizing the delivery of community amenities, park space, public infrastructure, childcare service, and heritage building retention while commensurately facilitating economically successful real estate developments for the private sector.

When the city bought Woodward's, there was a lot of mistrust and, obviously, a community that was boiling over. So our first task was to come out with a set of guiding principles that were firmly rooted in the community—from, by and for the community. We did a whole series of workshops and developed what we called "The Woodward's Road Show," where our technical staff and I would go out and meet with anyone, at any time, who wanted a meeting—individuals, business groups, charities, non-profits, activists, housing associations, you name it. We had hundreds of them. We gathered their feedback which was fed into a community visioning exercise around Woodward's. It was a very powerful weekend because it was open and we had thousands of people come through.

We had a whole series of architects—there must have been close to a dozen—that were the hands drawing the visions and the aspirations of the people who attended. Those visioning boards absolutely served to inform the process that unfolded as we filtered through those ideas. It set the roadmap for how we would move forward so that everyone's interests were respected in the process.

There was a point where people weren't having meetings; there was no discussion, there was no public vision. The idea prevailed that backroom deal-making was going on and that the local interests of the residents were being sold out. There was a lot of hyperbole in the community and it fed on itself to the point where it erupted in the seizure of the building, the "Woodward's Squat."

This was all going on at the same time when funding for non-market housing and support services dried up. You had huge facilities like Riverview closing, and a lot of those patients were being left to their own means in New Westminster and in downtown Vancouver. It was all done with good intentions but, unfortunately, it was a perfect storm.

It's very interesting because we wouldn't have had much of a response unless we came out with a coordinated marketing plan for how we were going to take this project forward. There was absolutely no interest from the private sector to participate in Woodward's. They'd look at you like you were crazy. Their attitude was, 'I'm making so much money building glass condos in Yaletown and around the city, why would I ever come down there?' And then the news story broke about people in the community making threatening calls to developers. We responded with a very well-coordinated effort. We convened a steering committee comprised of the department heads for planning, real estate, engineering, social planning, cultural affairs, facilities design and housing. All the department heads were on this committee so that we could make sure there was a coordinated and seamless effort within the departments.

These were all the respective interests that folded into this project, which we had to break down, component by component, to make sure that everyone was being brought along, that they were informed and part of the process. One of the first things we did was to come up with a set of guiding principles that we ended up taking to council and endorsing for the public. They were the rules of engagement.

I don't know how many council briefings we did, but I'd always start with these guiding principles. They all carried the same weight: it was to be financially viable and self-sustaining; it was to be developed in a timely manner; it was to include at least the 100 units of non-market housing that were part of the original transaction—we ended up with 200 at the end of the day; it was to be open and inclusive; it was to be a catalyst for urban revitalization; it was to maintain and enhance the existing community; it was to incorporate the talents, visions, and desires of the Downtown Eastside community—this was echoed time and time again at our community workshops; it was to play an important role in the economic revitalization of the community; it was to provide employment opportunities for local residents in both the construction and operation of the building; and it was to provide opportunities and create synergies for local owners and businesses—all boats rise on a lifting tide. We were concerned to incorporate user-group involvement throughout the design process and it was very important that it be done in an open and transparent way. We also wanted to celebrate the symbolism of the important building—that's the 'W' sign, the building facades, the Christmas displays, the things that were near and dear to people's hearts when they remembered Woodward's. And very importantly, we wanted it to be a model of environmental sustainability. We wanted to create a lively street front with animation at grade to bring back the pedestrian customer to the area, not just a black box. We wanted to accommodate and encourage pedestrian circulation in and through the site—you'll see that in Gregory's design. We wanted to provide appropriate parking, not an oversupply, but certainly enough to accommodate the demands the project would create. It had to be accessible, and by that, we meant universally-designed accessibility for people with handicaps. It was to take advantage of heritage opportunities. Having been developed in numerous phases—starting in 1903, then 1908, 1918, 1920, 1921, 1923—it's unbelievable how this building morphed. And, finally, it had to be respectful of the heritage context around it, which was Gastown.

It was extremely important for us to take these guiding principles and merge them with the vision that came out of the Ideas Fair. We had some very difficult decisions to deal with even before we went out to talk to the developers. They centred around how to deal with the commercial business interests around the project, the non-profits that expressed a desire to be involved, and the low-income community that would be living at and using Woodward's. We had to select a non-market housing partner that was going to manage and operate these units and help us in the design for the first 100 units, which became 200 units. At the end of the day, we got two non-market housing sponsors.

The Portland Hotel Society will manage 125 singles units and the Affordable Housing Society will oversee the 75 family units. Housing was absolutely key. We knew that if we were going to bring the community back to livability, if we were going to encourage some sense of normality, that Woodward's was the core in the hub. Woodward's was a challenge for two reasons. One, it had failed up to that date because it couldn't sustain a commercial, viable presence in the community. Two, we were pushing the envelope to have market and non-market housing built together for the first time in Vancouver. A lot of eyebrows went up. We brought the development community in very early because we recognized that we wanted to transfer the development risk from the city to the private sector. At one point there was some political pressure for us to actually be the developer of Woodward's, to get into the business of retailing condos. We're in the retail business already, but in a much larger scale. We don't get involved in housing.

One of the beautiful things about Vancouver and as any developer will tell you, one of the reasons why they like doing business here is that we understand their challenges and their risks. They don't have to educate the city about what it is to be a developer in this market. I was a developer and I was brought in from the private sector to run real estate, and we have almost an embedded private sector development firm in the city that can help embrace the challenges when these projects come along. That's been very, very good because we can quickly align the developer's needs with the city's needs, and through that alignment create a great deal of shared public equity: roughly 70 percent in the city's favour and 30 percent to the development community. That 30 percent is to mitigate their risk and it's compelling. I think it has led to the massive development that is currently underway.

At the competition stage we were excited to get the proposals, what we called 'Four Gifts' to the city, because we knew that we had projects we could work with. We could have worked with Concert or with Westbank. We were also thankful that the Millenium proposal came in because, even though their project was too massive for the community, they made it a very exciting, lively debate.

I'm 100 percent convinced that this project is going to work. I wouldn't say it if I didn't believe it. Here's why I believe that to be the case: it's based on decisions we made very early on. The first one was coming out to address the developers' fundamental concern about why they should participate in Woodward's. We had to manage their risk and we had to give them some certainty that if they came to the table, they would meet a city administration willing to work with their proposals. So we went out and hired an independent architect to come up with a set of urban design guidelines that helped to inform everyone what the redevelopment of Woodward's would be. It looked at heritage retention versus demolition, it looked at heights, density, massing. We came up with about eight options at the end of the day for developers to consider. We said, "If you guys come in under these parameters you've got a project that will go forward."

Council also made a key decision early on that was very creative. It addressed not only the concerns of the low-income community but, ironically, the concerns of the developers as well. What we did was we classified ourselves as a participating investor. We said to the successful developer, "We're going to trade you the land in return for an air space parcel that you're going to build at your risk, your cost, your expense, and you're going to give that back to the city in exchange for the land." So the developer gives us back an amount of square footage and the value of that square footage. In this particular case, 31,500 square feet was going to land in our books at over $13 million in construction costs alone. Remember, that's for our five and a half million dollar investment. Council immediately said it was going to allocate the city's space to non-profit uses. So that created this huge volume of space that could then be programmed for community services. That gave a lot of comfort and confidence to the low-income community. We don't see this as gentrification at all. We see it as revitalization without displacement, and that is a key message we've echoed to the community.

We ended up getting 12 developers to the table, which is an amazing accomplishment, considering that at the outset, no one wanted to touch this project.

We rolled out the red carpet. I was phoning developers saying, "You guys definitely want to come to the table, it's going to be good." We cultivated that interest. We short-listed the 12 developers down to four. We decided that SFU was a critical partner in this project because it did so much to address the fundamental problem about commercial activity at grade. If we could get SFU in there for a 100,000 or 120,000 square feet, it would be a catalyst to make everything else work. SFU was very serious about committing, but they said, "We need Treasury Board approval; we need to know who the developer is; and we cannot give you any guarantees whatsoever that we are going to be able to sign a contract for a long time."

So we crafted the RFP as a two-pronged proposal and we went to the developers and said, 'You've been short-listed to do not one, but two proposals'. The challenge for the developers to solve was whether it could be done without SFU's participation. If you didn't have SFU, what would you put in? We had a proposal for a day-and-night market; we had a mix of other commercial retail; we had another large office user partnered up with Vancouver Community College. So some legitimate and bona fide interest came out of it. We could move forward with both options, so in the event that SFU was not able to deliver, we weren't back at square one again. We were down the path. Council actually awarded both projects to the same developer.

The question of SFU's involvement was complicated by the fact that the chancellor of SFU also happened to own London Drugs and had an interest in wanting to open a drug store in the project as a legitimate catalyst for bringing back retail. As a philanthropist in the Downtown Eastside, he has a vision that goes well beyond Woodward's. So it was timely that the key anchor tenant with which the developer was dealing was also the chancellor of SFU. Apparently, there was a very important phone call that went from the chancellor to the premier's office. Important and highly confidential. A marketing campaign was launching at the same time for 536 market condos that were sold as an intellectual property, which assumed SFU's presence. Let's face it, the entire success of this launch was firmly rooted in SFU's participation.

But it worked. People were calling us saying, "My mom used to work at Woodward's, I'd love to buy a unit in her memory." We had people mistakenly calling us thinking we were the developer and we would just refer them to Westbank. A lot of people bought because of the synergies of the non-market and the market, and the symbolism of what Woodward's was for the community. They put their money where their mouth was. Over 4000 people wanted to live there. We had to manage crowd control outside the launch where you got a wrist band, which gave you a half-hour window. I don't know how many deal writers they had, but the way they marched people through the sales centre was extremely well done. Woodward's was unique because, in this particular development, the FSR exclusions for storage didn't apply. So Gregory was able to design very innovative units which appealed to buyers who liked that edgy, artsy feel. All 536 units sold in one day.

I don't know if Gregory's bragged about this yet, but he and Ian Gillespie decided to make the top two penthouse levels of the W Building into ammenity space as opposed to a Ritz-Carlton-style $28 million penthouse.

FOLIO III

MARKETING BROCHURE
Letterbox Design Group

TEL 604.781.7109 TOLL-FREE 1.866.500.7109

woodwardsdistrict.com

TIMING IS EVERYTHING. INVEST IN

A COLLECTION OF MODERN LIVING ENV

SUBSTANCE AND CONFIDENCE IN THE HEART OF DOWNTOW

AND SET IN AN AESTHETICALLY A

THIS IS TRUE VANCOUV

an intellectual property

IGINAL VANCOUVER ADDRESS, WOODWARD'S.

MENTS AND CLUB W, DESIGNED WITH STYLE,

ATURING AMAZING VIEWS, CONNECTED TO SFU,

TISTICALLY ATTUNED COMMUNITY.

TH INTELLIGENCE AND SOUL.

The new view of Woodward's and downtown Vancouver from the North Shore. Photo taken January 12, 2006, at 5:45 p.m.

escape

YOUR PARENTS' RUMPUS ROOM NEVER LO

CLUB W IS ALL YOURS. OWNERS HAVE FULL ACCESS

INCLUDING A GLASS-FLANKED GYM, STACKED MEDIA ROOM A

DOUBLE-HEIGHT SPACE. READ. FLIRT. MEDITA

DINE OUTSIDE ON THE DECK. GET STEAMY OR WET — THER

PLUS, CLUB W IS RUMOURED TO HAVE T

club w

ED LIKE THIS. REMARKABLY, THE PENTHOUSE-LEVEL

AMAZING ARRAY OF ROOFTOP VIEWS AND AMENITIES

AMOROUS LOUNGE. LIVE LARGE IN THE SOARING

VITE YOUR FRIENDS TO A MOVIE OR BARBECUE.

EN A GIANT HOT TUB (YES, IN THE SHAPE OF A W).

XIEST RESTROOMS ON THE CONTINENT.

d

ertion 304.1 opening 265.7 door doorway
302.6 entrance cast a spell 1036.7 delight
entrance access 306.3 entrée (Fr) in (informal) entry entrance 302 access opening
open door open arms channel 396.1 entrance-
Day 302.5 foyer 192.19 ingress 302.1 in-
sertion 304.1 opening 265.7 door doorway
302.6 entrance cast a spell 1036.7 delight
865.8 fascinate 650.6 captivate charm
spellbind cast a spell beguile intrigue enthral
enrapture transport enravish
tize mesmerize entranced asto
dreamy 535.25 overjoyed 86
alluring 650.7 fascinating
charming glamorous exotic e
ful spellbinding ravishing enravishing intriguing enthralling attractive interesting appealing engaging fetching (informal) catch-
ing winning winsome prepossessing exciting
charismatic seductive seducing beguiling en-
ticing inviting come-hither (informal) flat-
atous coquettish coaxing cajoling tempting
tantalizing provocative provoquant (Fr)
piquant (Fr) irresistible hypnotic mesmeric
bewitching 1036.11 pleasant 863.7

YOU ARE HERE

PUSH THE ENVELOPE

Here's the start of your art collection. Each Woodward's owner will select
a signature private entry door from a group of 10 artists' works in limited
release. Exclusive to Woodward's, the designs were collected via an
open call, juried by the interior designers and development team with
selections based on artistic merit, contribution to the project's philosophy
and overall aesthetic.

IN EVERY SUITE

Graphic entry doors

Exposed concrete ceilings

Sleek AEG, Panasonic and LG appliances

Custom Eggersmann kitchens

Glass feature wall tiles in a choice of five colours

IT'S IN THE DETAILS

In the bathroom, underfoot and on the walls, an impressive setting of 12 x 24 in. porcelain tiles. To punctuate the space, a deluxe wall-hung Eggersmann vanity with polished stone slab top, sexy mirrored cabinets and a feature wall of custom linear glass tiles. The frameless glass shower, custom oval tub, semi-inset sink and sleek fixtures complement the ultra-modern, playful look.

IF YOU'VE LIVED IN VAN[

YOU MAY THINK OF WO[

BUT IF YOU'VE MOVED TO [

10 TO 15 YEARS, OR HAVE RES[

IN THE WORLD LIKE NEV[

YOU WILL RECOGNIZE THE INCREDIBLE POTENTIAL — THIS[

NEIGHBOURHOODS LIKE THIS ARE RARE AND OFFER A CREAT[

THAT'S WHY THE INTELLIGENT BUYER WILL GET IN EARL[

BE BOLD OR [

UVER ALL YOUR LIFE

DWARD'S AS EDGY.

NCOUVER IN THE LAST

ED IN ANY OTHER MAJOR CITY

'ORK OR LONDON,

AUTHENTIC AREA, NOT A SANITIZED ENVIRONMENT.

OF CUTTING-EDGE CULTURE, HERITAGE AND CHARACTER.

S IS THE FUTURE. THIS IS YOUR NEIGHBOURHOOD.

TO SUBURBIA.

3

THE TEAM

The Woodward's Redevelopment Group consisted of well-established, locally-based enterprises committed to building and strengthening Vancouver's communities. Past accomplishments in developing large-scale, financially-viable projects combined with experience in non-market housing and community services in the Downtown Eastside were of great value in redeveloping the Woodward's site. Not inclined to celebrity-status architecture, the design team consists of urban idealists trying to mend the city's urban fabric.

Henriquez Partners Architects, established in 1969 by Richard Henriquez, has greatly contributed to shaping Vancouver's urban environment with the typologically innovative Gaslight Square (1973); the major renovation of a city block that unified several distinguished heritage buildings, including the old Vancouver post office, with a central atrium to form Sinclair Centre (1985); and a series of luxurious condominium towers overlooking English Bay and Stanley Park, most prominently the Sylvia Hotel Extension (1984) and Eugenia Place (1987), which were the first towers to fully maximize their sites' panoramic views with all-glazed façades. The Woodward's redevelopment was the kind of project Gregory Henriquez had been working towards since joining his father's firm in 1989. Community-sensitive projects like Bruce Eriksen Place (1999), the Lore Krill Housing Co-op (2002), and the Gastown Parkades (2004), gave him street credibility. Proportionally larger than his previous projects, the scale and complexity of Woodward's made it a watershed in his career, in the history of the city and in the longer narrative of urban design in Canada. As a pragmatic utopian full of ideals about the integration of ethics and aesthetics in community design, Gregory was finally positioned to practically test and develop those ideals in built space.

In the summer of 2003, after the city of Vancouver had acquired the Woodward's site from the province, Henriquez Partners approached Westbank Projects Corporation to enter the competition for the Woodward's redevelopment project. Having worked with Westbank on the unconventional Dockside Live/Work building in Coal Harbour completed in 2002, Henriquez Partners appreciated the architectural excellence and superior, detailed quality that Westbank achieved in their work. Ian Gillespie, head of Westbank, is design-oriented and appreciative of design's marketing potential. Established in 1992, Westbank had, in its first 15 years, developed $4 billion in projects consisting of over one million square metres of retail, mixed-use, residential and office projects. Westbank's innovative and entrepreneurial approach to development has led them from primarily developing shopping centres in Western Canada to becoming a large, multi-disciplined developer with prominent developments across North America including Shaw Tower and Living Shangri-La in downtown Vancouver, Century Park in Edmonton, Shangri-La in downtown Toronto and Azure in Dallas, Texas. With a specialty in high-density, mixed-use developments,

Westbank Projects Corporation/Peterson Investment Group was well-suited to be the project developer, project manager and property manager of the Woodward's redevelopment project.

The Portland Hotel Society (PHS) was established in 1993 by Jim Green and Liz Evans, now Executive Director of PHS Community Services Society, to provide permanent, semi-private accommodation with responsive services for people living with concurrent disorders in the 70-room Portland Hotel, named after Portland's progressive movement to turn the management of single-room occupancy hotels over to non-profit societies to prevent their redevelopment. The program moved to a new building in 1999 and expanded to the Stanley/New Fountain Hotel, Sunrise Hotel, and Washington Hotel. Their advocacy for adults in the Downtown Eastside poorly served due to their physical health, chronic mental illness, chronic home-lessness and substance dependencies led them to initiate a community dental clinic, the Interurban Art Gallery, North America's first supervised injection facility called InSite, and an eatery and catering service called Potluck Café. Henriquez Partners invited PHS to be a community partner early in the competition for Woodward's to provide input on their design, to advise on its appropriateness based on intimate knowledge of the needs and interests of the Downtown Eastside, to build community support for the project, and to liaise between the developer and community members during the competition's public consultations and meetings. In the hour-long presentation of the final submittal made to the city council, the city planning department and the Woodward's Steering Committee in July 2004, Liz Evans of PHS publicly endorsed Westbank's proposal, noting its strong commitment to the Downtown Eastside and its embodiment of the community's aspirations. After fulfilling its role as community advisor to Westbank, PHS submitted a proposal to be a non-market housing sponsor for Woodward's and was selected in January 2005 to manage the 125 singles non-market housing units.

TEAM 'W'ORK
IAN GILLESPIE

Ian Gillespie
Developer
Westbank Development Corp.

Ian Gillespie, President of Westbank Projects Corp., has been redefining the concept of mixed-use real estate development across North America. He founded Westbank in 1992 and quickly became a leader in shopping centre development. Mr. Gillespie then turned his attention to residential and mixed-use projects where he created some of Vancouver's boldest and most innovative developments.

Under Mr. Gillespie's leadership, Westbank Projects Corp. is currently developing over 4.5 million square feet of real estate exceeding $2 billion in value. This includes the development of luxury condominiums, hotels, urban infill housing, Class A office space, shopping centres and rental apartments. With his roots firmly planted in BC, Mr. Gillespie is now using his expertise to branch out to markets across Canada and North America.

Mr. Gillespie possesses a Master's of Business Administration from the University of Toronto and a Bachelor's of Commerce from UBC. He currently resides in Vancouver with his wife and three children.

What are your earliest memories of Woodward's when it was a department store?

I grew up in Port Coquitlam, which is about an hour's drive east. I remember shopping at Woodward's to get my school supplies. I have these quite vivid memories, so I specifically remember where we got off the bus. Port Coquitlam was a separate village at the time and not a suburb of Vancouver. In the last 30 years it has all filled in, but in those days it was the big trip into town and Woodward's was the reason to do it. It's not like we went anywhere else when we came into the city. We went to Woodward's, bought our pencils, rulers and binders, and then we got back on the bus and went home.

So what made you get involved in this project in the first place?

Gregory called and said we should do this deal, and at that point I hadn't given it a lot of serious consideration. I think I looked at it as something that could turn out to be an incredible amount of work, and then we might not even end up doing it. And maybe ending up doing it would be the worst part. So I really wasn't that interested, but Gregory got me interested. Then I started having a conversation with Ben Yeung, my partner on the project, and he was actually quite keen. So the two of them in combination talked me into it. I was probably a bit reluctant because of the amount of work I thought it would take, in comparison to the amount of return that would come out of it, and I think those fears were justified. At the same time, I am very, very pleased that we made that decision because it has been really rewarding from an educational perspective, and getting to work with Gregory has been especially rewarding. Prior to the Woodward's project, 80 percent of my practice had been with Jim Cheng, and a large part of my business is still with him. So expanding to work with a new architect has been good and the result is that we are now doing two, maybe three, other projects with Gregory and that is important for my business. I think we also got some currency out of the project that will only grow when the project is finished. It's hard to put a number to what that goodwill is worth, but I think in the long run it is worth something. Of course, the fear is that there is so much change at the city of Vancouver right now, that you wonder if any of the people you did business with are still going to be there. That is a bit of a concern, but at the end of the day, all you can do is the best work you can and hope that the rest takes care of itself.

You said you learned something doing this project. You're a pretty savvy guy, so I'm interested in knowing what was the educational portion for you on this one?

You learn something on every project that you do. On the big ones—when you're doing a 700-foot tower in Toronto—you learn because you haven't done business in Toronto before. You just learn from that perspective. Woodward's is over one million square feet going up at once, with three levels of government involved, with Simon Fraser involved, with all these interest groups and the community involved, and all of them wanting to have more involvement. Whether you paid them or not, everyone in town wanted a part in this movie. So just juggling all those interest groups was very time-consuming. I think managing all those expectations was a rich learning experience and then, of course, every deal has its intricacies. Just from a legal point of view this deal was incredibly complex, so it's also a learning exercise from that perspective.

Have you been kept apprised of everything from macro to micro issues as the project has developed?

Yes. If there is one issue that distinguishes our firm from other developers, it's that I am much more hands-on. I am always amazed at how removed other developers are from their projects. They put the deal together and then they move onto the next one. I am there for every single detail and it becomes incredibly time-consuming. But it's all those details which I find interesting. My reward is building the building. I like building buildings. I like the creation and design of it. I don't want to say I'm equally responsible with the architect on what they look like, but I have a lot to say about the building from inside and out.

The aesthetics are important to you?

It's why I'm here. It's why I get up in the morning. Otherwise I would be doing something different.

Have you ever been involved in anything this complicated from the point of view of the number of people and agencies involved?

No. The truth is there isn't a deal that is this complicated. It doesn't exist. Four of the six biggest buildings ever built in this city are mine and I can tell you that the complication on Woodward's is more than the other three combined. It's not a little bit more; it's double what the other three are combined. Take a look at the Shangri-La, which is going up at the same time here in Vancouver; it's the first time a building ever went over 450 feet. We've got the Vancouver Art Gallery's Curated Art Site; we've got a heritage building needing to be restored—none of them are even close. The irony is that if you look at these other projects from a time-for-money perspective, Woodward's makes no sense at all. But it doesn't matter. I'm really proud of it and I think that when it's finished I'm going to be even happier than I am today.

I know you started digging a hole before Simon Fraser was even in on the deal. What made you run that economic risk on this project?

That's one of the pitches we made to the city. We basically said there is going to be a bunch of hiccups on this project. We don't know what they're going to be but there will be dozens, and one of the reasons to go with us over someone else is that we will see our way through them. Whether that was solving the problems, or whether it was moving on despite the problems, that's what we had to do. You've got to remember how many times Woodward's failed before it got to where it is today. I just felt that if we didn't keep moving forward—it wasn't even a matter of stopping—then we'd be moving backwards, instantaneously. There was no middle ground where we could say, "Let's put it on hold for a month and solve this problem." The minute we did that it would have slipped out of our hands. So we took some huge financial risks and I honestly can't think of another developer that would have taken on that kind of risk. To the credit of the city and guys like Michael Flanigan, we had many conversations where we all said, "We're going to do this together," and they said, "We're going to be there for you at the end of the day." And they delivered on that commitment, which doesn't happen every day.

It's a very sophisticated ecology you have here, layered, complex and potentially divergent?

Yes. I work in a lot of other communities and nothing even comes close. Of course, one of the fears we have is the fluidity with the Vancouver city staff right now. We fear we might lose some of that. But working here is so different than working anywhere else. You really do have an amazing level of sophistication.

When you were approached with the idea, did you think this thing would fly? Was there a point where you thought it was a mad idea?

Obviously, going into something like this, you have more trepidation than you would on a more typical site. The thing is that you always assume you can solve problems with price, and the fear on Woodward's was that maybe price wouldn't solve the problem. Maybe people just won't buy, period. Price either works or it doesn't. But if you drop your price to the point where you don't make any money and people still don't want to buy, that's where the problem presents itself. From that perspective, there was a bit of fear about whether the market would ever get there. I guess we talked each other into that. I think in this business you have to have a lot of faith or an equal amount of stupidity. There are definitely times when you talk yourselves into things. But at the same time, another characteristic of this firm is that we've probably done 34 or 35 projects, and every one of them has been a success. So you build up a certain level of self-confidence. And without sounding cocky, I never really had a doubt that it would be a success. It was just a matter of how much work for how much money, and how many resources we were going to have to put into making this a success, not whether it would be a success.

Were there doubts in your mind that you would be the firm chosen among the four finalists?

Absolutely. I think the market was definitely betting heavily that Concert would get the project. We were probably second because we felt we had the best thought-out proposal and we certainly had the best team. I remember standing in front of city council saying, "If you don't go with me, I'm okay with that, but tell the other developer to go with Henriquez." In this case, Gregory's firm assumed some of the role that the developer would typically take in getting into the community. They took more of an activist's role than a purely architectural one. I think this project has the ability to be a milestone in Gregory's career and they only come along so often. I think he realised that and said to himself, 'Okay, I have to do this. I have to make this work and I'm going to do whatever it takes to do it.' Gregory is a little bit like I am. We are really passionate about what we do, and I think passion is probably the reason we were chosen more than anything else. I think people knew that's what the project needed. I like to think that was the reason. It was certainly why I thought we were the right team to do it. I will also say that the city of Vancouver picked us despite the fact that the economics of our deal was not as attractive to them on the surface as some of the other deals. We didn't pay as much for the land as some of the other proponents were offering. At the end of the day, the city will probably do better as a result of picking us, but when they made the decision they didn't base it on economics. They based it on which team was going to ultimately get this thing across the goal line.

You talk about this as being a milestone in Gregory's career. Is it also a milestone in the redevelopment of Vancouver and the way the city will be perceived? You must also have a certain degree of pride in being involved in this kind of project?

For sure. It was important for me. I am very competitive, so when Gregory talked me into it, the one thing I said is, 'If I go into it, I have to win. Because if I don't win, I lose. And that's not acceptable.'

My guess would be that's the kind of talk an architect wants to hear from his developer?

And that's my curse: if I go into something, I can't let it go. I have to really go for it. I can tell you we spent way more money than the other proponents did on their proposals. Some guys were risking tens of thousands; we were risking hundreds and hundreds of thousands. It wasn't a question of whether we could lose; we had to win.

How do you see this playing into the larger architectural and redevelopment future of the Downtown Eastside, Gastown and Vancouver generally?

I think Woodward's is unique, I think that the SunLife building is unique, the Army Navy is unique and so on. We have to be careful in not becoming formulaic. What's important is that each project is looked at for its own characteristics and its own particular reasons for being redeveloped. Woodward's will be what it is for many reasons and I'm not sure you can make it an example. If there is anything to draw from it, it's the process more than the outcome. I think a big part of that process was an architect who was willing to roll up his sleeves and really get into it. And get in with so many different interest groups that all felt they had a voice in it. We didn't necessarily agree with or take their recommendations, but we heard their rationale. Sometimes it was good and sometimes it wasn't. One of my faults and one of Gregory's strengths is that I'm not sure I would have the patience… No, I take that back. I know I wouldn't have had the patience to do that; Gregory has and that is a virtue.

What will be the measure of success? How long before there are measurements in place that will allow you to say confidently that Woodward's wasn't just a noble social experiment, that it has actually effected desirable change in the Downtown Eastside?

The first thing that comes to mind is warm bodies on the street. People with money in their pockets going to London Drugs; or going to the grocery store; or students going to Simon Fraser; or real people living in real condominiums; not a bunch of speculators or people going to the plaza. I think the neighbourhood misses a sense of normality. Everything is always in crisis. It's not a matter of pushing people out; it's a matter of bringing new people in. Normality may be the wrong word, but that is one of the reasons we pushed so hard to finish the deal with Simon Fraser. I think it will be one of the important legacies to come out of this project. I really believe in this comparison with NYU: the whole idea of dropping a campus in the middle of this neighbourhood and having it change the neighbourhood for the better. It's not a bunch of GAP Stores, it's a bunch of kids who aren't freaked out by a different kind of neighbourhood, who have the ability to bring positive energy to a place that desperately needs it.

What made you decide you wanted Stan Douglas' photomural of the 1971 Gastown Riot, such a dramatic and significant piece of art, in the atrium?

The reality is that the city of Vancouver has its public art program and we have done a lot of public art. We really believe in the program. If you look at our typical budget, it might be somewhere in the $500,000 to $600,000 range, whereas we probably spend two or three times what we're required to spend. We spend what's necessary to produce the piece. I don't care whether the costs are two or three times over budget. Woodward's is turning out to be that case. We'll spend triple what we told the city—no, triple won't even get us there—but Stan was the right artist to do it. Stan lives in the neighbourhood, he knows it and he is incredibly smart. What turns me on about working with different artists, whether it's Liam Gillick next door, or Diane Thater, or Rodney Graham, or Stan Douglas, is this incredible intellect. We spend so much of our day having interactions with people and it's so refreshing when the person you're having this interaction with is so much smarter than you are. It's really intimidating.

Do you mean that?

I do. I'm really turned on by their intelligence and every good artist I've gotten to know has been way smarter than me. It's somewhat humbling and that's good, because this isn't a very humbling business.

Gregory has told me that you want a better quality of housing as well. Your aesthetic sense will make you spend more money because you don't want your name on something that doesn't look as good as it could. Is that accurate?

When Gregory says that, he's trying to make me out to be a good citizen. That's bullshit. It's really a good business plan. There are people who manufacture housing and people who develop housing, and we're not manufacturers. We're not General Motors or Ford; we are Mercedes or probably better, Porsche. If you're going to build a Porsche, you have to put a lot more into it. A lot more time, a lot more work and more money. That's our business model. That's not to take anything away from the business models of people who want a Chev. In fact, more people want a Chev, and more people can afford a Chev; that's just not my model and I will never change it. I had to take that business model to a sale at Woodward's and, of course, that's where you get a challenge. Because you want to do great design for a low price, and that's a lot harder than doing good design and selling it for $2,000 a square foot.

Were they under-priced? The units were less than they would be if the market were operating at full throttle, right?

The market was operating at full throttle and when we sold, we did better than our expectations. Things sold at a higher price for that neighbourhood than we could have ever forecast. The crazy thing is it's literally three blocks from the Fairmont but that is a long three blocks. It's another world. One side was selling for $550 per square foot and the others were selling for $2,500 per square foot.

Have developers bought up most of the buildings down in the area?

There was a ton of speculation. Once we got going in the planning process, everybody dived in. For us, the speculative nature isn't important. We've never been speculators. That's just not what we do. I have never bought a site and not built it. It probably would have been smarter financially to have bought some of the land around it, but it feels like all the sharks went feeding. Now some of those same sites are coming back to us, and the owners are saying we want you to pay triple what we paid for it. What's really crazy is that the sales packages from brokers all reference Woodward's. You know, half a block from Woodward's, and one or two blocks from Woodward's.

Are you a better developer because of the context in which you've been able to operate?

For sure. There is an argument that sometimes the planning controls can be too much, that you're not given the flexibility you might otherwise have. But I think the positives far outweigh the negatives and more to the point, for us and for a handful of other developers, once you've gained a level of trust, you're given much more freedom than other developers would be given. So we get accused of benefiting from favouritism. But it isn't favouritism. It's called trust and if you earn that trust, you should be given more latitude than if you haven't. I think that's exactly the way it should go. Other people think it's not fair. Well, what the fuck is fair? What has fairness got to do with anything?

Why do you keep doing it? You've already changed the face of Vancouver, you've made all the money you need. Why bother now?

At some point over the last couple of years, it changed from building buildings that interest me and making money to building a business that I can bring my children into. It never started off that way, it happened accidentally. So that's now the motivation, and everything we do—in terms of geographical or product diversification, amount of risk, or any number of things—we do with that in the back of our minds. We're building a business for the next generation.

THE HEALING PLACE
LIZ EVANS

Liz Evans
Co-founder
Portland Hotel Society

Liz Evans is a graduate of the Ottawa University nursing program. She moved to Vancouver 18 years ago, pursuing an interest in helping the mentally ill and socially disadvantaged through the health system. Through her work with the Vancouver General Hospital, she began to believe that the emergency room was not the way to deal with the problems many of the people she dealt with every day were facing, and instead signed on with the Downtown Eastside Residents Association (DERA), to run one of their hotels. As a trained nurse, many of the people with more complex care requirements came to live in her hotel, which prompted the formation of the Portland Hotel Society.

I'VE BEEN IN VANCOUVER FOR 18 YEARS and my only experience with Woodward's was I shopped at the closing-down sale. I think I bought towels. There was an awful lot of talk about Woodward's, especially when it was closing down. It was interesting to understand how significant it was as an icon for the neighbourhood.

When I started the Portland Hotel Society in 1991, I was a nurse. I had done my nursing degree at Ottawa University and while I was a student, I worked at a couple of homeless shelters. I went to work in psychiatry because so many of the people I saw on the street were mentally ill. I became interested in the fact that the people in the hospital system who were mentally ill were additionally poor and socially marginalized, street-entrenched and drug-addicted. These people presented a cross section between mental illness and the gravitational pull to poverty and social exclusion. When I moved to Vancouver, I started working at Vancouver General Hospital in the Psychiatric Emergency Department, and I started seeing the same pattern; the overwhelming majority of the people in acute crisis who were mentally ill were also socially disenfranchised, poor and homeless. I realized that the Emergency Department was the wrong instrument to remedy what I saw as the contextual issues around people who are suffering.

I didn't really have a background in social activism. When I was 14, I became super-passionate about *Strength to Love,* Martin Luther King's book of speeches, so maybe it started there. Here in Vancouver, I volunteered at the shelters, recognizing that it doesn't make sense to be in the hospital sector because my image of what health care was—doing good for people in a big way—didn't fit what I was experiencing. So I left the hospital to move into the community and then I applied to work with what was then the Downtown Eastside Residents Association, DERA.

In those days DERA was considered the voice of the people. It was 'the' group in the Downtown Eastside. I had heard about them through social workers in the hospital who were interested in dealing with poverty issues. They had told me about Jim Green, the guy who ran the organization. So I met him and he said he had an idea for this hotel but nothing was firm, so I said, "Okay, put my name on the list and call me when you're ready." I took six months out, went traveling to Turkey and to Europe and when I came back, I popped in again and asked Jim what was going on. He said, "Let's have an interview because we've got a little bit of funding and we've bought this hotel."

It actually was a hotel, a 70 room, SRO building in the Downtown Eastside. It was owned privately, but DERA got a contract to run the rooms upstairs. The reason they called it the Portland is because Portland, Oregon at the time had a very progressive mayor who was getting non-profits to run SRO hotel rooms, primarily to prevent gentrification. It wasn't necessarily what we did with it; they wanted to rescue the housing stock and to prevent it from being developed.

So I got hired. I took a dip in salary. I was earning 40 some grand and at Portland, I started earning 12 because it was a three-days-a-week half-time position as a mental health worker. I never actually worked less than an 80-hour week from the day I started. So I went to Jim one day and said this isn't a half-time job. This can't be done in two and a half days because I have a hotel full of 70 homeless people who are extremely sick.

I was doing everything, changing toilet rolls and painting doors. I vacuumed all four floors of the hotel every single day. I had psychiatrists come in to do home visits and they'd say, "What are you doing vacuuming this floor? You have a degree in nursing!" I'd just laugh because that's what it takes to build trust in a community that is extremely marginalized and in crisis all the time. To actually make a difference, you had to be with people.

As soon as people found out there was a nurse running the hotel, I got sent everybody: complex personality disorders, drug addictions, mental illness. I was shocked to find there were hotels that had quiet old men. Jim's sense of the Downtown Eastside was always much more the bearded logger version. We used to joke with him about how he never saw this group I helped. I was immersed with them from day one. In the early '90s we were dealing with heroin overdoses. We were dealing with CPR every day. We were dealing with deaths and burials and the police. Our view was very different, which is why we split from DERA and formed our own organization. DERA was happy because we were going in a very different direction. Our mandate was to protect the housing rights of this group that was always being kicked out and was in constant crisis.

HIV was also a huge problem. I think we were hitting the peak of our HIV conversion rates in 1997. One in four drug addicts was becoming positive. We reached saturation point in '98, which means everybody who could become HIV positive was. We had the highest rate of HIV in the Western world. The reasons were complicated; some were moral, some were political and a lot of it was fear. Not to mention bad policy. You could easily write a Downtown Eastside version of *And The Band Played On*. One study blamed the hotels in the housing stock. I could equally blame needle exchange policy and city politicians. There were a million things that happened at that time that led to conversion of HIV. It wasn't simple.

We saw ourselves more as a community development group than an institutional-focused program. Our objective from day one was just to be in the community, to be its voice and to facilitate programming, supports and housing that would be what people needed. We've always lived in the Downtown Eastside. I've lived eight blocks from the Portland for the last 20 years.

I consider many of the residents friends. A lot of the people I housed back in 1991, the ones who haven't died, still live in the Portland. So we have created a tremendously stable population, but a lot of them are very sick. I think many of them were kept alive by the fact that we gave them stable housing. We became the only place which would take injection drug users into housing. For almost eight years there wasn't anywhere else the hospitals could send somebody who had a drug addiction, was HIV positive and homeless. Seventy percent of the people living with us were HIV positive, which is why we had so many funerals. We kept some of the HIV-positive injection drug users alive so long that they ended up developing cancers that weren't previously seen in people with HIV. We thought, "That's an interesting social experiment!" I'm sure we housed the person who lived the longest with HIV, an injection drug user who was one of the early converters in the '80s.

He got it because of drug use and he only died two years ago. He lived with HIV for almost 20 years.

From day one, we were dealing with people with concurrent disorders. I remember the first meeting I went to where people started talking about dual diagnosis and then they realized HIV was there too, so it was multi-diagnosis. They came up with all these labels: 'hard-to-house' and 'multi-diagnosis'. These are just people, they're people who have a lot of shit going on. A lot of them have been abused and a lot of them are poor.

The biggest deal for me was going to work everyday, hearing more and more intimate stories about people's lives, and then coming home and crying my eyes out. For the first two years, I don't think I went to bed one night without weeping. I couldn't handle it; it was just so painful. Like the aboriginal woman whose husband killed her seven-year-old daughter, went to the federal pen and when he was released, the social worker gave him her address in Vernon. He went there and tried to kill her. She and her other daughter were sex-trade workers and coke addicts. She eventually died of an overdose. She used to hold on to me and wouldn't want to let me go; she'd break down, saying how I was like her daughter.

I was only 26 when I started, so I was relatively young. People would say, 'Oh, you're a young kid, so I can share these things with you'. I wasn't a guy and I wasn't powerful. I didn't intimidate people. It was unbelievably emotional. I guess I was pretty arrogant and naïve and I thought I could probably fix some stuff. Not long after, I realized, holy shit, I can't do anything. All I can do is be here and being here is better than not being here. But it's also not a cure. I can't do anything, ultimately. I can advocate, I can lobby, and I can try and build some housing and bring some care. I can scream and cry and fight and kick, which we do, but we do it because we know something is better than nothing. Not because we think we can stick somebody in one end of a program and have them come out the other end the way we want. I guess my view on life is that no one person or thing or program can create an outcome. What we do is up to us as individuals. So if I've been fucked over until I was 18 and I start coping by using injection drugs when I'm 13, and I'm suicidal by the age of 15, if that's my life story, what's it going to take for me to stop believing the things about myself that I started believing when I was 5 or 6? What is it going to take for me to ever be able to live in a world that isn't defined by self-hatred and self-blame and a lack of trust? Can any number of years of therapy recreate safety in that individual's life? And what are we going to do as a society to take on the thousands of people who feel that way? Not only do they feel they are garbage and do things every day to destroy themselves, but we as a society reinforce that by allowing them to be homeless and die of HIV. We incarcerate them and tell them they're criminals. The whole thing is set up for failure.

So all we're doing is saying, "Let's give these people some breathing room and some space." Let's tell them they have the right to that at least. Then maybe, just maybe, after 20 years of stable housing, and in most cases much less, we can give them some dignity, and they can feel a little bit better about themselves. But you can't predict which people are going to find the strength to heal and to move on. Some people do and it's always fabulous when you see it happen. But as many, if not more, don't because the pain is so ingrained. And it's hard to change, right? It's hard for me to change bad habits. I still bite my nails and I'm 42. It's relatively minor, but it's a ridiculous thing to do. And I have a home, I have resources, I have good food, I have a marriage, I have two kids, I'm well-off. So it's a lot to expect and if you set yourself up with the assumption that you are going to do anything to anybody, you are flawed. It's really about offering windows and offering hope and offering love and offering some sense of place. We don't boast about successes, but we also don't define ourselves by failings. Because if we define ourselves by their suffering, how can we then take on this very damaged group of people?

You have to be in a state where you understand exactly who you are as a human being, knowing your flaws and your weaknesses. To be with other people in that community, without your suffering becoming part of it, you have to understand exactly your own humanity. If you're going to be a vehicle for change or hope in any way, your role can't be about healing your pain, it can't be about meeting your unmet expectations. That's not a zen thing, it's more about self-awareness. I've learned over 17 years, every day, painfully, to be more and more self-aware about what parts of me want to engage in certain things. It's a process of letting go. So for that reason, and in that way, it's a very healing place to be.

I think all these community processes are the same. They can't be about you, because if you want people to join your team, if you want to work collaboratively, then your ego needs to be isolated. One of the problems we've had in the Downtown Eastside is that certain people have wanted everything to be about them and they push others away and then there's more fighting.

For a long time we didn't have anything to do with the fight for Woodward's because we were busy doing what we were doing. But it went on and on and on and nothing seemed to be happening, so at some point we decided we should try and do something. The province put it out for proposals and those of us in the community wanted to fight for as much as we could possibly get, which is itself fairly nebulous. I mean, how much is enough? Is something better than nothing? At some point we managed to convince local developer Michael Audain to line up with us and a friend of ours who is an architect, Sean McEwen. He did some draft plans and models, which we took to Michael and said, "We think you should put in a bid to buy this and help us out here." So Michael wrote something up and actually approached the premier and said we were interested in doing this as a partnership. But in the midst of this, the city took over ownership of the building and Michael came to us and said, "We don't need to do this. The city has it now and they're going to make sure there's a certain amount of social housing."

It was out of our hands at that point. We figured out who were the interested developers and met with almost all of them individually and talked to them about how we thought the community's interests could best be served. Then we decided to meet with Gregory and he asked us if we'd like to join their team. The proposal that Gregory and Westbank had come up with, if you compare them to the original concept drawings we had with Michael and Sean, was not that different. So for us, it was a good fit. We just wanted to make sure that we had the maximum number of social housing units. And Gregory is such an incredible person, it's hard not to want to work with him. It just felt like it was a personal mission. It didn't feel like it was this inert business deal. He had such passion. Of course all of us had a huge amount of fear and trepidation about what it would mean for the future of the Downtown Eastside. We still have that fear.

I don't actually think there are good guys and bad guys in this development. There are purists who would say that to work with any developer is courting the enemy or sleeping with the devil. Maybe this is a flaw, but I was raised in a very liberal home. In some ways my father was the quintessential 'avoid-all-conflict' kind of person. He was a doctor and nobody was bad; everyone was just doing their best. I'm a humanist and I recognize we all have pain, we're all fucked in some way or another. But if you're only looking at that then you can never make anything of these opportunities. So developers are making money off the developments and their objectives are totally different from ours, and you can argue the capitalist system has created this poverty in the first place, and that it's all wrong. But if I'm going to do anything about any of that, couldn't I take some value from building good relationships and getting some of that money channeled into something that's going to make a difference?

It's hard to know what your influence is in any of these things, but I think our presence on the Westbank proposal was helpful. I think the city was happy that somebody who supports the Downtown Eastside community was involved. The other thing was we weren't arrogant enough to say we were speaking for the community. Because that's always an issue. How do you speak for 5,000 or 16,000 people? All you can do is say that I'm in the community and from the work we've been doing, we think these things would be beneficial. We did distribute hundreds and hundreds of questionnaires asking people what they wanted from Woodward's and the biggest thing for everybody was the volume of housing. That was the over-arching issue.

From our perspective, 200 housing units was the minimum. That was the breaking point. We fought about it internally, too. The whole thing had been going on for so long, and there was so little momentum for any of it to change. We weren't sure if there was even a chance to get the 200 because the Feds hadn't ponied up. It wasn't until the city moved in that we were in a position to do something about this problem.

We were involved in the very beginning of the Squat. We set people up with tents and bags, and we helped the first handful of people break in. So we were very supportive of that as a mechanism, but then it got taken over and the whole thing went haywire. There were many different messages spun around the Squat. People tried to make out that it was just these few angry young men who were deliberately trying to fight with the police and create tension. That was true of a handful, maybe five at the most. But the other 200 were sincerely sick. We moved a pregnant woman into one of our hotels when we had to clear the Squat. We had somebody who went missing and died three days after we got him off the street because he was so sick. We tried to get him into the hospital, we called in all these resources. About 80 percent of the people that we took into our hotels directly from the Squat didn't even have welfare. So they didn't exist in the system. They didn't have social insurance numbers; they didn't have MSP numbers. It took us almost one full year to get them reconnected. We were dealing with street youth that were crystal meth addicts. About 80 percent of the people we housed were addicted to crystal meth and we had one staff member working 24-hours a day to deal with all that.

When they were marketing the condos for the Woodward's project, our advice was just don't lie. Put the homeless people on the advertising posters, put on the guy with the guitar and the bottle in his hand. It's stupid to pretend otherwise. Try and attract people who want to be in a diverse, urban community, people who get how amazing this community is. There is Gastown with nice, clean shops; you're really close to downtown; and you're within walking distance of everything. And the Downtown Eastside community is a poor community, which you don't have to be afraid of. But if we start filling 600 new condos with people who are going to call the cops every time they see a homeless person, then we've failed. We've created a total nightmare for the community.

For some strange reason we're afraid of the poor in North America. We want to hide them away; we want to create these sanitized, suburban developments that look exactly the same. We have a problem with conformity in this country. I don't get it. I think the need for conformity defines a lot of how we gravitate to the social models we use in our plans for cities. Everybody wants conformity and I think it's wrong. Look around. People are different and that's what's great. We don't need to be afraid of difference.

Woodward's needs to be successful for everybody who partnered in it. We see it as our high-end housing. That might sound bad to people in the community who want to argue for housing the group that we have at the Portland. Because we do take the ones that are completely homeless and marginalized and difficult and who can't live anywhere else in the entire city. They come to the Portland and the Stanley and we've got a couple more projects on the go that will be targeted for that group. But there are people who can live more independently, and we're going to aim for that group. Because some of the people we've housed at the Portland for 16 years are really excited about moving into Woodward's. That might freak Gregory out but these guys are very stable now. They've lived in one place for long enough that they can actually graduate. I only have three that I can move for sure but for those three it's going to be incredible. They're going to have great mountain views and they're excited about the roof garden. I think there are people in the neighbourhood who are stable enough to be able to handle it. People come up to us all the time and say, 'Can I get a room in Woodward's? Can I get a unit in Woodward's?' It's going to be a difficult process to make sure everybody feels they've had the opportunity to apply.

Our whole notion is that if this group of people has been so pushed to the margins of society because of who they are, then we need to re-embrace them, draw them into society and create some space for them. We can only do that by creating places where they're welcome and that they feel comfortable using, where there aren't a million rules and a million expectations about who they need to be to come there. Once you've done that, there's no reason why people like you and me won't also want to share those spaces, as long as you're open-minded enough about the fact that somebody beside you won't look the same as you. We've done things to say, "Here is an example," and Woodward's could be another example of that, on a much grander scale, and at a much higher end. Unfortunately, it might also be potentially a much more exclusive version. We've got this little café on the corner of Columbia and Hastings called Sunrise outside the Sunrise Hotel and it's got a radio station café in there and we've got internet and we've got cappuccino. It's run by really nice people who work with anybody and everybody in the Downtown Eastside.
The cops come in and they can get a donut and a coffee, and so can somebody who lives in one of the hotels, and a prostitute can come in and get her coffee. That's my version of living under the rainbow. We need more of that. I don't know whether Woodward's will be that or not. Only time will tell how strict the security guards will be about kicking people out of the common areas. As a community, we'll have to be vigilant about making sure that looking clean doesn't become a marker for using public space like at Tinseltown. I don't know but it's certainly not going to be easy.

IMAGE BREAKER, IMAGE MAKER
Bob Rennie

Bob Rennie
Realtor and Marketing Consultant
Rennie Marketing Systems

Born in East Vancouver, Bob Rennie has been selling real estate across Canada and America for over 30 years, and has built an extensive resume of achievements. At the young age of 19, he began working for Bus Norman in a real estate office in East Vancouver. In 1988, Mr. Rennie branched out on his own and started Rennie and Associates Realty. Under his guidance, his firm of over 90 realtors developed a strong presence in the market and became a household name in the community.

Building his experience in project marketing and eventually becoming the city's top project marketer, Mr. Rennie is now the principal and director of Rennie Marketing Systems. Every year, he has maintained his presence as one of the top marketers in Canada including the title for Top Sales in Dollar Volume and Units Sold from the Real Estate Board of Greater Vancouver for 2003. Mr. Rennie is a very committed contributor to many charities, most notably the Vancouver Children's Hospital, Burnaby Hospital and the fine arts community.

This year, Mr. Rennie's dedication to the community and various charities has earned him the Queen's Golden Jubilee Medal, which recognizes citizens for outstanding and exemplary achievement or service to the community or Canada as a whole.

You must have memories about the store prior to your engagement with the Woodward's project?

My mother would take me to the lunch counter downstairs just off the food floor, and we'd have fish and chips. There were two or three large, round horseshoe bays where you would sit and wait for a table. There were counter seats and the dining room was behind, but the dining room was fancy.

Were the fish and chips good?

The fish and chips were great; the hamburgers were good, and then just off the food floor, they had a donut counter where they made really bad cake donuts with brightly coloured icing that everybody's copying today. And they had elevator ladies, and all of the counters had a one- or two-inch stand of glass. The mother of a friend did nothing but cut and replace glass for the little credenzas that were typical of the place.

Was Woodward's a special place, or was it just the only place in the area?

I think it was an early model for what Nordstrom's and Macy's and everybody else has become, but it just didn't survive. It was working-class. The walk was from the Army & Navy to the east, then you hit Woodward's, and finally you'd walk up to Eaton's and the Bay. I think there was a class structure all the way down—Army & Navy being affordable, Woodward's was all-encompassing. As you moved to Eaton's and the Bay, they probably were closer to a tie for high-end stuff. But Woodward's was a family department store.

Was it an anchor for that area?

I've been in the real estate business here for 33 years, and when Woodward's stopped, that was the break, that was the great divide.

Were there lots of signs that it was in trouble? Did people know that something was amiss at Woodward's?

Woodward's was up at Oakridge too, so the myth carried on. But nobody realized the financial difficulties that it was in. Was it mismanagement? Did they move with the times? Was the market too fractured? Parts of what they were selling was available at Zellers; other parts were at London Drugs. Woodward's didn't have its own identity.

Let's talk about your involvement with the Downtown Eastside.

I grew up in East Vancouver, so I tend to have a little bit more sympathy towards the area. I bought the oldest building in Chinatown, the Wing Sang

Building. I'm building a 27,000 square foot heritage restoration—6,000 for my office and the rest for a contemporary art collection. Chinatown has been forgotten, and I can't promise people the old Chinatown, but my way to save the area is to get the fortunate living with the less fortunate, people with jobs walking along with people without jobs. I have a lot of empathy for what's going on in East Vancouver. I was probably the right one to handle the marketing and sales and the branding that it needed. Everyone told me it was suicide to take on Woodward's. With Chinatown, they think I'm crazy. I'm just five years too early.

Why did they regard your involvement with Wooward's as suicide?
The December newsletter of Canaccord Capital said that I'd lost my mind in thinking that I could get people to move into hell. They call it "Wastings and Pain," instead of Hastings and Main. I thought we should go for pure affordability. The rich aren't moving there. So we're just going for IKEA-and-less in finishes, and smaller suites. I said, "Let's hold our head up high. Let's deliver a mainstream, lower-priced, Yaletown-type downtown product." I figured we might as well be transparent and tell the truth. Take pictures of everybody in the area, show what the area looks like, and sell it as an emerging area and an intellectual property. If you've lived in any other major city in the world, you would look at the Woodward's district as emerging, but if you lived in Vancouver all your life, you look at it as questionable and forgotten. So there were a lot of challenges to get Woodward's to move along. I spent four and a half million dollars on the proposal. And we sold all the units in a day.

I guess the people who thought you were committing an act of suicide were wrong?
Yes. But we were very purposeful. We came along with an advertising campaign in October 2005, knowing a municipal election was coming up in November; Ian Gillespie and I wanted it to be an issue. So we started then and by the first week of April, we had 6,200 people in our database. Then we got going with our sales program on April 21st. Over two and a half weeks, we had 4,500 people through the presentation centre. We opened phone lines up, and you had to say whether you could come in between 9:00 and 10:00, 10:00 and 11:00, 11:00 and 12:00, or 12:00 and 1:00. I think we had about 150 to 200 people per hour and 90 agents writing offers. Of the 1,600 that phoned in, 1,100 showed up to claim the wristbands that allowed them entry into their hour line-up. The first hour slept overnight; the second hour arrived early in the morning and the rest is history.

You were purposeful, but were you also surprised?
If you asked me on that day from October, I wouldn't have been conscious. But I watched it mount. "I don't need 30 people writing; I need 50; I need 90 people writing," and you start to fill in the holes. But it took everybody by surprise. We were very careful to let architects and consultants in early and the night before opening, we allowed 100 units to go to residents of the Downtown Eastside. We promised we would acknowledge local residents by giving them the first opportunity. The problem is, there are already developments in the area, and many of the people who came along were speculating because they already owned a condominium in the area and they could afford to get in. But we had a few people who scraped every penny together, helped by family, and those ones you really felt for.

This project mattered to you?

My career and the future of my company are based on trying to find affordable solutions. I'm doing the Olympic Village where I've got 250 non-market units. We did Robson and Richards where the city sold off land in 2003 next door to two crack houses. So I went to the developer and said, "I have a choice. I can sell luxury Robson projects next to crack houses, or you buy them, rebuild them, and I'll get you taller buildings." So I'm trying to find that win-win where the developer has a gain, and the city replaces its housing.

How much of an experiment in a social utopia is the Woodward's project? Is it going to work?

Yes, because Portland Hotel Society is managing the non-market component and they're going to be judged on this. I'm being really cruel, but on a scale of one to ten, they're not going to put their worst crack whore in there. They're going to put in their best cases to prove that the model works. I bank on that. I bank on everybody's secret agenda. They'll make sure the model works so they can prove that it should be duplicated over and over. Maybe on their fifth one, they'll say, "To hell with you, we have to put this drug addict somewhere and we have to put this drug dealer somewhere." But right now I think we're going to get people for whom life has really given a bad turn. That's who they're going to put in. But you'll never again see a 42-storey tower built with small and mid-size suites and those protected views. You go nine blocks down and anything facing the water is 2,600 square feet, and then you go to Woodward's and you can actually buy 600, 700, and 800 square feet with great water views.

You certainly don't hold back, do you?

I am willing to say that the community groups in the area have a love/hate relationship with me. I delivered them 200 units. I helped clean up the area. We'll get a food store and a drug store, and Simon Fraser University will be there. But the area is becoming gentrified and that's not what they wanted. But this isn't Soho or Chelsea, where following artists around is your best real estate investment. In New York and in any city, artists move to depressed areas where rent is cheap. Then the coffee shops move in, you start to see sustainable life move in and the artist can't afford to stay. It happens over and over again. But our social housing structure is legislated and zoned in place. We were careful to tell everybody buying, "This isn't going to become Yaletown. This is going to be a mixed demographic area forever."

This is an unusual city in a lot of ways. It has an intense market, and lots of money can be made. Then there's an equally intense activity in social responsibility. It's a rich, strange city in that way.

It's unbelievable. We'll drive down East Hastings with our foot on the gas pedal to get to Stanley Park to write a cheque to save fallen trees, yet pass all these fallen people on the way. I don't understand it. Because if you write your cheque for trees, it sounds good at dinner and you understand that there's a solution. It's attainable. But if you drive through hell, and look at United We Can—where people are bringing in their found cans and pop bottles and the drug dealer is capturing the money as soon as it's turned around—it looks like *Night of the Living Dead*. It's embarrassing. I was invited to dinner with Adrienne

Clarkson. I very seldom go to organized events at night. VanCity phoned and said, "It's just a few people and you really should come." I was in the middle of doing Woodward's, and I said okay. We met at VanCity, right down Main and Terminal, got onto a bus with Adrienne and eighteen people. The bus turned into Columbia behind Pigeon Park Savings, which is by the Portland Hotel, and there was some commotion as we turned onto Hastings. We realized Adrienne Clarkson wasn't prepared to walk across the street. So we had to circle around Cordova and come back on the south side of Hastings right in front of Pigeon Park Savings, so that she could get off the bus and walk directly into the reception, catered by Bishop's Restaurant, which was all shrouded off so nobody could see in. And she talks about how we have to embrace our new immigrants. I left the minute dinner was finished. I live a very privileged life and I'm as bad as she is, but I'm down there talking to these people and I understand what's going on. There are a lot of Milton Wongs of the world who are trying to save the Downtown Eastside. But I told him the other day, "A bunch of rich guys meeting and easing their conscience isn't going to do it."

Is being down there part of your sense of duty?

Let's judge people by their actions and not by their words. So I'm down there and I've got my employees. It wasn't a lot of convincing, but they had to understand that we're doing our part. I own the real estate, and there will be financial gain down the road, but not for years. I think we need more people like Peter Busby who said that Woodward's should have been our new city hall. He's right. That would have been a real statement that the city is part of the solution.

What kind of statement is the Woodward's project making?

I think the food store/drug store combination is great. So is the Toronto-Dominion, the non-market housing, the market housing. I think we need a three to one ratio to absorb the non-market. I haven't put them in the same elevator, Gregory hasn't and Busby hasn't. We're not there yet. But what happened is that Simon Fraser University felt that they had the machine and the backing to raise money to do this. We got down to last September and they were unable to raise the money. My understanding is that one of the board members went to the premier and said, "Either you give us $4.7 million a year to cover the lease and the tenant improvements, or you're going to look bad."

There was already a hole in the ground, wasn't there?

Yes. It was under construction. Ian Gillespie found this out. If we lost SFU, we would probably lose our retailers, and we'd lose the financing for the project and then you could stick a fork in the Downtown Eastside forever. Seeing what Rich Coleman's been doing for the Downtown Eastside by buying these SRAs, I phoned him, knowing him from previous movies too, and said, "Will you take a meeting because we're about to lose the Downtown Eastside." So I got together with Rich who said, "The provincial government is right. They're tired of universities coming and going. So my problem is now your problem." I said, "This one's different. We're exposed, we're in trouble, play the Olympic card;

play the humanity card." So the provincial government, through Rich Coleman and through Ian Gillespie's great mathematical mind, reduced the yearly shell rent down to about $2.2 million and the provincial government put in $32 million. It saved the project.

Without Simon Fraser, was it really dead in the water?

For this part, Simon Fraser becomes the most important component. If Simon Fraser was there and we lost the market condos, that would be the most important. It's so sensitive. About a month before opening, the city phoned and said, "We want your support for an AIDS-related resource centre," and I said, "No way." I don't own this thing, but I handle the market. And they said, "You have to." It came out of city hall that I was homophobic. I'm gay. I also said, "I won't put in a Starbucks because I can't have anything at the extreme market and non-market ends. It's a paper plate and it's full. I can just go away and you do what you want after I've accomplished the sales, but you have to leave me alone now." And they did. But people are always going to picket me, or worse. There were the three ladies that represented different community groups at Blake's Coffee Parlour on Carrall, and they were going to rip my head off. I said, "I'll meet you on a Sunday," and we went and had coffee. I said, "You have to understand this analogy." I pointed to Bill's Convenience Store across the street on Carrall Street off Cordova, and I said, "You know what this area is going to look like five years from now when Woodward's is done? Bill's is going to have clean windows, a new awning and a new front door. He'll sell more bottled water because tourists are going to make the walk through Gastown, past Woodward's and over to Chinatown." And they said, "We don't want it." I said, "You know what? Poverty is not a sustainable enterprise. It can only go downhill. You don't want it, but Bill needs it for his kids. They're going to take over that store and sell bottled water to tourists and it's too god-damned bad. I'm not giving you a 7-Eleven and a Walmart." They listened and they all backed off. It was a real turning point in that they understood we're going to gently change. We're not going to turn it into Yaletown.

What is going to change the Downtown Eastside?

I think honest conversation. I think people go to a meeting with those three ladies and figure out how I am going to sell them. That's over. We all have access to too much information and I think we need brutal honesty. I went to a meeting with ten community group leaders from the Woodward's Advisory Committee and explained to them what I'm doing. They said, "We need you to come and see each group three times." I said, "No, that's your job. First of all, you know my hourly rate." I don't have an hourly rate. Then I said, "Do you understand what it costs to get me out to a meeting where for which I had to decide between being with my kids and friends and being with you? Do you know the cost of that? I'm not doing it." And they understood. But had I said, "Okay, let me look at my schedule. My people will get back to your people," —they've heard all that before. I think that's why Rich Coleman is doing a good job. He goes in and quietly buys ten SRAs, announces it, and says, "I'm helping solve the problem," rather than standing on a soapbox going, "I'm the guy."

Brutal honesty describes the problem. Is it also a way of finding a solution? What's the best possible scenario that will emerge from a successful Woodward's project?

I think we'll find the flaws. The awful part would be if those non-market units go to 200 friends of influential community group leaders. That's a disaster because then we haven't done anything. This is a business. Poverty is a business. How does it exist in such a vibrant, prosperous city? One, because we have such a moderate climate, people can live outside. Try this in Winnipeg. People from Calgary come here and say, "It's so cold." But I say, "Yeah, you're outside. In Calgary, you're always covered." I think this model will show there is a market demand for the fortunate and the less fortunate living together. All these kids on Facebook are not expecting to live the way their parents live.

Well, they're certainly not going to be able to in Vancouver.

They can't afford it. Vancouver real estate is so buoyant and non-desirable as an economic model because I'm selling to local rich guys, to empty nesters from Iran, Korea, Europe, China, and the rest of Asia. That's what our city really is— we're a resort city. Our city planning department goes crazy when you say it, but the biggest pressure on our real estate prices and why nurses, doctors, clerks and other wage-earners are not buying is our city's restrictive planning policy. You have to find a polite way to say that.

How will you measure whether or not Woodward's has been successful? Will its influence leech into other areas?

I think the developers are buying up all around the area, assuming that it's going to work. The city seems to have a "let's take a breath and understand it" attitude. I also think that we either have to take all the poverty and move it out of the Downtown Eastside or we can absorb it through occupants, renters and home-owners. I prefer absorption to displacement which just makes it somebody else's problem.

In the scenario you imagine, the role of the developer is critical, isn't it? It's not going to be done by social service agencies and the good graces of government.

Without profit, nothing gets done. Let the developer make some profit, but let him give something back. Because without the developer making a profit, we don't need a planning department. Our government's not going to fund everything anymore. The most successful Olympics was LA in 1984 and it was all done commercially, so we have to start looking at that same model to solve our social housing problems.

What are the benchmarks to consider when we look at Woodward's five years from now? How will we know if it has worked?

In a utopian society, if every one of the 536 residents of Woodward's adopted one person on the street, it would all be done. But that's not going to happen. If I have my cast of street people I buy coffee for and you get food for, it's going to happen that the young lawyer who lives in Woodward's buys that same down-and-out person a cup of coffee every day on his way to work. And that person might just start to stabilize a little bit. I think it's about eyes watching each other. You'll drive down Carrall and off Pender, you'll see somebody laying in a lane-way and you'll keep going. If that's on Robson Street, you'll dial 911. But once you live in the area and you always see that person standing up, and they're laying down, you're going to think, "Something's wrong with Harry," and you're going to call for help. I think it's those simple gestures. You can't describe that in a marketing program, and you can't convince people. You look at Salt Tasting Room in the laneway behind Blood Alley. There are people walking into hell, to a restaurant with no kitchen, to have wine, cured meats and cheese. It's packed. When I see that, I realize I didn't even understand that would happen. So it's all moving along. The young couple will go there for dinner on Valentine's and walk through hell. His parents won't, his lawyer won't and his doctor won't, but he will and he's my new demographic.

Jim Green genders the problem. Or makes it a family affair. He looks at 95 percent single male occupancy in the Downtown Eastside. Obviously the demographics have to change, but he says you need mothers and kids.

Families are a hard one. Everybody says we should build towers for families, but a family living in a tower is an alternative lifestyle. Then when you try to homogenize an alternative lifestyle, it doesn't work. I've had so many people say, "Let's put up a gay building on Davie." But unless it's a halfway house, or helping people out, the biggest struggle with the gay population is that they want to be at the Four Seasons. They want an identity, but they also want to fit in, and you know what happens when you have a gay tower: then all the negatives are going to come on—AIDS tower, Vaseline tower—and everything that goes along with it. We have to be careful with these family models. I think it's a bit too early to say, "Let's have kids running down Hastings Street." But it is going to change. If you live in Tinseltown on Pender, and you walk over to shop at Woodward's food floor, or you live in Gastown and you walk over, that's what's going to fix it. The drug dealer is petrified of those people, so he'll go elsewhere, because his customer doesn't want to walk down the street with people like that. So those shifts will take place.

FOLIO IV

SALES DAY: APRIL 22, 2006
Jonathan Cruz

4

THE COMPETITION

AFTER THE CITY OF VANCOUVER purchased the Woodward's building from the province, city council adopted a project framework for the redevelopment to evaluate potential civic and other uses for the project, to consider design options, to address financial oversight, and to develop an inclusive community consultation process. In July 2003, the Woodward's Steering Committee, co-chaired by Jim Green, issued a Request for Expression of Interest for the Woodward's site, inviting proposals from interested developers, tenants, non-market housing sponsors, and non-profit community groups. Some of Vancouver's largest property developers submitted credentials including Concord Pacific Group, Concert Properties, Holborn Group, Westbank Projects/Peterson Investment Group, Columbia Housing Advisory Association, Millenium Properties and Kingswood Capital Corporation.

Proposals ranged from razing the existing building to creating a 'superblock' project by incorporating land west of the building. Various plans combined creative program elements, such as an arts and crafts market or a West Coast longhouse, with a mix of social housing, rental apartments, condominium units, arts complexes, social services, information-technology spaces and native healing centres. Many of the proposals recognized that the scale and allowable density of 55,700 square metres on the Woodward's site offered a rare opportunity to create a new neighbourhood hub on the downtown peninsula.

Developers were asked to present their visions at two public meetings in November 2003. The Woodward's Steering Committee short-listed Concert Properties, Holborn Group, Millenium Properties and Westbank Projects/Peterson Investment Group in February 2004 to participate in the second stage of the developer competition, the formal Request for Proposals, which presented guiding principles for the Woodward's project based on information gathered from the city's public consultation process. The Affordable Housing Society, Columbia Housing Advisory Association, and PHS Community Services Society were short-listed as non-market housing sponsors and also invited to participate in the Request for Proposals.

Since all short-listed developers were deemed capable of financing the Woodward's redevelopment, which at that time was estimated to cost approximately $150 million, the second stage of the competition would be decided by the best architectural vision and financial package. The developer-led teams had 10 weeks to refine their concepts. The Request for Proposals required them to present schemes with and without SFU's School for the Contemporary Arts.

Holborn Group, a Malaysian-based development company lacking development experience in Vancouver, had chosen to partner with architecture firm Davidson Yuen Simpson, whose principal Ron Yuen had presented, with Jim Green and the Downtown Eastside Residents Association, plans to the provincial government in the late 1980s to convert the Woodward's building into co-operative housing. Holborn's scheme, called Woodward's Square, proposed carving a public plaza from the centre of the heritage buildings that would act as the heart of the project and surrounding community. Two weeks into the competition, Holborn Group requested an amendment to the Request for Proposals that would allow them to include two lots they owned adjoining the Woodward's site, effectively enlarging the project footprint. Because the city wanted to test whether a larger site would benefit the project, they approved the amendment to the consternation of the other competing teams.

Concert Properties was a union-pension-backed developer who had 20 years of local building experience and made political contributions to the left-leaning COPE party. They partnered with architecture firm Musson Cattell Mackey on a proposal called Woodward's Place, which was centred on a publicly accessible open space similar to Holborn's scheme. Concert saw the advantage of Holborn's two adjoining lots for bringing more light to the centre and creating a less imposing project. They joined forces with Holborn, and the two groups worked on unifying their architectural visions. The final proposal accommodated 135 loft-style market housing units in the heritage structure and added a tower whose first 10 floors would house SFU's School for the Contemporary Arts with the remaining floors dedicated to 100 units of social housing. Vancouver Community College would establish its Contemporary Design Centre and School of Music on the ground floor and basement of the heritage structure facing Cordova Street. The 1903/08 building would be refurbished for uses designated by the city.

Millenium Properties, a local developer partnering with architecture firm Gomberoff Bell Lyon and urban consultant Chuck Brook, based their proposal on a 163-metre tower articulated in three offset components. The tower would create a vertical street for 300 market housing units interspersed with sky parks accessible to residents. If built, the tower would have been the second highest in Vancouver. One hundred five units of social housing would be accommodated in the heritage structure. The neon 'W' sign, considered to be of historic significance to the site and a central icon for the Downtown Eastside, would be located in the courtyard.

Westbank Projects/Peterson Investment Group, a development company specializing in high-end projects such as Vancouver's Shaw Tower and Living Shangri-La, was convinced by Henriquez Partners Architects to enter the competition. Westbank's proposal centred on razing the site save the original 1903/1908 Woodward's building at the corner of Hastings and Abbott, and incorporating the program in one tower, two mid-rise buildings and the heritage building. The fracturing of the site into different components would allow pedestrian access through the project and define better linkages between the various communities surrounding Woodward's. Having also chosen the Portland Hotel Society as an advisor and community partner, Henriquez Partners was aware of the demands from the Downtown Eastside community for more social housing than the 100 units for which provincial funding had been secured. Although the RFP only required 100 social housing units, Westbank's proposal identified how up to 237 units could be accommodated in their design. The proposed housing considered the needs of a wide population from families with children to seniors.

In early July 2004, the teams submitted their final proposals and made hour-long presentations to the city council, the city planning department and the Woodward's Steering Committee. During the next two months, each proposal was judged on the degree to which it maximized benefits to local residents and the city at large, the economic viability for the developer and the financial return to the city of Vancouver.

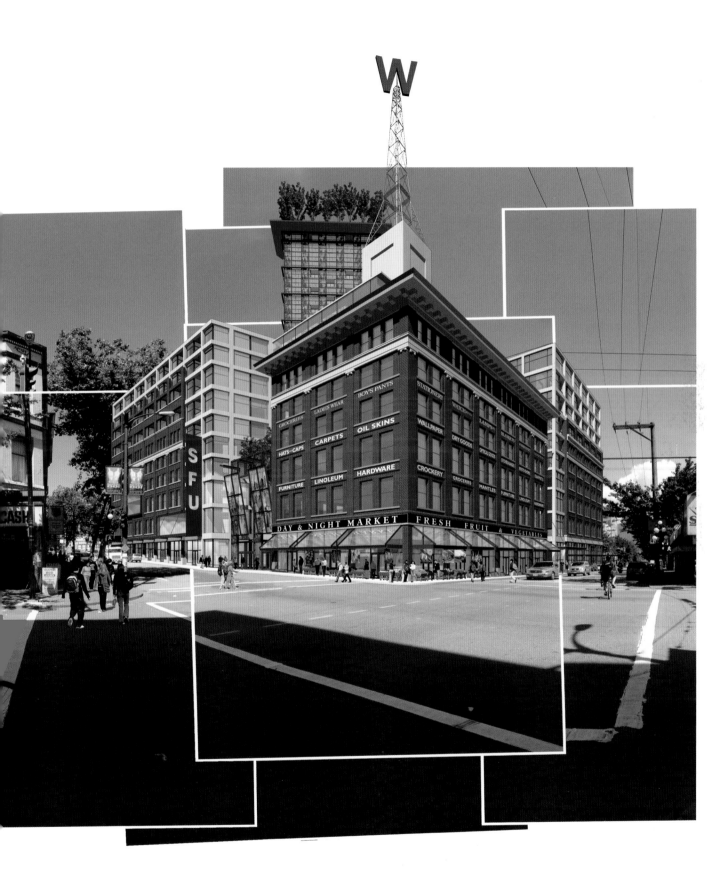

An Evaluation Committee was formed to conduct detailed evaluations in accordance with the terms and conditions of the RFP and eleven evaluation criteria: overall quality, urban design and architecture, sustainable development, heritage restoration and retention, financial performance, retail and commercial impacts, social goods and community linkages, non-market housing, engineering and transportation, project schedules and community feedback. The Evaluation Committee reported their conclusions to the Steering Committee, which then made a recommendation to city council.

The proposal from Millenium Properties offered the best financial terms of the three proposals and would provide the city with $20 to 22 million, but was contingent on gaining significant height and a floor space ratio over that specified in the Woodward's Urban Design Guidelines. The financial incentive was attractive, but not sufficient to overcome the urban design and architectural challenges the tower height posed. Overtly iconic, the tower was deemed to challenge the height, form and scale of the rich, established historic context and therefore sent an inappropriate symbolic design statement. While Millenium expressed willingness to work with staff and community to revisit the design, all agreed a full redesign would compromise the proposal.

The financial structure of Concert/Holborn's proposal was contingent on a transfer of 37,100 to 43,400 square metres of bonus and heritage density valued at between $40 million and $47 million from the Woodward's and adjacent sites to a distressed construction site on West Georgia Street, which Holborn later attempted to develop into the Ritz-Carlton Condominium Hotel designed by Arthur Erickson. Concert/Holborn would only cover the cost of the non-market housing shortfall of $6.1 million if they were permitted by the city to transfer most or all of the density to West Georgia requiring both properties to be successfully rezoned. The proposal charged the highest price for the city parcel and contained uncertain returns in the profit share for the market housing to cover the city's land cost. Concert/Holborn would require the city to fund, and thus take financial risk for, the entire 1903/1908 building restoration. While the Concert/Holborn proposal garnered the strongest support from the city's planning department and offered the preferred heritage and

urban design solution, the contingencies related to its financial performance were deemed too risky for the city.

Like Millenium, Westbank's proposal was also contingent on being granted a height and density allowance, though more modest than that required by Millenium. Westbank proposed a straight trade of the land for the city parcel located in the 1903/08 heritage structure, accepting all risk associated with upgrading it and providing a tenant improvement allowance to finish it. Significant tax and levy allowances were requested totaling $8 million. A transferable off-site heritage density bonus would provide the developer with a further $8.4 million to $10.1 million. Westbank assumed that the province would fund the non-market housing shortfall of between $5.6 million and $7.3 million. In contrast to Concert/Holborn's proposal, Westbank demonstrated a commitment to place a larger amount of density on the Woodward's site to achieve a critical mass of people and facilitate the revitalization of the surrounding neighbourhood through much needed retail and commercial activity. The proposal expressed confidence in the local marketplace through the amount of dedicated retail space and the provision of a food market; the retail and commercial component garnered the most support from the business community, including the Gastown Business Improvement Society. Responsive to calls by community members for ongoing participation in the project's further design development, the proposal requested that the city establish a Community Advisory Council of neighbourhood representatives.

The proposal received favourable community support with its economically viable, flexible, and sustainable urban design and also because Henriquez Partners had previously worked with Jim Green, as had the architects on both the other teams, on several successful community-based housing projects in the Downtown Eastside. While the project's height and provision of exterior open space would need further consideration, the Woodward's Steering Committee, including then Co-Director of Planning, Larry Beasley, appreciated the proposal's possibilities for urban revitalization through an ambitious mixed-use program and the diagonal thoroughfare coursing the plan. The committee was unanimous in its recommendation in September 2004 to have the city of Vancouver enter into negotiations with Westbank Projects/Peterson Investment Group as Woodward's project developer.

The Project Manager, Michael Flanigan

FOLIO V

DEMOLITION: SEPTEMBER 30, 2006
Shawn Lapointe

5

Woodward's is a project that started as a community development dream and it has become the biggest single site development in the history of Vancouver. It is a landmark project that is very different then any other major project in the city because it was created out of social concern.

Jim Green

THE COMMUNITY

PUBLIC PARTICIPATION was essential to the vibrancy, relevancy and achievements of Woodward's as a community-based development project. As early as June 2004, the Westbank project team recommended the formation of a Woodward's Community Advisory Committee (WCAC) to ensure the ongoing participation of the public, the Downtown Eastside and adjacent neighbhourhoods in an advisory capacity. In March 2005, as the Woodward's project entered detailed design development, the city, with input from Jim Green of the Woodward's Steering Committee, appointed area residents, community advocates, and business stakeholders to the committee and administered it until January 2007, when the city issued a building permit for the Woodward's site and the committee's mandate ended. Participating in an ex-officio capacity were representatives from the city of Vancouver, the project team, SFU, and the non-market housing sponsors.

The WCAC was charged by the city with providing guidance and advice to the development team, city staff and the Woodward's Steering Committee on issues related to the Woodward's redevelopment, including overall design, non-profit uses, integration of the non-market housing, and accessibility. Its recommendations would aim to improve the social, cultural and economic well-being of area residents and neighbours. The WCAC would also ensure that the project respects the Guiding Principles, a distillation of the community visioning process in 2003. It would advise on ways for the project to incorporate community talents, visions and desires, and develop options for how to implement the advice within resources limitations. To increase meaningful public input into the development's process and content, the committee would consult with external groups and the public at large.

In May 2005, the project team presented WCAC with design changes that were conditional to the city's selection of Westbank as Project Developer. These changes included lowering the W Building by 15 metres and creating a second tower on the Abbott Building to accommodate extra density from an additional 100 units of non-market housing and SFU's confirmed presence. While the committee accepted the new design, it did not agree with the planning rationale for limiting the tower height, which was to avoid setting a precedent for violating view corridors. Many committee members preferred the W Building's previous height of 134 metres and the resulting massing on the remainder of the site. Confirming that the atrium and public plaza would not be gated but be owned and operated by the city of Vancouver to ensure public access, the committee supported the expanded public realm. The committee also voiced general support for replacing the existing structure, except the original 1903/1908 building, with new construction.

The WCAC advised on the selection criteria and process used to determine the non-profit groups that would occupy the city parcel. The city requested committee members sit on the Selection Advisory Panels to evaluate applications for

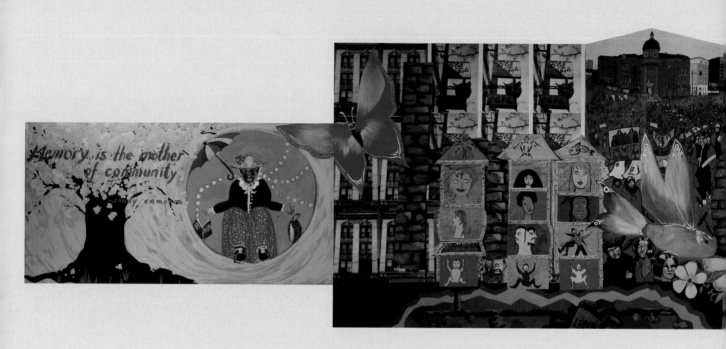

the non-profit and childcare spaces against the evaluation criteria and provide a vehicle for community input in the selection. The committee was able to nominate other community members who could represent the childcare sector and the three categories of non-profit organizations being considered—social service, health and culture—to participate on the selection panels.

As the Woodward's redevelopment entered the construction phase in early 2007, the WCAC was instrumental in compiling a list of Downtown Eastside businesses and organizations that would serve to maximize local hiring for catering, security, cleaning and other services needed during construction. The city issued the Development Permit for Woodward's on January 26, 2007, ending the role of the WCAC as an advisory committee to the city, but it suggested compiling a reconstituted committee.

Lee Donohue, co-chair of the WCAC and long-time Downtown Eastside resident activist, believes that continuing to use the participatory process that the Woodward's project has defined is imperative because it gives the area residents a voice. Rather than betraying his principles as some have accused him, he feels his participation on the committee was a way of engaging and learning about the development process. He would like to see Woodward's setting a precedent that required all housing projects in the Downtown Eastside to incorporate a community advisory committee.

BladeRunners

An important community partner of the Woodward's redevelopment was the BladeRunners organization. BladeRunners is an award-winning employment program for at-risk and disadvantaged women and men aged 19 to 30. In September 2006, two weeks before demolition of the old structure save the original 1903/08 store, bricks from the Woodward's building were sold, raising $19,000 to help support BladeRunners. BladeRunners secured many construction jobs on the Woodward's site for youth enrolled in their program.

The Woodward's Mural

In the fall of 2006, I was asked to come up with a proposal to create a mural for the construction hoarding around the Woodward's redevelopment. Workshops began in the spring, and the mural was installed in the summer of 2007. The project involved 36 artists and residents of the Downtown Eastside. We incorporated all the ideas into one image, and much like a collage, the work had structure as well as space for improvising. Many hands, many ideas, and many hours. In the thousands of square feet of murals that I have helped coordinate, the painting of this one in the DTES has been the most meaningful. Maybe because it was the last one, or because Woodward's has meant so many different things to people, and maybe because it's beautiful.

Sharon Kravitz

Mayor Gregor Robertson with Gary Jobin and Gilbert Morvin of BladeRunners

Woodward's Community Advisory Committee

Committee Members

Lee Donohue	Area resident, Co-Chair
Lou Parsons	Area resident
Wendy Pederson	Area resident
Anne Marie Slater	Area resident
Dean Wilson	Area resident
Linda Mix	Housing advocate
Albert Fok	Chinatown Merchants Association
Jon Stovell	Gastown Business Improvement Association, Co-Chair
Judy McGuire	DEYAS
Susan Tatoosh	ACCESS
Paul Tubbe	Advisory Committee—Disability Issues
Joe Wai	Joe Wai Architects
Sean McEwen	Architect

Ex-Officio Members

Michael Flanigan	City of Vancouver, Project Manager and Director of Real Estate Services
Nathan Edelson	City of Vancouver, Senior Planner
Christina Medland	City of Vancouver, Assistant Director of Cultural Affairs
Vickie Morris	City of Vancouver, Senior Social Planner
Anka Raskin	City of Vancouver, Social Planner
Christine Tapp	City of Vancouver, Planning Assistant
Helen Ma	City of Vancouver, Planning Assistant
David Leung	Westbank Projects
Gregory Henriquez	Henriquez Partners Architects
Bob Nicklin	Affordable Housing Society
Jim O'Dea	Consultant–Affordable Housing Society
Mark Townsend	Portland Hotel Society
Tom Laviolette	Portland Hotel Society
Owen Underhill	Simon Fraser University

Woodward's Mural Project Participants

Project Coordination Team
Sharon Kravitz, Sara Ross, Quin Martins, Rose Spahaan

Artists
Adrienne Macullum, Amber Shara Dell, Barbara Allan, Beatrice Starr, Betty Morris, Bryce Rasmussen, Calvin Bradbury, Derek Mehaffey, Debbie Leo, Diane Jacobs, Diane Letchuck, Doris Angel Ponkey, Donna Gorrill, Elizabeth Cheng, Frederick Cummings, Hendrik Beune, Hermes (Daryl) Williams, Karen Lahay, Madeline Arkley, Michael Frazer, Montana King, Muriel Williams, Patricia Harram, Jeska Slater, Richard Shorty, Robin Johnson, Ron Solonis, Selina Barton, Sharon Burns

Documentation
Yun Lam Li

Workshop Leaders
Richard Tetrault, Guinevere Pencarrick

STREET SMARTER
Lee Donohue

Lee Donohue
DTES Activist and Co-Chair
Woodward's Community
Advisory Committee

Lee Donohue is a native of Vancouver and grew up in the Mount Pleasant area. As a child, he recalls coming to the Woodward's store with his mother; the store was a working-class environment, relaxed, pleasant to spend time in.

Mr. Donohue has been a volunteer in the DTES community for more than 18 years, and has been involved with efforts to redevelop Woodward's since its closure in the early 1990s. He considers helping to change the government's perception of housing from a luxury to a basic necessity for mental and physical health as one of his greatest accomplishments. He hopes that the Woodward's project may become a template for mixed-market housing developments across North America.

I'M A COMMUNITY ORGANIZER. I've been a volunteer for 18 years in the Downtown Eastside, so I've been involved in Woodward's since its inception. I didn't shop at the store, but my parents did. My mother would drag me down there and then leave me at the downstairs counter. Everything was much safer in those days, so I could just stay there. I'd have ice cream and she'd go shopping. My father was a logger who tended to frequent the hotels and the bars in that part of downtown. So it was an area not unfamiliar to me.

One of the reasons I think that my family and people in our neighbourhood used to go there was that we actually knew the employees. It was a very working-class, relaxed environment. Hundreds of people would go to the Vancouver Library, get a coffee and sit there all day and read. They weren't necessarily homeless, but they lived in single-room occupancy hotels, SROs. The library was at Robson and Burrard, which is now a music store. The top floor of the Bay was another place people would go because they made fresh scones everyday at 3:00 and they were cheap. So it was a social hangout for some people.

When people talk about the marginalized class, it really gets me going. I don't know what that means anymore, but I think in 2008 it's certainly different than it was in the '60s and '70s. I'm one of those poor, working-class people. Were we marginalized? I don't know. There were only two people in my 10-block square area who went to university. It was primarily working-class. Yes, we were marginalized in an economic sense. But compared to today, no.

The people who lived down here were mostly single males. My stepfather knew lots of them. They were loggers. They'd go out and come back in, have a binge for a couple of weeks, and then go back out. Or people like my stepfather would binge before he went home. That was what the hotels down there were for. And there was a liquor store at Main and Hastings for many years. Actually, I ended up working there when I went to university.

The history of developing the Woodward's site goes back a long way. I don't know where to start. There have been lots of players. We often suspected that owners bought the property so they could flip it.

I was present when the "Squat" happened, but I wasn't living in it. I had been involved in other things before. The city of Vancouver was starting to develop the Downtown Eastside and one of their projects was called the Van Horne, a building that went up without much community consultation. At that point we realized we should have been involved and that we had to get it together. So a bunch of us, who were already activists in the community, formed this group. We decided we were going to concentrate our energy on these big developments that were coming. We called ourselves the Woodward's Co-op Committee. On one hand, we were trying to legitimately negotiate with the city by going to all the planning hearings and, on the other, we were staging protests at the offices of developers.

The Portland Hotel Society and I are kindred spirits in lots of ways, especially in terms of the political side of things. I was on the board of the Carnegie Community Centre in those days and we created the Carnegie Action Project. We organized paint-ins at Woodward's. We tried to keep ownership of the building and keep it in the media. The membership changed over the years, but I'd say we had an average of nine to a dozen members.

The most important thing to realize about what we were doing was that we had nothing. We were just a bunch of people who lived and worked in the neighbourhood and who cared about it. No developer or city councillor wanted to talk to us. They didn't know who the hell we were, and they thought we were a bunch of bums. We had to convince them that not only were we worth talking to, but they didn't have to be afraid of us. We could actually work together, and we could learn mutually. For all kinds of political reasons, some people didn't want to work with us at all, and some people wanted us as a token. Over the years, we met with many different developers and looked at many plans. It would often get to the blueprint stage; we thought it was going to happen and then it came crashing down again.

It got to be depressing after a while. People asked me if I really wanted to get involved with the housing issue. I had been doing other stuff in the community, but I knew that housing was important and it was going to be a major issue. Our group always wanted the same thing. We wanted to learn how to deal with developers, so we could teach other people in the community. Most of them just wanted us to go to hell. But because of Jim Green's connections, we were able to get a bit of tokenism. Now, Jim is not the kind of guy who likes meetings. He's pragmatic; he likes to get things done and go. We had to haul him in and say, "Look, we have to work together and we do need to have meetings and you need to communicate with us. We actually want to learn what you know." He wanted to do it, but he didn't want to do it. Time wise, it's a huge thing to teach people. But eventually he agreed and so the Woodward's Co-op was created.

We were looking for people interested in developing the site. We met with famous architects and with budding architects. One thing that became clear to us right away was that while we were teaching ourselves about what they did, we had to teach them about the community. None of them would admit it, but most of them were afraid. It took us a while to realize that our community wasn't part of their perception; it wasn't part of their world. They didn't know how to deal with people sleeping on sidewalks, getting drunk, beating each other up—all that stuff. It was too dirty. They were completely freaked out by the notion of mixed-market housing. I live in a co-op that's mixed and it works really well. But there were lots of people who said, "It will never happen; no one will ever support mixed housing in the Downtown Eastside. It's got to go high end or nothing. Or else, they've got to build slum things." Our position was, "It can work, and it will work." We just kept saying that over and over and over.

There are two areas where we did make a big difference and I'm especially proud of them. We started telling all these organizations, at the federal, provincial, and city levels, that housing was a physical and mental health issue. They said, "What the hell are you talking about?" Now everybody talks about it as a given, but in the early '90s they thought we were crazy. They said, "This is just another con by people who have nothing and are trying to make us feel guilty." It was bizarre.

We had several organized delegations go to city hall to take over council meetings. We used stuff like that. At one of the meetings, there were some nurses, some retired and some practicing, and none of us knew them. They stood up and started saying to the councillors, "I want to live in a mixed housing place like Woodward's; I have enough money. I'm single and I don't want a house, but I would be really proud to buy a place in a community environment like that, knowing what I was doing was helping to support that kind of venture." That was a big beautiful day for us.

You could see certain councillors were really nervous. They didn't believe that these people existed, but now they couldn't say no to us. They had been arguing that we have to negotiate with the developer, and the developer's scared because he knows he can't sell the units if there's Downtown Eastside people in there. They were really blatant about it at first but now they're saying, "We're really not that way at all."

Once we were established as a committee, the city gave us official advisory status. There were lots of reasons why that happened and Gregory was probably one of the biggest. He's such a generous man, he would say, "If you want to get involved in the process, I'll let you get involved. We'll sit down and talk about doorknobs." He thought it would bore us to tears, but everyone loved it because we'd never been asked that kind of stuff. And people, of course, had lots of ideas about how hallways should be designed, what kind of rooms would be practical, about sizes and lengths.

When Glen Clark was premier, the provincial government agreed to give us 200 units of social housing, but there was no developer for Woodward's yet. There was also fear amongst our group. First of all, they offered us money and we said, "We don't want the money; we want the units because, by the time it gets built, who knows what it's going to cost." We were surprised, but they agreed to it.

One of the points of change in the group came about because we were spending a hell of a lot of time and energy in meetings. So we had to decide what we were going to do. Some people on the committee said, "Look, let's take 200 units now. We might never get anything else, so let's take them, look for another site, and try to build them." A few of us said, "We don't think that's a great idea. We're not letting go of Woodward's, we're going to stay." So the group split; one side fighting for the Woodward's site, and the other forming the Lore Krill Housing Co-op. They found two locations and they got them built. The 200 units by Lore Krill were a consequence of Woodward's.

At that point, there were individuals in the community who were getting pissed off at us and saying, "We wanted 400 units of social housing in Woodward's and you guys have sold out." Our response was, "Give us a break, we're not selling out, we're making this sell. We've got to do something because this thing isn't happening." Communicating and working with these guys was so intense. You have to be careful not to lose touch with the grassroots. What happens is the group becomes an entity in itself, and the government doesn't want to have to recreate all this again; so once they decide they like you, that they're not afraid of you, then they'll deal with you. Then the people in the community start to distrust you. They were asking us, "Why are you hanging out with those guys?" None of us were getting piss all; none of us were working. It was all volunteer work. We didn't get honorariums; we got nothing. We had to scrounge to have coffee at our own meetings. But there was so much fear and distrust in the community.

One of our goals was to show so-called outsiders that we could have valuable input in the process. Another goal was to show the community itself that they could be positively involved in the process, that it wasn't all terrible, that we could actually learn by working together. But I can tell you that, for years, it was pretty hard to pull that off because the city, the government and the developers weren't being very good to us. And the community was getting frustrated because people were dying, people were still trying to get housing and it was getting worse.

When I started out, the big thing was getting social housing for single women with children, people who needed two- and three-bedroom places. That was a big need in the Downtown Eastside. You'd meet kids whose bed was the drawer of the bureau in the room. A lot of them were Native. I remember, at Carnegie in those years, we had ongoing debates about getting social programs for Native people in the Downtown Eastside. The demographic had changed a lot. The community had gone from single, white working-class guys—loggers and fishermen—to a community in which there were lots of Native kids. It was a strange time in the '60s and '70s, when the government allowed families to sell their children's status in the hope that they would get a better start in the city. The federal government had come up with this idea that they would buy the children's status. So Native kids would come to the city and, of course, racism was rampant and they weren't getting hired and there was all kinds of trouble. It was a whole other kind of melting pot, and our group wasn't successful in reaching out to that community. It's frustrating because we still don't know how to deal with the problem.

There are other problems. All these people with "dual-diagnosis"—another phrase that has only been accepted in the last five to ten years—are being dumped here from Riverview, a nearby psychiatric hospital, due to funding cutbacks. They have addictions. Then there's this whole new class of young, middle-class white kids getting thrown into the mix. They don't feel attached to the community; they're only here because of the drug scene. They'll eventually go back to their neighbourhoods because their commitment isn't to the Downtown Eastside. They're not really part of the neighbourhood in the way the Native community is, or the loggers were before them. They're here because there's nowhere else for them to go.

If you go to some drug or alcohol meetings, you can hear these guys. They are banker's kids, teacher's kids, middle-class kids who grew up in environments where there was alcohol and cocaine. Cocaine was more a part of that environment than it was in the Downtown Eastside. Heroin was big in the Downtown Eastside, but cocaine was really a middle-class thing. There were repercussions from this migration. The police had this stupid policy of pushing everyone to the Downtown Eastside. For years, they denied it; now at least, they admit they did it as a means of control. Their theory was, if they had them all in one area, you could control the problem. It was just ridiculous. You don't want the police doing social engineering.

The question of our power and the precedent we established is a complicated one. Even though we accomplished a lot, I think it was never enough, and it still isn't enough. The need becomes greater and greater, and society doesn't really want to deal with its problems. It was odd for me to suddenly realize that the people I was working with were actually middle-class, they weren't working-class anymore. It was a shock. I'm talking about the street guys, the addicts and the dual-diagnosis kids. They weren't poor, but they had been totally rejected by their families. In the Native community, fetal alcohol syndrome was a big thing. But in the white community, there were different buzzwords—attention deficit disorder; kids who'd had Ritalin shoved down their throat for years and who learned that drugs are just part of life; kids who were watching their mothers. It's like that Rolling Stones song, "Have You Seen Your Mother, Baby". It's a whole societal problem.

There were also by-law problems. There were different categories, like housekeeping rooms or SROs, and each category gave you different rights; you could have a fridge and a stove, or else just a hotplate. The city had wanted to save the housing that existed. But we don't want it saved; we wanted homes. They were talking about rooms slightly larger than the size of your bedroom which would include everything, the kitchen and the bathroom. Is it better to have people living there instead of sleeping of the street? Sure. But it's not a home and it's not mixed housing, especially when they're effecting this huge demographic change to the area. They're changing all kinds of things by encouraging development for young, middle-class workers, but they're not helping the people who are in the community. They buy these SRO hotels and they say they won't kick people out, but I've seen a couple of them and there's nobody living in them. What are they doing? Are they renovating them?

We lobbied the city to relax some of their by-laws so that the people in the SROs and the so-called housekeeping rooms would be allowed to cook and have fridges in their rooms. To do that, they had to change the square footage rule because that's what it was all based on: the amount of square feet defines what you can do this in the space. So they had to relax that. Man, you couldn't believe how fast the developers ran. They ran to False Creek and started building these 225 square foot spaces and selling them for $300,000. That's how they dealt with the issue. We had a few of these guys come to our meetings and say, "I want to build a place full of these little units for people. It'll really help them. It'll have murphy beds and they'll love it." Well, it's just cheap crap. We said, "We don't want that, we want to build mixed social housing." And they just keep trundling out the same speech, over and over and over.

In the meantime, there is pressure in the community because we were beginning to see more homeless people, more people sleeping on the streets. There used to be so many hideaways in Vancouver; Stanley Park, underneath the Burrard Bridge, a couple of lots where they're building that new Olympic Village. There were actually people living in those areas, who had lived there for years. They had dug these elaborate nests, and the city came and dug them up and kicked all those people out. They were always there; you just didn't see them. Now they go places where they can sleep in a doorway, or in the back of a shop—some place where they're not going to get bugged. There used to be a lot more bush areas, and those have all gone. They were well-used. A lot of the old guys would tell you that you don't screw around in the summer; you screw around in the winter, because then you go to the can where you're okay for the winter. Those guys actually lived that way.

There were also corrupt landlords who would rent one room to five different guys on welfare. To be eligible for welfare, they had to prove they had a residence. So the landlords would stamp it. What they were actually doing was pilfering 50 to 100 bucks from each guy's cheque and they weren't even living there. They were living on the street, and the landlords had four and five people listed as living in this one room. A couple of them finally got caught. But I know it still goes on.

Gregory really changed a lot for me. I was getting depressed by the in-fighting in our own group. It just gets on your nerves, putting in all this energy and thinking you're doing the right thing, and then wondering, should we have done this, or maybe done that. Then a guy like Gregory comes along and treats you with such respect and honours you. It was wonderful.

I think Gregory's a puzzle to the other developers. I mean, you get used to cons living in the Downtown Eastside, and you know most of them yourself. Maybe not the multi-million dollar ones. But Gregory, he's just one of the guys. He was immediately really helpful and sincere. I don't think anyone ever felt he was being condescending or patronizing. It definitely gave us another step of power with the city because now, we had another person to lobby for us, not just Jim Green, but Gregory. And Gregory had connections to the development community that Jim wanted.

I took a stint on the Gastown Historic Area Planning Committee because they hated us; they hate the soup lines; they hate places for people to sleep; they hate everything about us. But because of Lore Krill Housing Co-op, which was on the edge of Gastown, we were considered homeowners. We were allowed to send our reps to the Committee. They didn't like it, but we got the city to make sure that we went. So they got used to us and realized we weren't so bad after all. I think there are a lot of people out there who are really nice, but they just buy into a stereotype. And we're equally guilty of stereotyping. Once we actually got together, they realized we weren't so bad. There's this heroin addict Dean Wilson. We were all joking because he and John Stovell were speaking for the housing projects up at city hall. John even commented that he never thought he'd see the day. But it worked. Although the most boring fucking job I ever did was on this committee.

I'm still worried about Woodward's and I tell Gregory about it once in a while. I'm worried about it becoming a gated community and not being part of the Downtown Eastside. I'm not convinced we're there yet. We still have to get a user agreement with the city, Simon Fraser and the community. There are lots of things to do and the Woodward's Community Advisory Committee hasn't met for over a year and a half now. I keep trying to get meetings but I know that the role of the committee as a city advisory body has changed and the people from the city really don't give a shit. They don't want us. There are lots of people who didn't want Woodward's to become a success under any conditions

I've been trying to promote the process as much as I can, but there are just no ears for it right now. People aren't interested. I really want to promote Gregory because I think he is the real key to the thing. I think the Portland is really important; I think what we did is really important. But I think the key is Gregory and the respect he gets from the community for his work and from the circles he travels in—I think we have a long way to go into that community. And Gregory is going to be swept away by other jobs. He's not going to develop every project in the Downtown Eastside, and I haven't seen anyone who is even close to him. So maybe the ball has started to roll, but slowly. But I think it could stop; it could even roll backwards. It could screw up that easily.

I'm tired but I believe in the process. It's the way I learned to do political and community activism. I know it works, I've seen it. You sit down and you say, "This is my position, this is what I want. Now what do you want?" And then you compromise. And so far, especially since Gregory's been involved, it's worked every time. The worst thing I learned in university was how to read between the lines. It's bullshit and it's a waste of time. You shouldn't have to read between the lines. But I'm concerned about it becoming a gated community. I really want to get on Simon Fraser's case. No one likes to talk about this, but, many years ago when Simon Fraser was going to get involved, they wanted us to support their application to the city. I said, "Great but you could do something for us too. In exchange you could say you're not going into that site if there isn't social housing." They refused.

So I said to hell with them. They hate it when I bring that up, but you do have to be vigilant. They move quickly. And if you're not there, not having meetings and not having interaction, you don't know what the hell these guys are doing. I don't know what's going on there. I know that Simon Fraser is scared of us. I think they're scared shitless. They've got 125 units of dual-diagnosis housing sitting on the roof of their institution. I said, "Look, what we want from you guys is to set up programs, early entrance qualifications for people who live on the Downtown Eastside—single women, mothers, Native people—just let them into your programs as mature students." We even found support within Simon Fraser for the idea and they took it to the Board of Governors who turned it down. So we don't want anything to do with them.

Woodward's is barely the beginning. Even though it's a $250 million project, it's still really just the beginning. It's a good start, but it needs security. It's not secure at all. Even the 31,000 square feet for the community is not safe. We don't really have a community-use agreement with the city, even though we're supposed to have one. They could kick people out—give them five-year leases or three-year leases, kick them out and put city offices down there. We're still fighting to make sure that the entrance to the non-profit community space is accessible just like all the other entrances. They didn't want it. They want a separate entrance on Abbott Street to keep "those people" away from "these people."

I love the project. Even with all these problems, it's fantastic. I don't think people realize that there is nothing like Woodward's in North America that has a university, social housing, private business and market housing, all in this incredibly cramped area. Sometimes I can't believe it.

GROUND LEVELLER
Mark Townsend

Mark Townsend
Executive Director
Portland Hotel Society

Mark Townsend immigrated to Canada from England in the early 1990s. Having intended to stay temporarily, his volunteer work on a housing project led him to remain in Vancouver on a permanent basis.

Executive director and co-founder of the Portland Hotel Society, Mark believes that founding the Society with Ms. Evans was less a conscious decision than something that just happened in response to the situation in the DTES, and the sheer number of people who needed the support. He hopes that Woodward's will become a mini-city and integrate some vital services into the DTES by providing sufficient people to keep them in place. While it was, in many ways, a compromise, he hopes that it will turn out to be a good one.

I WAS BORN IN ENGLAND and came to Vancouver in 1992. I shopped at Woodward's myself. Everyone in Vancouver says they shopped at Woodward's. From the CEO of Concert, David Podmore, to Michael Audain, the CEO of Polygon, everyone has some story, from actually working in the store to sweeping Blood Alley outside of it. Jimmy Pattison didn't have a direct connection, but he had stacked hymn books in the mission on the corner.

As an outsider, it almost seemed like a joke. In Britain, would everyone have a story about British Home Stores? No. There isn't the romantic, teary-eyed, Jim Green-ish kind of story there.

I initially came here because my partner was Canadian, and I ended up not leaving. I was going to work on a housing project for a year to help Liz out and time drifted on and I was helping more and more. I sort of got tricked.

At PHS Community Services, we operate as a team so we don't really have titles. Technically, Liz and I are the executive directors and the founders of the PHS. We would be the main people in charge, but it doesn't really come out like that. I'm just a person in the community trying to do something in the best way I can with what's in front of my face. I can only deal with what I see.

My mom and dad have recently come here because we've got kids and they wanted to be nearer to them. In England, my parents grew up in what would be seen as the slums, so they come from a rough area and they have a simple perspective. They couldn't believe the Downtown Eastside. My mom actually cried. She just thought, "How could this exist in North America?"

That view is echoed by most Europeans. Ultimately, there aren't that many homeless people in Europe, and while the housing there is inadequate, they're not in a 100 square foot room where they share a bathroom and toilet with 20 or 30 other people.

It's funny how things don't change. Just the other day, I was reading an editorial in The Province that said, "The Downtown Eastside is a blight on the community and rampant development is the cost of it and the city needs to have a plan." The editorial is from 1954. So these things are always with us, especially in North America. There's a lot of naïveté about there being simple answers to the problems. There aren't.

When we started the Portland, our perspective was that you needed to meet people where they are, and make them as comfortable as you can. That's a simplistic version of what we were trying to do. But in trying to make people comfortable, you get involved in all kinds of different things, whether they're dental clinics or banks or grocery stores. People here don't have the infrastructure that the rest of society has. It doesn't exist.

I could see that people weren't getting any medical care. HIV was shooting through the community like a wave, and people were saying you could only exchange needles and not distribute them. This was a significant public health issue; an individual would only be allowed three needles but 12 people were using them. So we basically grew a needle distribution. We got needles from somewhere and we distributed them. The system had cost a lot of people their lives, and it continues to cost lives. It also meant that the Downtown Eastside had the highest HIV conversion rate in the Western world. But nobody listened because junkies and people with addictions are seen as less than human, like they're not as good as you or me, but bad people.

We weren't political, we were just pragmatic. I was speaking recently to a woman high-up in Gordon Campbell's government and she was saying the Portland comes up a lot. They say we're political and they'd also say, "But if we give them money, they'll actually get something done; they're good at getting things done." Unfortunately, we're not achieving any fundamental change. We just get a little more bread and butter on the table for people.

It is like being in a refugee camp. It's little kids who went through the foster care system, had 25 foster parents and were sexually abused by five of them. They have brain damage, but now they're too old for us to care about anymore, so that's the end of them. They are our society's refugees, and they're scapegoats for all of our pain.

The refugee camp is a model to learn about how we can deal with the people here. If you see it as anything else, you can become judgmental and you become angry when people are ungrateful for the good work you're doing. And people are ungrateful for the good work you're doing. Not because they are evil, but because they've been treated like animals for years and years. Just because I give them a burger one day isn't going to suddenly make all that pain go away. You have to see their humanity, and also your humanity and your own weaknesses. People get very high and mighty when they deal with addictions. But we all have them, and some of us are lucky that our addictions don't cause us to be in the Downtown Eastside prostituting ourselves.

I think my attitude probably goes back a long way. I grew up in a similar sort of culture. My nan lived in a house that was declared unfit for human habitation. She was a sitting tenant, a type of tenancy that doesn't exist in this country. It meant that her rent, which was £1, could never go up and she got to stay there for the whole of her life. The trick was the landlords never did anything to the property, they just let it deteriorate.

Some people might look down their nose at her, but she was fun and she had a good life. And Mr. Cox, the multi-millionaire butcher who had a swimming pool in his back garden—an unheard-of thing in England because heating an open-air swimming pool cost so much money—used to hang out with my nan. So Mr. Cox, with his Rolls Royce and pink Mercedes convertible and open-air swimming pool, just seemed like a regular human being to me. In the Downtown Eastside, there's a giant community and you can't walk down the street without people saying hi and chatting.

The community's concurrent issues just make it that much more complicated for people to see the whole picture. On the whole, people view the mentally ill as more deserving than the junkie. Some people are scared of the mentally ill, but the vast number of people in society feel sorry for them, and want to see them afforded some help. But when you turn into a junkie, it's a different thing. And if you're both, then it's especially hard to get the social service system to respond. And some of these people have serious health issues, HIV or hepatitis, or chronic infections that look horrible. Some who were sexually abused have personality disorders coming from that and they can be tenacious and very aggressive.

The whole Woodward's story is a long one and for us, it was about housing. Housing makes a huge difference. We would have liked to see 400 units, but we knew that if we didn't compromise, then it was going to be all condos. We wanted to at least engineer that compromise. It was key for us to get Simon Fraser in there. Milton Wong was saying he wasn't interested in Woodward's because the space there isn't that big and he wanted a much bigger space for the Asian community. But we wanted Simon Fraser because when we looked up the road, we saw that Harbour Centre hadn't been an agent for gentrification. So for us, Simon Fraser was a key part of the thing, as was a grocery store. That's why we asked Jimmy Pattison to put a grocery store in there. We didn't want an Urban Fare; we wanted a normal grocery store.

For the rest, we didn't really mind as long as there was some balance. We did want Simon Fraser; we wanted the grocery store; and we wanted the maximum number of units for social housing. Unfortunately, Woodward's will be an agent of gentrification, but in our mind, it will be less of an agent of gentrification than had there been no interference. So it's a compromise. We believe the addition of Simon Fraser's art school, the addition of the "lower level" grocery store, the family housing and the social housing, and space for groups in the community, will make it workable. We want to see groups like AIDS Vancouver in there. As long as we can hold the line on having those groups, we believe it will help.

When people look at Woodward's and think that it has initiated gentrification, they're just twits who don't really know what they're talking about. Gentrification had already come. If you analyze who bought the land in that area, you'll see it was purchased by relatively big developers. The issue is, can you repeat that compromise on other developments in the Downtown Eastside? So far, that hasn't happened because you needed all the potent things you had in the Woodward's project to work together.

The thing about a city is that all these different people live in it. So all we're doing is creating a smaller city. The exciting things will be housing for people with low incomes and the grocery store. Ultimately, the redeveloped Woodward's will make the community look nicer. It's stating the obvious, but people don't want to live in a rundown building.

We're stuck with fundamental needs, with malnutrition, poor housing, and with no access to health care. Even though millions of dollars are spent on health care, this group of people don't use it because it's not done in a way that works for them. They're very, very sick. Some areas of public health have improved: HIV is better under control, and not just because it reached saturation point; needle exchange has improved; access to methadone has improved; the rest of Vancouver has a high rate of TB and ours is low. So there are some improvements. But the fundamental issues remain; those of poverty and oppression, and those issues, ultimately, are not about health.

SQUATTER'S RITES
John Richardson

John Richardson
Executive Director
Pivot Legal Society

John Richardson founded Pivot Legal Society with Ann Livingston in 2000 while articling at Sierra Legal Defence Fund. When he completed his articles in January 2002, he began working for Pivot full-time as its executive director, a job that has changed constantly as Pivot has evolved and grown. In November 2005, Mr. Richardson elected to the Ashoka Fellowship for his vision of strategically using the law to advance the rights of the most marginalized members of society.

Before starting Pivot, Mr. Richardson attended Lester Pearson College of the Pacific, where he obtained an International Baccalaureate degree. From there, he obtained his B.Sc. (Hon) in Mathematics and Philosophy at the University of Toronto (Trinity College), and his law degree at the University of Victoria. While a member of the Environmental Law Centre at the University of Victoria, he co-authored *Civil Disobedience: a legal handbook for activists*. During his time at law school, he spent two terms as a co-op student at the BC Law Institute.

Mr. Richardson is the lead author of *To Serve and Protect: A Report on Policing in Vancouver's Downtown Eastside*, and has played a supporting role in many of Pivot's other publications and campaigns.

WE WERE INVOLVED IN PROVIDING LEGAL INFORMATION to the people who were squatting and on a couple of occasions, we represented them in court. There was a whole sequence of events that happened around the occupation.

The first stage involved occupying the Woodward's building when they actually got inside to the second floor. I knew a bit about civil disobedience because I had done a book about it in law school. They were trespassing, so we went up there to give them basic legal information about what their rights were and what they could expect.

Then the police came and everyone got kicked out of the building. Did they have an injunction at that point? I don't remember. Basically, they all got arrested and we represented them in court, myself and another lawyer named Noah Quastel. We bailed them out that same day. I think it was a Saturday or Sunday. That's when they all camped on the sidewalks. People donated mattresses and tents, and it became a very big protest. They had these awnings that would go over the sidewalks, so it was quite sheltered. It was a tent city and covered a lot of area. There were probably 100 people there. At this stage, we were giving them information about their legal rights as far as camping on the sidewalk was concerned. They actually had more rights than they did when they were inside the building because municipal by-laws came into play. We advised that they could be ticketed for impeding the flow of pedestrian traffic. They were creating structures on the sidewalk, so it was a ticketable offence, but not one you could be arrested for.

I guess it was about 11:00 on Sunday night when I got a call from Ivan Drury. He said, "John, you've got to get down here. Get down here quick. The police are beating people. They're trashing and beating us with sticks." I could hear all the noise in the background, and then the line cut off.

I put on my suit, miked myself and got in a cab. At Cambie and Hastings, the police had cordoned off the whole area. So I got out of the cab and walked past a police officer down to the intersection of Abbott and Hastings. There was a big crowd on the south side of Hastings and on the north side of the street, in front of Woodward's, there was a police blockade. There were police cars and vans everywhere. You could see people running, and the activity of the police was clearly visible. There were big dump trucks with trash compactors, and the police were putting people's possessions in the compactors, which crunched them up.

People were being arrested. I could see some of my clients; these were the people I had just represented in court a day earlier. So I said to a policeman, "I want to talk to your supervising officer because I have clients here. I want to see if we can deal with this some other way. This is not my understanding of the law around what the police are empowered to do." The officer wasn't very responsive or interested in letting me through, and he wasn't interested in letting me talk to anybody.

They were more concerned with keeping us in line. So I crossed the line, and they arrested me.

There were TV cameras everywhere, and the police were arresting a lawyer. They kept me overnight in jail, but the Crown refused to press charges. They didn't see it as something they could succeed in prosecuting. But it did raise the stakes. People saw the injustice. I guess there were eight or nine of us, and we were released the next morning.

The police definitely destroyed people's possessions. It was all extremely well-documented and it was also extremely illegal. They didn't have any right to do that. People lost valuable possessions. There were homeless people that had all their stuff in their backpacks, and the police were tossing them in the compactors. Wallets were lost. Personal heirlooms. Lots of things were destroyed.

The unfairness and the high-handedness of the police action really seemed to galvanize the public, because the next day, a mass of support poured in. Even though the police had destroyed all the mattresses and camping gear, there was a little kitchen set up. By the middle of the next day, trucks were coming down, inns were donating mattresses. Tents were being donated en masse. By the evening of the next day, the squat was rebuilt better and bigger than the day before. The police realized they had lost it. And that was really an amazing reaction. Then it became a much more protracted legal battle because they weren't willing to use the same tactics again.

At that point the city applied for an injunction to remove people and we got into the whole process of fighting it. It went to the Court of Appeal and we eventually lost. They got their injunction, but they got it a week or so before the municipal election. Along with the injunction, the city also obtained an enforcement order. But it was clear that the Coalition of Progressive Electors, COPE, was going to take over city council, and they had a completely different approach to dealing with the situation. They wanted to negotiate and put people into housing after the election. We submitted affidavits arguing that they should not issue the enforcement order until after the municipal election based on the different statements being made by the two competing political parties. The court refused to withhold the enforcement order, but members of the city staff said, "We'll just hold our breath and wait. Because it looks like COPE is going to win and if it does, then we better not have done the wrong thing." So they decided to hold out until after the election. It turned out that Larry Campbell of COPE was elected with a majority, and they did a number of innovative things. They moved a whole bunch of people into the Stanley. And Jim Green was very invested in neighbourhood appeals about social housing.

The Woodward's building had been promised for social housing, for which there was a massive need. Commitments had been made by the New Democrats, who were not the government at that time, about Woodward's being redeveloped as social housing. The Woodward's building had been empty for about a decade. People were sitting on the street, looking at this giant building that they were not allowed to go into, and thinking, "What the hell is with all of this?" Then the provincial government started talking about creating a technology centre, or some kind of industry centre in the building, and there was no more talk about social housing. It was all about industrial redevelopment.

Not surprisingly, people got really choked about that. It triggered a lot of resistance. Obviously, Woodward's is an icon in the city with the big W, so it became the focus point of a campaign for social housing. It was emblematic. It symbolized the fight for social housing and the government's recalcitrance on that crucial issue.

Housing is critical. Everything flows from it. If people don't have housing, there's not much we're able to do. You can't effectively be in treatment if you have nowhere to go home to. You're not going to turn your life around. You're not going to find a job. You're not going to be able to pursue an education. You're not going to be able to do anything if you're sleeping in the streets.

So housing is what we do first. Don't worry about programs. All we have to do is get these people in a space. Then we go from there, then we can start to add things on. Because people start to stabilize, they feel comfortable, safe. Then they can start to think, "What do I do now?"

There is a mystery to the Downtown Eastside. You know, the most beautiful city in the world and the worst postal code in the country. So you have these intentions, and you ask, "How can we make progress and fairly integrate communities? How can we be innovative and look to principles?"

Woodward's definitely makes a good foray into that. I think there's a lot of buy-in to some basic principles, like there shouldn't be displacement of the current community, that it is a community worth preserving.

Then there's the arts community. The Eastside Culture Crawl is a big arts event during which 200 studios open up to the public. There are a number of environmental and eco-density initiatives. Some of the more interesting ones will incorporate this need to house and ensure healthy lifestyles for marginalized, addicted, ill people. I think there's an important cultural and artistic element that needs to be preserved. It's an interesting playground.

The sort of things that have come out of the demographic concentration are also interesting. Obviously, there are negative aspects, and the concentration of the drug market down there aggravates the problem. But that same concentration allows people to have their voice and create a community. If Woodward's hadn't happened on the edge of the Downtown Eastside, it never would have happened. Because people got together; they talked to each other. They got active and socially engaged. It's a very powerful thing to have a community of poor people advocating for themselves and participating in very powerful processes.

In many ways, they speak on behalf of other people who are in the Downtown Eastside. Social housing is being built in other places, but it's because of the Downtown Eastside that these other things are happening. The demographic concentration also allows for more sophisticated projects. There are economies of scale in everything. When you put together treatment facilities, health service centres, food and low-income housing, there are efficiencies in those linkages that are not negative. You can call the drug market a negative consequence of having so many poor people concentrated in a district. Or you can call it a consequence of the criminalization of addiction.

My position is definitely that criminalization is the cause of the rapid drug market and the spiraling of addiction. All the social and personal harms that occur as a result of this are because we've taken a certain path. We have to treat it as a health issue that needs to be addressed constructively, rather than shutting these people out or throwing them in jail.

I think it's an issue of how we relate emotionally to the things we're afraid of. I always come back to this, but in each of our daily lives, things come up that disturb, scare or threaten us. We can shut it out, cast doubt, deny it or totally ignore it.

Or we can open up and try to have a positive emotional relationship to it. These things happen in our own minds, but I also think as a community, we have these types of emotional relations to darkness and pain and suffering. The Downtown Eastside provokes all of these reactions. It has people that we'd like to smash and crush and make it go away. We want to block it off and make a wall and not go there and just deny it. There are people who don't even want to acknowledge its existence. And then there are people who want to open it up, find the vitality that's there, and make it into something that's integrated into the rest of the community. I think that's what is happening in people's heads in the Downtown Eastside.

The theory underlying Pivot is that everyone's life improves when the lives of the marginalized are improved. We address those things in a structural way, using the law and rights. Gandhi said that the test of a civilized society is how it treats its most marginalized people. People don't necessarily see how they benefit when the lives of marginalized people are improved because the effects are often indirect. We've created an Us/Them dichotomy and it's a delusion, because in this community we're all interconnected.

A RESOURCEFUL SOCIETY
Ken Fraser

Ken Fraser
Executive Director
Vancouver Resource Society

Ken Fraser is the executive director of the Vancouver Resource Society (VRS). Born in Vancouver, British Columbia in 1958, he graduated as a Certified General Accountant from UBC in 1992.

Mr. Fraser has worked at VRS since 1982 and has been the Executive Director since 1987. VRS has operated as a non profit society since 1972, providing independent living opportunities in the community for people with disabilities. VRS will own 9 units in the Woodward's redevelopment project. The units are fully wheelchair accessible and will accommodate wheelchair-bound tenants. The VRS owns and operates 26 properties in Vancouver and Burnaby and provides housing and support services to over 150 individuals.

WE'RE A NON-PROFIT SOCIETY. We've been around for about 35 years and we provide independent living opportunities for people with significant disabilities. Not only do we build, acquire, and manage wheelchair-accessible housing, we also provide the 24-hour attendant care support needed to allow these folks to live in the community. I would say we're midsize. We have an operating budget of about 10 million a year, we have 130 clients and about 300 employees. We sometimes get grants from the city but not that often. We're predominantly funded by the provincial government. We have a membership because we're a not-for-profit society. All non-profits have a board of directors and a membership.

We have two kinds of clients. If you have good upper body strength and can live on your own, that's one thing; but then there's another group that is more significantly disabled who needs home-care support. The clients we focus on are those that require supports 24-hours a day.

Woodward's will be our first presence in the Downtown Eastside. We were part of the proposal call with Millenium. We basically took what our role was going to be in Millennium's project and presented it to Westbank and said, "We'd still like to be part of this even though our proponent never got the deal." We told them what we were looking for. At the time, we were pretty ambitious. We thought we were going to buy the first four floors of the W Building. We were going to buy these units at cost minus land value. The city was providing density bonuses, and we thought there was an opportunity for us to acquire a fairly significant number of units. Then as the numbers crunched out, they got more and more and more expensive and we had to peel back our ambition a little bit. We wound up getting one floor with nine units.

Our plan is to have six of the units modified to our client's specific needs. We also have the option to sell off three. They're not modified, they're regular market units. We could keep those and maybe people who are deaf or blind and who don't require wheelchair access could live in them. So we've still got those options. If we can come up with the right financing and the numbers work, we'll keep all nine. If we need some more equity and there's no other way to come up with it, we have the option to sell.

Our negotiations with Westbank were sometimes heated. Things tend to hit rough water from time to time and in some of the more heated conversations, they told us they didn't need us. They could quite easily go forward without us, and it was simply by their good graces that they kept us involved. We said, "That's all well and good, but we think we're there for a reason." Ian Gillespie is a pretty solid guy and I think he wanted to do this.

What we had to do to our one floor was significant. There were probably many days when Westbank and the architect questioned whether they had made the right decision in getting us involved. Part of it is we're a non-profit society. Our day-to-day work is doing other stuff, so we would leave the floor plans for the Woodward's project sitting on a desk for another week after. They asked us for our input. We gave them a bunch of input and then they came back to us, saying, "Okay, this looks like it's going to be the final take." We responded with a huge number of changes. They figured we were going to tweak a few things, but we came back with some pretty significant stuff. It was because of our lack of attention to detail in the beginning. We said, "We're sorry, the units you have given us are workable but we've got an opportunity here to make them perfect. So let's make them perfect." And that's what we went after.

We didn't mess with structural concerns because we couldn't. But we completely reconfigured the kitchens. A lot of the kitchens originally had islands in them and we said, "Those don't work. Get rid of them." We went with counters along the walls and an L-shaped kitchen. We literally blew the walls out of bathrooms and made them two and three feet bigger and wider. We narrowed some hallways and literally moved walls over. We didn't have the flexibility to mess with the windows. So those were the kind of things with which we came back to them afterwards.

Their sense of humour had somewhat waned by the time we were all done. We worked with Peter Wood from Henriquez Partners. He took the brunt of our changes, and he finally got fed up with us. At the end, he said, "That's enough. We're not going to be doing anymore. That's all we can do for you guys." And that was fair enough. We were going after more because we wanted perfect units, but we got a lot out of them.

These are some pretty darn nice units here. We have some that are 1,209 square feet, some at 981 square feet, and the smallest is 643 square feet. Some of them are two bedrooms so some people will live with somebody, while others will live on their own. SFU is in the complex so our target population is going to be people attending university. If they need accessible onsite housing we can provide it. We think it will be a huge attraction.

FOLIO VI

WOODSQUAT 2002
Murray Bush

6

THE SITE

As defined by the Request for Proposals in February 2004, the Woodward's site initially consisted of the easterly portion of the city block at 101 West Hastings Street bounded by Abbott and West Cordova streets. It was occupied by the Woodward's department store, constructed in nine principal phases between 1903 and 1957, and was acquired by the city of Vancouver in March 2003. During the developer competition to redevelop the site, Holborn Group obtained an amendment to the RFP that allowed them to include in their proposal two lots they owned adjoining the Woodward's site to the west at 149 West Hastings and 150 West Cordova, collectively known as the Holborn Lands. The final joint proposal submitted by Holborn Group and Concert Properties involved transferring a large portion of the three sites' allowable density to other projects, including a 183 metre tower planned for a distressed construction site at 1133 West Georgia street, and was to be the Ritz-Carlton Condominium Hotel until cancelled in the 2008 economic downturn.

After Westbank Projects/Peterson Investment Group won the competition, a complex deal was struck whereby Holborn sold their westerly lands to Westbank in exchange for Westbank conveying to Holborn approximately 9,300 square metres of the heritage density that would be created through the heritage restoration of the 1903/08 Woodward's building. Holborn needed the density to build the West Georgia tower. The larger Woodward's site was necessary to incorporate SFU's School for the Contemporary Arts and to create an enlarged public realm. Changes to the Cambie Street/Cordova Street lane configuration in September 2005 and an amendment of the Downtown Official Development Plan in February 2006 to include the Holborn Lands in the Woodward's site increased the final site area to 10,071 square metres.

Zoning

Excluded from the Gastown (HA-2) zoning district through the Woodward family's political influence, the Woodward's site was part of the Downtown District (DD) zone. In May 2006, it was rezoned to a Comprehensive Development District (CD-1) to facilitate the proposed large and complex mixed-use development. The original site of the Woodward's store had long served as a community gathering place, so the city identified two public amenity qualities required to ensure a lively, open, and inclusive development scheme. The first was the creation of a diversely mixed-use project including a significant component of non-profit space to address the unique needs of the community. Second was the provision of a major public gathering place, both indoors and outdoors, available to all citizens and useful for activities that contribute to a healthy community culture. The rezoning secured a well-focused neighbourhood centre to support and encourage community social activities. The allowable floor space ratio (FSR) was increased to 9.5, of which 1.68 FSR was transferred off-site, and the building height was increased to 45.72 metres with Development Permit

Board discretion to extend it to a maximum of 137.16 metres. The CD-1 zoning permits all uses proposed in the Woodward's redevelopment, including cultural and recreational, residential, commercial (retail, office, service), and institutional.

Surrounding Character Areas

The Woodward's site is strategically positioned at the convergence of the Downtown Eastside, Gastown, Victory Square and the Hastings Corridor. These areas provided clues and guidelines for the appropriate form of the Woodward's redevelopment.

Gastown

As the location of John "Gassy Jack" Deighton's saloon serving millworkers and the Granville Townsite, Gastown represents the city's historic core. Gastown served as Vancouver's earliest commercial and warehouse district, so the majority of its buildings were built between 1886 and 1914 of masonry construction. The buildings extended to the front property line and their height varied between two and seven storeys.

During the 1960s, protests against proposals to turn Carrall Street into a freeway and community support for the protection of heritage buildings galvanized. The designation of Gastown as a historic area by the British Columbia government in 1971 directed considerable public and private investment in the rehabilitation of buildings. Over 200 Gastown properties were designated as historic and a series of public squares, heritage paving, cast-iron bollards and chains, globe street lamps with flower baskets, and a Victorian-style steam clock were installed. Buoyant market

conditions supported the rehabilitation of manufacturing buildings and warehouses to retail, office and residential uses. While creating a historically-themed tourist area, the beautification erased some of the existing authentic urban character and divorced Gastown from the rest of city life. Less favourable economic conditions in the 1980s required most projects to seek added density and relaxations to make them viable, gradually eroding the heritage character of the area. The 2002 Gastown Heritage Management Plan attempts to overcome the complexity and expense of renovating heritage buildings relative to rents and the difficulty of accommodating a wide range of tenant types by implementing administrative and financial incentives to encourage rehabilitation of heritage buildings. These incentives include grants for preservation of façades, property tax relief, density bonusing for transfer off-site, allowance for building one additional storey, and a streamlined approval process. The plan includes Design Guidelines to guide the rehabilitation of historic buildings and the construction of new buildings.

Because Woodward's edges Gastown, its built form respects Gastown's neighbourhood character, particularly the "saw-tooth" block profile resulting from the accretion of individual, purpose-built structures erected prior to zoning regulations. While the original Woodward's building was larger in scale than typical Gastown buildings, the new project has been massed into four separate buildings, allowing for movement through the site and the creation of a central public space.

Hastings Corridor

The Hastings Corridor from Cambie to Heatley Streets was the principal shopping street and hub of commercial activity in Vancouver between 1900 and 1920. A significant number of the buildings on the street were designed by prominent architects. Merchant families commissioned these buildings after Vancouver surpassed Victoria as British Columbia's principal port of entry in 1899 by offering a lower transfer cost of freight to the provincial interior and better regional commercial connections. With Woodward's anchoring Hastings Street, Pierre Paris & Sons opened nearby in 1907, followed by Army & Navy Department Store and Pappas Furs in the 1920s and Wosk's Furniture and Goldman Men's Wear prior to World War II. Often, businesses chose to begin modestly with a Hastings Street storefront, then expand with manufacturing facilities or chain stores.

The Hastings Corridor, zoned as Downtown District west of Carrall Street and Downtown Eastside/Oppenheimer east of Carrall, is characterized by structures of

varying widths and heights built to the front property lines, forming a richly diversified streetscape. To combat the current lack of business activity, storefront vacancies and deterioration of older buildings, the city extended the Federal Historic Places Initiative Program and the façade improvement incentives, property tax exemption and bonus density already approved for Gastown and Chinatown to heritage buildings on Hastings Street in July 2003 for a five-year period. Extending the heritage incentive program increased the number of heritage buildings rehabilitated and contributed to revitalization of the Downtown Eastside.

Victory Square

The Victory Square area, defined as Hastings and Pender Streets bounded by Richards and Carrall Streets and Beatty Street from Pender to Dunsmuir, was part of Vancouver's main downtown commercial district for the first half of the twentieth century. The city's major department stores and numerous retail shops, banks and restaurants were located in the area prior to the southward shift of retail activity in the 1970s. More than 40 percent of Victory Square's buildings are designated heritage and many of the structures have historic stone facades. Victory Square itself is the only significant open space in the neighbourhood, best known for its ceremonial function on Remembrance Day. The 1990 Victory Square Policy established a maximum floor space ratio of 3 and a height of 21 metres. Aside from residential and commercial uses, the area's zoning encourages a broad range of cultural, educational and light industrial uses and formalizes live/work suites in the area's flourishing artists' community.

As commercial activity moved out of the Victory Square area in the 1980s and 1990s, pedestrian traffic decreased, contributing to a cycle of decline. The city worked with concerned community stakeholders in 1998 on an area concept plan, from which a policy plan was developed in 2005. The primary objective of the planning effort was to develop a strategy for revitalization that would bring investment back into the area without displacing the existing community or compromising the area's heritage value. The plan emphasized heritage building rehabilitation, street-wall developments, fine grain frontages and varied building heights while envisioning

a wide supply and range of housing types, particularly for low-income residents. The Woodward's redevelopment responded to the four key planning principles of the Victory Square Area Concept Plan: revitalization without displacement of the existing low-income community; retention of low-income housing; retention of the area's heritage buildings, scale and character; and partnership with the community. With the Woodward's redevelopment and the extension of heritage incentives approved for Gastown and Chinatown in July 2005, a range of activities is expected to re-occupy vacant storefronts in Victory Square.

The Vancouver Agreement

The vitality of Gastown, the Hastings Corridor and Victory Square are key to addressing the economic and social challenges of the Downtown Eastside. The Vancouver Agreement is an integrated urban development initiative between the governments of Canada, British Columbia and the city of Vancouver to increase economic development in the Downtown Eastside, improve the health of area residents, and to increase public safety. Signed in March 2000, the agreement commits the government partners to work together with communities and businesses in Vancouver on a coordinated strategy to promote and support sustainable economic, social and community development such that the city is a healthy, safe and sustainable place to live and work for all residents. Four strategies were developed to achieve the agreement's goals: economic development and job creation through revitalization of the Hastings Corridor; dismantling of the area's open drug scene; ensuring hotels offer safe, clean places to live; and making the community safer for women, youth and children. Under the agreement, the three levels of government contributed finances, staffing resources and coordination to redevelop the Woodward's site.

BEACH STORMER
Peter Wood

Peter Wood
Architect
Henriquez Partners Architects

Peter Wood was born in Calgary and moved with his family to Vancouver in the 1970s. His father, a developer, was heavily involved in Richmond and Delta, and he believes this may have everything to do with why he became an architect.

He graduated with a Masters of Architecture from UBC, and joined Henriquez Partners, becoming project architect for the Michael Smith Laboratories at UBC, and is currently Associate-in-Charge of the Woodward's redevelopment project.

Mr. Wood is a talented designer who, prior to joining Henriquez Partners Architects, headed his own architectural studio and gained extensive experience designing art galleries. In 2002, he received a Prairie Design Award of Excellence and his work has been published in Azure, Canadian Architect and Western Living magazines.

I HADN'T WORKED WITH LARGE TEAMS before being put in charge of the project. I have a fear of public speaking and I had to chair these weekly meetings. I'd walk in, and there would be 25 consultants in the room. This happened every Monday for almost two years. Every Sunday night, I wouldn't sleep. I was terrified going into these meetings and once in them, I would all of a sudden hear someone leading and I'd realize—it was me.

I'm a lifer. I was there from the first sketches. Working on this project is like surfing a huge tsunami. Once you're on that wave, you're committed. There is only one direction and that's forward.

Had I known the architectural profession was going to be like this, I would have become a dentist. Every day is humbling as everyday presents something new. Every time you think you understand what's going on, something happens where you realize you don't understand everything, or you've just simply forgotten the vast amount of information you are supposed to remember. But you become an incredible problem solver. I think that is what makes a good architect, that at the end of the day, you're able to distill a tremendous amount of information and come up with a simple solution. I find that the most challenging, yet most rewarding, part of the profession.

Most people are under the impression that when you design a building, you put your ideas on paper and the builder simply builds it. And every once in a while, you grace the site to point out something that compromises the integrity of your art. This is as far from the truth as you can possibly get.

Every day brings new problems and everyday, a new fire has to be put out. At the beginning of the project, when things were new, we quickly realized that the first way to resolve a problem was to determine if there was a problem at all. More often than not, it was just miscommunication. As we became better communicators, the construction became more complicated and the real problems multiplied. Particularly because we're building Woodward's during a tremendous building boom. Not only are there new towers cropping up at every corner, but we are pre-Olympic. There are hundreds of projects going on: the Sea-to-Sky highway, the Vancouver Convention Centre, the Richmond Olympic Oval. Everybody is busy, and there are fewer products out there, and an even smaller number of trained workmen. If you go to the Woodward's site, very few people are speaking English because so many of the workers are Filipino and Mexican.

We're pretty realistic architects. We realize that we work for Westbank, and they've got a big bill and a tremendous amount of risk. The bottom line is always there. So we do our best to make decisions regarding the bottom line without taking on that risk of liability. Everyone has heard the term "value engineering," but very few people in the construction industry know what it truly means. If you ask a contractor about value engineering, his first response is to delete something. But any idiot can delete things, right? The whole idea is that you keep the value, and engineer the cost out. I think that's what we've been doing, but it is a tremendous battle. And Gregory is a smart architect because he realizes that you have to be prepared to give and take. But you also have to be committed to fight for those things that are important.

Recently, it was something as simple as the custom tile shower membrane for the residential units. We had specified one product, and the trade had signed a contract for some other product that was profoundly cheap. With 736 units in the project, there is tremendous exposure for liability here. It took us a month to figure out that we were talking about two different products. We finally came to an understanding; we provided options and it was priced. Over, right? No. I looked at the mock-up the other day and everything was wrong. They had installed another cheaper product and it was built completely incorrectly. You name it, it was wrong. We all thought we had consensus, only to start over again. My life right now is a form of hell. In the nine descending circles, I'm at eight.

The problems also jump scale. You start with something small and innocuous as a shower membrane, that most people don't even know exists, and you end up with issues regarding the whole building, such as the Heritage Building. The contractors are saying it will cost us an additional $7 million beyond the initial estimate to keep it standing . Is it really worth saving? As an historical entity, it's not. It's a horrible structure. You can see that it was put together by ad hocery. But we had to preserve it because we'd removed so much of Woodward's already. We have to restore that building no matter how horrible it is, no matter how impossible it is. We're still coming to terms with how to do that today. We are under construction all around it, and we still don't know how to structurally hold it up.

We've built about 22 storeys of the tower and we're still designing the other buildings. So it's a huge leap of faith. From the outset, the schedule has been challenging; there's a reduced timeline to fast track the project. In response, we've broken the project into pieces, releasing the documents for one building at a time to the contractor. Obviously, the process is fraught with problems because the drawings for the whole project aren't 100 percent complete. The other motivating factor for the speed is to tie down the trades right away. Because the cost of construction in Vancouver is escalating by one percent a month, you're pressured to sign a contract and ensure that someone will be showing up on site to do the work.

I make the joke that I'll exhale in 2009. Every day I go into the office with the fear that the elevator core needs to move over two feet after we've poured its footings, and I wonder, "Did we make a mistake?" To counter that kind of thinking, there's the internal optimist in me that thinks, "If we do make a mistake, we have people with enough talent to figure it out."

There's a tremendous leap of faith that everything will work in the end. In our office, I've tried to establish a culture of watching each other's backs. If you make a mistake, I'm not going to chastise you. There's no finger-pointing. People aren't punished for making mistakes. We're all under a tremendous amount of pressure, and there's an acknowledgement that we all make mistakes. When we find one and resolve it, that's what we celebrate. Considering the scale, complexity and speed at which we are moving, I am endlessly surprised by how few mistakes we actually do make.

I don't know how I feel about the success of the project. Right now I'm too close to it. For the people involved early on in negotiating the interests and terms of the project, they've hit their great victories. It's as if now they're in England having tea with Churchill while I'm storming the beaches at Normandy. At that moment, it's difficult to say what the war means to you; you are simply reacting. I'll be able to tell you after the war. Generally, I think Woodward's is a positive thing. I know that it has already affected people who have worked on it. I've never had this level of cooperation between the developer and the city on any project I've worked on. That has carried through onto the construction site. We battle a lot, but there's so much goodwill. I think the people who are working on Woodward's understand that it's an important thing for Vancouver, a meaningful thing. When you walk around the perimeter of the site, a whole range of people, including the drug addicts and the homeless, stop and watch. I think everybody is excited.

When it's all done, like most buildings I've worked on, I'll spend two or three hours with it just before it opens to the public. I will have my time with it. Then I'll walk away to the next project. It's funny, but when you're involved in a project from the first sketch to the last lightbulb being screwed in, all you know of the building is a series of battles involving endless meetings and rivers of emails. When you look at the building, all you see are mistakes. It takes a couple of years for you to look back and to realize how incredible it was to build something. To start with nothing and end up with something, and actually have it be part of the landscape of the city, is a profound thing to do, because you impact people's lives. Those thoughts and ideas that you've worked on—and worked very hard on—that you've had such an intense emotional investment in, become a space that people occupy and it becomes meaningful to them. It's a pretty powerful experience.

STRAIT TALKER

Dave Leung

David Leung
Project Manager
Westbank Projects Corp.

David Leung originally came to Vancouver in 1982 to study, starting with a Bachelor of Arts (Geography), between 1982 and 1986, converting to a Bachelor's in Architecture which he received from UBC in 1990. Prior to joining Westbank in 1998, Mr. Leung was an associate of Annand Burton-Brown Architects. He is a licensed architect and a Member of the Architectural Institute of British Columbia (MAIBC). He currently serves as a Board Director for the Downtown Vancouver Association.

Mr. Leung is Development Manager for Westbank Projects Corp., which is managing the Woodward's redevelopment on behalf of the Ownership, W Redevelopment Group, Inc. (Westbank Projects/Peterson Investment Group in joint venture). He also acts as the owner's representative and project director of the Woodward's redevelopment. The projects Mr. Leung has managed for Westbank vary in type from retail, office, hotel and industrial to residential with emphasis on mixed-use developments.

THE DAYS WERE VERY HECTIC and very long with the Woodward's project. I represent the owner's interests: Ian Gillespie for Westbank and Ben Yeung for Peterson Group. Obviously, I'm not the sole person working on the project in the company, but my primary responsibility was shepherding the design approval process through the city, getting the construction manager involved, basically being the liaison between ourselves and the various parties, and managing the various parties. It was a daunting task.

Most of the projects we do are single-use projects. With Woodward's, you have multiple users and many more stakeholders than on any other project that we've ever encountered, including the Shangri-La and the Fairmont Pacific Rim. It is probably the most complex project we will ever do. There was so much economic, social and political history involved. My favourite saying is that it's not politics with a small "p" but Politics with a capital "P." But because of all that history, the will was there to make it happen from all parties. I've got to say that for a project of this complexity and this significance, it actually went very smoothly. Projects of this kind can get bogged down in problems and issues of self-interest. That didn't happen. It was very well-handled.

One of the big issues with the Downtown Eastside is getting community involvement. The Westbank/Peterson proposal definitely was inclusive. We wanted community representation from all facets—business, Chinatown, Gastown, residents that lived there. The city was the guiding force in bringing all those interests together, and I think we very wisely tried to include all the stakeholders we possibly could and incorporate them into the project and the program itself. Ultimately, we're not a panacea for all ills. We can't solve everyone's problems, nor can we make everyone happy. But if you can make the bulk of the people happy, then I think you've done a pretty good job.

Anytime you get different uses together, there is inevitably a conflict of interest in terms of ownership, cost allocations, maintenance and operating. You have to get down to who pays for what, who's responsible for what, who's liable for what. Definitely when you have non-market and market users, that becomes a little more "illuminative," for lack of a better word. Typically, in terms of marketability, not to sound elitist, but people who buy million dollar condos don't necessarily want to live with people who are renters or living in subsidized or affordable housing. What we tried was to separate the users on the site as much as possible, knowing full well that there is going to be integration of some sort, but trying to minimize it as much as possible. So they have separate elevators and separate lobbies. You try to remove most of those issues and you try to incorporate that in the design. One of the things the city of Vancouver wanted was to really marry those two users.

In one of the early meetings, we argued that it wouldn't be as successful if you were to mix them completely. In the end, I think they agreed with us.

I think Woodward's is going to be a prototype for a lot of municipalities, especially in the larger urban cities. I've no doubt that it's going to be very successful. It's already turning around the area locally. If you go around Gastown, there's been a lot of revitalization. People are actually investing in the local area, which for years wasn't very successful. At one time, a number of people thought Gastown would become much more successful economically and it would be revitalized, but it never seemed to turn a corner. One gentleman who has had a furniture shop in Gastown for a long time noted in the newspaper not too long ago that he felt this was the time. He's seen phases of revitalization, but he actually thought this one was finally going to take hold.

I think some properties have changed hands. There are developers who have taken advantage of Woodward's coming on board and the accompanying increase in property values. Gentrification will be real. We're not going to deny the fact that people buying into it are not going to turn over the area. I'd be naïve to say there won't be some displacement. But I think what Woodward's offers is some inclusion, some accommodation for people to stay in the area and that's why we have 200 non-market units.

One of the things I've learned through this process is that economic revitalization occurs when residents start coming back into an area. Commercial opportunities come after that because now you've got the consumer base to help service the commercial aspects. If the commercial is successful, then a lot of people originally living in the area have a place where they're now employed, and they can actually remain in the area. The 75 non-market family units and 125 single units represent an opportunity for many of the residents who might not be as well-off to actually work and stay in the area.

Personally, I don't know how long it will take for the commercial ventures to make a profit or break even. One of the beauties of these large retailers, like London Drugs, is they were prepared to take that chance. They were initially going to take only one level, and now they've taken a second one. So we've added a mezzanine because they grew more and more confident that they could do well. Then you have TD Canada Trust, the first major bank to come back into the Downtown Eastside since the early 1990s. That whole area used to be redlined by financial institutions, so they definitely see the area changing.

I think you need wide demographics for an area to be totally revitalized. That was evident in the Concord Pacific lands and the creation of the first elementary school in a North American inner-city in 20 years. What astounded the city planners was the number of young couples that were choosing to remain in the downtown and start a family there. Woodward's is probably no different. You need that wide demographic, you need the kids to help support the childcare. If you get that mix, you get stabilization and the area will become much more livable.

When we went to market with Woodward's, there was definitely a discount of the unit price because it was Downtown Eastside. It was the very fringe of downtown. To be honest, we weren't 100 percent sure how the market would receive Woodward's, given the history we were fighting against. It's one thing to market a product that you *know* will do well, but it's another thing to market a product that you *think* will do well. Part of our marketing approach was to start selling the idea that the area is really changing. It's changing for the better and it's changing permanently. So we got out there with Rennie Marketing Systems and started marketing Woodward's six months before we even got development permit approval, which in itself was quite a gamble. But we knew we needed time to convince people that this is happening and if they didn't get in early, they were going to miss the opportunity. It turned out to be a very successful strategy.

I was in the sales centre on the day of the marketing frenzy and it just blew my mind. I couldn't believe it. The reception that it received, the confidence, and the fact that people bought in, showed it was ready to happen.

The people who did buy-in cover a wide spectrum. There are singles, entry-level buyers and married couples. I talked to a couple who was selling their house in Burnaby to move back down there. Having that mixed-use complex with the food store and the drug store made it much more desirable to come back down to Woodward's. And SFU's participation supplied the body heat for the project to be successful. With 800 or so students and 200 administrative and faculty members, there will be a lot of people at Woodward's, and that in itself is enough to support the commercial aspects. Any time you can bring that many people into an area, it's bound to filter down.

Woodward's is unique and it sets a precedent, but it's not a precedent that will be often repeated. The city of Vancouver was very clear about that. They don't want other developers coming in and saying, "Woodward's got a 400-foot tower and this much density, why can't we?" I think that because Woodward's was so unique and there was such a need to revitalize the area, the city was willing to bend over backwards to make it happen. But it doesn't necessarily mean that they're going to make concessions for every subsequent development. Basically, it was the kickstart that the area needed.

My running joke is that before Woodward's, I was 6 foot 2 and 250 pounds and now I'm nowhere near that. I had left Westbank temporarily and when Ian asked me to come back and look at Woodward's, I recognized that it wasn't a glamourous project in the sense of Shangri-La or Fairmont, but what it had over any other project was social significance. It was a project that you knew was going to make a difference to an area, and you can't say that very often, especially in an area as downtrodden and blighted as the Downtown Eastside. I think Ben and Ian have very strong social values and if it weren't for that type of guidance and direction, it wouldn't be as good as it is. In the end, I think a lot of it probably came out of altruistic motives. You don't often find developers willing to do that.

Woodward's was a project where we said, "There's not going to be money made here. There's going to be a lot of time, effort and, frankly, brain damage associated with a project like this." This project really sucked a lot of both Westbank's and Peterson's internal resources. The amount of resources allocated to this one project could have been allocated to a number of projects that were much more profitable. Simpler projects, where you're not having to deal with various users and ownership groups.

One of the criticisms we faced was that we weren't saving enough of the old Woodward's building. But we knew that it couldn't work functionally with SFU. They basically needed a very program-specific and design-specific venue and the floor heights just didn't work. The other argument about the old building was that it was the Walmart of its day—they just kept adding and adding to it—so it may not have any redeeming heritage value. But the original building was the start of Woodward's, so keeping that, even though it cost twice as much as we had originally estimated in our pro forma, is going to be a bit of a jewel in itself. With heritage restoration projects, you don't know what you are going to get into until you find it. One of the sad things was the 'W' sign and the tower on which it was mounted. We wanted to save them but as we were investigating the tower, and then later the sign, we realized that the tower was so dilapidated and the corrosion was so advanced, that it wasn't worth saving. It was also a safety issue.

I think one reason why Woodward's has been successful, and I don't think it's something we should overlook, is that we caught the market when it was still very good and was becoming better. If it weren't for the market, I don't think Woodward's would be what it is today. If you put it on the market today, how would you fare? I don't know. A lot of it was just fortunate timing.

THE PRINCIPAL OF CONSERVATION
Hal Kalman

Dr. Harold Kalman
Heritage Consultant
Commonwealth Historic
Resource Management

Harold Kalman grew up in Montreal and studied Art and Archaeology, receiving a doctorate from Princeton. He also studied the conservation and preservation of historic structures at York and Cornell universities. He has worked as a tenured professor at UBC, ran his own heritage consultancy in Ottawa, and is now the principal of Commonwealth Historic Resource Management Ltd. in Vancouver.

He is the chair of the Vancouver Heritage Commission, has served on the boards of the Association for Preservation Technology and ICOMOS-Canada, and was the founding president of the Canadian Association of Professional Heritage Consultants. Dr. Kalman is the author and co-author of many standard texts on conservation and architecture, including *A History of Canadian Architecture, Exploring Vancouver, Exploring Ottawa, Reviving Main Street, Principles of Heritage Conservation, The Evaluation of Historic Buildings, The Sensible Rehabilitation of Older Houses, Encore: Recycling Public Buildings for the Arts,* and *Pioneer Churches.*

I know from talking to Peter Wood that the 1903/08 building, which is the one you're involved with, is in some jeopardy. They're trying to figure out how to keep it from falling down.

We have lamented two decisions since the day we walked into the job: one, that there would be a new, double basement in the building; second, that there would be a childcare on top of the building. The sandwiching compromises the infrastructure. A consequence of the two new levels below is that it can't sit on its natural foundations, but has to be underpinned—basically suspended on skyhooks while they build the two levels of basement—and then put back down on top. Buildings don't like to be disturbed like that. If you were a plant, you wouldn't like someone giving you a root transplant in your older years. The consequence of the childcare is that it has extreme life-safety requirements because kids play there, and so the whole building has to have a two-hour fire-resistance rating rather than the usual one-hour rating, which means the wood structure has to be hidden under new materials. Peter is intimately involved in this foundation issue, and by cutting off its feet, the building is threatened with collapse. It needn't have happened. If we had been involved at square one, we would have argued that the basement should end at the perimeter of the building, which meant you might have to dig deeper to get the stuff in. It would mean the trucks wouldn't have the same turning radius. These would be very real constraints.

What are the politics of your having been brought in late?

We were brought on early for heritage consultants. In a typical heritage project, the architects and other consultants go ahead and then realize that they need some heritage help. Often by that time, all the decisions have been made.

I've always had a sense that Vancouver is a relatively heritage-conscious city.

It is, but what I'm saying is a subtlety that isn't realized. The reason you call in a heritage consultant is to recognize the consequences of making certain decisions. We discovered a lot of problems with the building, things that they weren't previously aware of that were causing more constraints and more issues.

And you wouldn't necessarily have been aware of them. This is what you discover when you go in?

This is us doing our job, conducting a proper investigation and discovering that they didn't build this as well as we thought they did.

*This building was grafted together decade after decade. It was a strange construction
sequence?*

Charles Woodward built his first department store on Main Street in the 1890s,
and then he needed more space. He was a genius in terms of understanding
the retail business. He knew that Vancouver was moving west, so he chose this
somewhat low, swampy spot to build a new department store. He built a four-
storey building in 1903, which is now the bottom 3 ½ storeys of the existing
building. In 1908, five years later, they added two storeys on top, rebuilding the
fourth and building a new fifth and sixth. Then starting in the late teens,
early '20s, the building grew like topsy.

Were they building on unstable ground?

Not unstable, just wet swamp. So they had to build better accommodations and
drainage. Charles Woodward is quoted as saying something like, "I wish I had
the foresight to buy the whole block," because it was very cheap. He was paying
ever higher real estate prices. But it was still good business and the store grew
until it almost filled the block. The last significant addition was in 1947 to 1949.
A sidebar is that the whole block, along Hastings Street had a real renaissance
after World War II. There was an enormous building boom from 1946 to 1950,
what I call the last hurrah of downtown shopping. Because just as Hastings
Street got to its 1950 appearance, Park Royal Shopping Centre was built in
West Vancouver, the first of the suburban shopping centres. From that point on,
it was downhill for the downtown.

Was there much that could be or should have been restored in the Woodward's project?

No. The decisions had been made before we came in that 75 or 80 percent
would be demolished. We challenged that decision, and Gregory totally
accepted the challenge. He said, "Fine, if you find a better solution, we'll keep
more of the building." We became absolutely convinced that the right decision
was made for two reasons: one is floor-to-floor heights. Having more height
than you need is an unnecessary expense, and in this paying-for-energy era,
people are very aware of that. Similarly, a lower floor height than you need
doesn't work. The floor heights were too big for residential and too small for
Simon Fraser. Gregory had already tried this exercise and we started all over
again. He said, "Here are all the elevations, all the sections, go to work on it."
The architects in our office and I spent the better part of three weeks trying very
hard. We finally threw in the towel and said, "We can't make it work." That was
reason number one. Reason number two comes out of an attempt in the 1990s
by Fama Holdings to do something at Woodward's. I think Fama was working
for the province and they did a great deal of destruction. Among other things,
they cut great big holes in the concrete slab, thinking they were building an
atrium or something. They also removed every detail of any interest from the
interior. Lord knows what happened to it all. At any rate, the concrete had been
compromised, and it was of very poor quality in the first place. We don't believe
in façades. We believe very strongly you should keep the entire integral structure, which is what's happening with the floors and columns of the old building. And we really hate it when floor heights compromise window levels. So it
just didn't work. Then on top of it—and this is more an aesthetic than a technical call—it's not much of a building. It wasn't good architecture. It was very

workaday, commercial architecture, done as cheaply as Woodward's could. It just filled the bill. Unlike Selfridges in London, which is meant to be an image-maker, Woodward's wasn't. There was a 1911 expansion scheme that did have a big classical façade, and I can just see Charles scratching his head and saying, "Why should I pay for that?" It never came close to execution.

It seems as though a lot of energy and expense went into getting down the 'W' sign.
We were very much a part of that. The commitment from the beginning was to keep the 1903/08 building, the so-called Heritage Building. I say "so-called" because in my business, everything is a heritage building. There were six major commitments in the development stage. Two of them are physical conservation and four are intangible conservation. The physical ones are to keep the 1903/08 building and the 'W' sign and tower, and the intangible ones basically boiled down to a very aggressive program of interpretation. Our ambition, no less than anybody who walks on that site—whether users, inhabitants, office occupants, students, or shoppers—is to know something about what that place was. In our way of thinking, that's as good conservation, if not better, than keeping the original walls standing. We are doing our best to conserve as much of the corner building as we can. There are a lot of competing objectives of which heritage is one. We don't win them all. My colleagues from Commonwealth and I sit around the board table and negotiate things; sometimes we win, and sometimes we lose and that's fair process.

In this process, why was it important to preserve both the 'W' sign and the tower which supported it?
This is when you start doing due diligence. We already had a technical report on the tower done by Levelton Consultants Ltd., who are basically engineers and testers. They had painted a really dark picture, which we didn't take at face value. Their report basically said that you can't do it. It's our job to be skeptics, and we sometimes drive our clients up the wall, but we feel we have to look into everything and be comfortable with it. We're not going to go up on a podium and say we did the right thing when we're not sure we did. With this one, we still weren't sure. Kevan Losch, among other things, likes climbing. He especially likes climbing when his girlfriend is watching. His girlfriend was watching that day. He went up by himself, because he wouldn't let any of his staff do it. I don't know what he was holding on with because he had a video camera in one hand and a hammer in the other. He was whacking away at things, and pieces of metal and lead were flying all over the place. Kevan and company cut the thing free and took it down. We looked at it, and it was in much poorer condition than we thought.

And the 'W'?
The 'W' exists. It's in safe storage somewhere in an undisclosed place. It consists of a steel structure with sheet metal on top, and all these incandescent light bulbs. The sheet metal is so corroded that we figured we'd probably have to replace 80 percent of it, which isn't keeping very much of the old 'W'. Also, water had been trapped in the bottom, so the lower part of the structure was corroded. The upper parts were fine. It came with some lovely mementoes, including two bird's nests. I have given out site instruction after site instruction

not to touch those nests. The 'W' in its current condition is going to be conserved so that further corrosion is retarded, then put into a transparent display case and exhibited on site in the atrium. It's going to be replaced by a replica 'W' and you'll be able to see both at the same time. You'll be able to see for yourself why it couldn't go back up there. It will be built with exactly the same dimensions, but with contemporary lightweight metals rather than steel. It will be lit with LEDs rather than incandescents. We have the general specs for it. Then there was the question of the tower, which was really interesting because the city's heritage planners were adamant that we should save it.

They put a lot of pressure on you?

That's their job. We worked very closely with them; we're advocates within the development team and they're advocates within the city's team. Unfortunately, they've been weakened lately because the senior planner in charge of the project left the planning department to go to another job, and the heritage planners who are left don't have his resolve or his clout. His name is Gerry McGeough. So Gerry led the charge, and we were put in the position of defending not keeping the tower. Again, we were technically satisfied that it couldn't be done. We didn't quite buy the construction manager's argument that no crane was strong enough to take it down, but we did buy the fact that you'd have to remove all of the lead paint, undo all of the riveted joints, probably replace 50 percent of the materials, then re-rivet or redo it, and once you'd done that, what was left was just a shadow of what had been there. And it might not be strong enough to hold anything. When it came over, a little more damage was done. It was toppled from below and hit the edge of the parapet, which bent it a little bit. Then the construction manager crammed it into a dumpster and did some additional damage. So now, we have a crumpled tower awaiting a decision as to how exactly it will be re-used.

Is it inevitable that it will be re-used in some way?

Originally, we were going to put the whole crumpled tower on top of one of the roofs of the Hastings Building, which would be visible from the high-rise and from surrounding buildings. But it doesn't really fit there, and we're not happy with the lead leeching out. So it may end up being just pieces under glass and shown in photographs.

Kevan will presumably be able to make an exact replica?

Except that instead of rivets he'll use welded joints. According to good conservation principles, new work should be distinguishable from old work. So if you go up close, you'll see early 21st century technology but from a distance it will be identical.

I gather the 'W' plays an important symbolic function. Is that why so much effort was expended to try and save it and then to reproduce it so accurately?

Yes. If you asked people in the community, "What is Woodward's?" they'd say, "It's the 'W' sign." The sign will revolve, but some interesting management problems come out of that because the people who live in the high-rise building aren't keen about having a brightly-illuminated sign revolving right outside their windows. So it may turn off after a certain time at night. We haven't dealt with the operational side of it, but it's an example of what I mean when I refer to competing agendas. The conservation agenda says it should be illuminated and rotate all night. The user agenda says, 'No bloody way because it's going to interfere with my sleep and my life'. We have to find a compromise.

What's your sense of the project itself? How complicated is the new configuration of Woodward's?

I've never seen anything nearly so complicated. I don't know that anyone has ever tested so many subsidized social units of housing and so many market units of housing in the same development. Obviously, Westbank and the city of Vancouver think it's going to work or they wouldn't do it. It's all an experiment—a very noble experiment.

Will Woodward's have implications for the neighbourhood?.

Property prices have already skyrocketed—people are buying old buildings they wouldn't have invested in before and holding onto them, hoping that something will happen. At a very superficial level, I expect it's going to move the drug trade away a few blocks, but I hope it does more than that. I hope it's one of the many things that's going to make the drug trade and homelessness less of a problem in Vancouver. I won't use the expression "War On…," but it is seen as part of the attempt to solve homelessness and drugs. So the people who bought into the neighbourhood are taking a gamble that it's going to work. If they have to fight people on the street every time they park their cars, then real estate prices are going to drop and they'll take a beating. If, on the other hand, it does work, then prices are going to rise until they are equivalent to prices elsewhere in town, and people are going to do very well. I understand that a lot of the purchases were made by people who want to live there, and some were bought for speculation. So when the time comes, there's going to be a hot market on Woodward's resale.

Is your best bet that it's going to work?

I think it is. In fact, my wife and I talked about buying there. We decided not to, but our reasons had nothing to do with the location.

One of your books talks about sensible rehabilitation of older houses. What's involved in the sensible rehabilitation of older neighbourhoods?

Interesting question. On the one hand, we have to retain those features that give the area its character, which means enough landmark buildings to have a context, enough traditional land use, enough street life, and so on. So if the lack of height is one of the things that give an area character, then we have to object to height. In Gastown, lack of height was definitely a feature. You had the Dominion Building on Victory Square and the Sun Tower on the periphery of Gastown, which were tall skyscrapers for their days—above 15 storeys. They were sentinels on the edge and we had nothing in the middle. So this is the first really high building within the Downtown Eastside. I think that's the objection.

Can we be overly sensitive to heritage issues? Is there a way in which it can get in the way of development?

The issue, which was resolved two weeks ago, which brought the question of competing interests to the absolute forefront was the windows on the Heritage

Building. The windows we inherited were, for the most part, built in 1903 and 1908. The 1903 building was well-constructed; the 1908 addition was poorly constructed. So we have very real problems. The windows and the brickwork on the top two floors are absolute junk. The best construction decision would have been to dismantle the top two floors, which is still a possibility, and rebuild them, but we put our foot down on this one, and said, "Look, so much of this building is eroded. One by one, the things we planned to keep are disappearing. All for good reasons, but the W sign has to get replaced and the tower has to be replaced. So we're drawing our line in the sand on the external brickwork." The project team recognized and respected this. There is a solution to reinforce it with shotcrete, sprayed concrete. But even then, the bricks are technically toast, so we're using some very high-tech sealants to keep the weather from destroying them further. We're doing things that those bricks don't deserve, all in the aid of making a statement for heritage.

The windows are a bit of a dog's breakfast. Many of them on the upper floor were replaced by metal windows, probably in the '40s. But on the second floor, the centre pivot windows with heavy wood sashes are in very good shape. On the next floor, the up-and-down sliders are in reasonably good shape. We had our window guy go by, and he found that a certain percentage would have to be replaced, a certain percentage would need pieces replaced—a lower rail here or a side rail there—and a certain number would only need the hardware fixed and the rest could be saved. But they're all single glazing, and single glazing gives neither the thermal nor the acoustic insulation that you want. They're old windows, so there's air infiltration around them. We argued to keep the windows and replace them when necessary, perhaps with double glazing. We were going for laminated glass, the kind we have on our windshields, which is better acoustically than double glazing, it's lighter and it fits the old sash better. But it's less than thermal. We argued the conservation thing. The old building is being leased back to the city and they're going to use it partly for non-profit offices and partly for other purposes. The Real Estate Services department is the lessor and they obviously want the best conditions possible for their tenants. They're not the heritage planners. They argued, quite rightly defending their interests and their subtenant's interests, that thermal comfort, air infiltration, noise, and ongoing energy costs are all important. They said those things trump heritage. Then, from the developer's point of view, capital cost was important. Additionally, you have to throw ongoing maintenance costs into the mix. It turns out that the wood sash windows with laminated glass or single glazing are much cheaper to maintain over a hundred years than thermal glazing. Thermal glazing breaks down in 20 years and you have to replace it. So these things were all taken into consideration. At first, it was a done deal that they would all be replaced, but we argued that it's not a done deal. We said we have to resolve this by due process. So due process happened. We had a meeting at the city and agreed upon the criteria: heritage, capital costs, maintenance costs, thermal insulation, acoustic insulation, air infiltration and energy consumption. We reached a compromise: some will be kept; some will be repaired; some will be replaced. We'd like to see a few more kept, but it was a due and proper process and I have no complaints. There was an immovable object and an irresistible force, and both backed off and reached a compromise.

It would be impossible to guess how complicated something as simple as what to do with windows could be. It's a fascinating exercise in a kind of democracy of building.

It's very complex at a technical level and it's also very complex at a personality level. Just like lawyers in a courtroom, the personalities that argue better often get their way. The people who hold the purse strings also have their trump card. When I reopened the window debate, Westbank was probably six inches away from firing us. They felt we had betrayed them. We had a discussion, and they told me they appreciated that I was doing what they hired me to do, to defend the best interests of the building. They said they didn't want the windows kept, but they weren't going to interfere with our trying to keep them. They just were not going to support us. "You're going to have to win it yourself," our Westbank contact said. When he finally realized that what I was doing was actually fulfilling the mandate he had authorized, he backed off and apologized for his anger, and I apologized for blindsiding him. We both behaved a little inappropriately, but the process was right.

You trust that the process has been working from a heritage perspective?

Yes. In this regard, there are two more things I have to tell you about the restoration of the building, and they involve fragments and wall painting. First, the restoration of the building. In the competition, it was decided the building would go back to its appearance in 1908. Here's the process: we have certain international charters that we follow in our business. One of them says that preservation—leaving a thing the way it is, showing the complexities and the continuity of history—is better than restoration, which is putting it back to a date. We argued for restoring it to 1950. Gregory and the architects looked at it and said, "The logic is right, but we hate what 1950 looked like. 1908 is so much more attractive." But they trusted us to make these decisions. We convinced the Heritage Commission that this was the right way to go. The heyday of Hastings Street was 1950, which was the last hurrah of Woodward's as a potent force. The two Woodward brothers, Charles' sons, had been running it; after one died and the other retired a couple of years later, it was downhill from there. It was the absolute climax of the power of the retail on that corner. So 1950 was fine and dandy until we started doing some investigation. You can see pictures of Woodward's interior where there are white painted wall signs under the windows. Department store meant there were departments. So one says "Caps and Hats" and one says "Boys' Pants" and "Toys" and "Drugs" which we all rather liked. One of the people in our office noticed that there was a little bit of a sign showing, so we did some tests and all the signs were there under the paint. They got overpainted and they've deteriorated after ten years but they're all there. What do you do when you find them? One of the rules we operate by is you can't restore something to multiple periods. You can't create a building that never existed in time. Which meant we couldn't do a 1950 building and show those signs. So we came up with this construct based on the fragment, where we were going to have two windows on the past: one on Hastings, and one on Abbott Street. Each one was roughly three windows wide by two high, where we were going to peel away 1950 and reveal 1908. You were going to get some of these paintings shown in complete words. It was a little bit deconstructivist. We were keeping "Diamonds" and "Drugs" deliberately because that's what that area was all about. They were side by side. We chose what we wanted, partly based on context, and partly on the architects saying what was good design and what wasn't. Then we sold that one to the city too. The brick would not be painted in those areas and we'd paint in other areas, and you'd clearly see the differentiation in colour and texture and you would understand that it was peeled back. That was fine. For the other signs, we were going to uncover them, then cover them with a clear sealant and paint over it. So if somebody said we had done a really stupid-ass thing, and we wanted to go back to the signs, we would not have destroyed evidence. Just like an archaeologist's backfill. They open it up, they look at the stuff and they put dirt back on it. We were going to open up the archaeology, look at it, photograph it, document it, protect it, and backfill the paint.

So there was the potential for pentimento?

Again, this is good preservation technology. It's what the bible says we're supposed to do. We were proud of ourselves. Then came the fiasco with the fifth and sixth storey brickwork. The brick is in bad condition. The technological investigation was done partly by other consultants: the envelope specialist, the paint specialist, and partly by ourselves; and we all agreed that the only way to keep the brick was with shotcrete behind it and with clear sealant in front of it. But the clear sealant warranty stated that if you painted on top of it, you voided the warranty. So we called the German manufacturer and he explained that you have to inspect it every 10 years to make sure you haven't broken it, and if you paint over it, you can't inspect it. So we accepted you couldn't paint over it, but our construct of 1950 was based on painting the whole thing just as it was found. We simply backed off and said, "We give up, 1950 doesn't work. We're going back to 1908." We had gone full circle: it was going to be restored to 1908, and Gregory was happy. I'm a great believer that when you get more information, you have to deal with it, and you mustn't take an inflexible position. There are people who call that "dithering," and they say dithering is a bad characteristic. We say it's responding to data.

What about this idea you have regarding fragments?

Gregory and I cooked up a concept. It was very deconstructivist, but we were going to save great portions of the exterior walls of the building we were demolishing. We saved portions 40 feet wide by 20 feet high, weighing 50 to 60 tons. We were going to take them off the building, store them, and then paste them back on the new building in exactly the position they had been before. We were choosing the fragments very strategically from 1920 to 1940. I think we had six fragments—pieces of cornice and pieces of store window—and they were going to get pasted back where they had been. Gregory and I were pleased with this. It was a lovely meeting of minds. The engineers looked at it and said, "We can do it." Ian Gillespie of Westbank said, "It's kind of neat. Nobody will walk by without noticing it—even if they laugh they will notice it." The person who didn't like it was Larry Beasley, who was the co-director of planning at the time. He said, "I trust that you guys will design it to make it look good," but he feared it would set a terrible precedent. So he basically put the kibosh on it. We could choose to continue despite him, and we might win through due process. But Westbank was trying to get all these concessions and amenities, and it's hard to bite the hand that's feeding you. So the decision was made to discard the fragments. At that point, Gregory redesigned the elevations. They had been quite planar to accept the fragments and once they weren't there, he said, "I designed boring elevations." So he made them much more plastic, much more three-dimensional. Now it's not possible to put the fragments there, but we did keep them. They're in storage with the 'W' sign and crumpled tower right now. They are going to get put back on site, but they're going to get reconstructed and deconstructed in the public spaces instead of on the building where they once were. They're going to be tame rather than outrageous. We had this idea which was too advanced. It was the avant-garde artist being dumbed down by a miscomprehending public.

I don't think anybody realizes how complex this whole thing is.
We were looking for models for interpreting multiple periods of buildings back when we were doing the fragments. There were very few but we finally found one, and it turned out it got dumbed down also. It's the Sony Center in Berlin, which is a very complicated mixture of old and new buildings. One of the old buildings had gunshot wounds from the two World Wars and it was being kept as a series of fragments. Two years ago on their website, they bragged about this and now it's not on the website. We think it got dumbed down somewhere in the execution. We think we're not the only ones who tried to come up with a slightly outrageous interpretation of the continuity of history. We want to say that property evolved for 100 years, and it's going to evolve for another 100 years. At this point we are witnesses, and we are telling you through our interpretation program and architectural program about the first 100 years of evolution. That has been watered down, sadly. We haven't talked about the interpretive program, but it's been diluted by all kinds of forces—partly by these competing agendas I've mentioned and partly by the force of cash. Collectively, we were breaking ground in terms of interfacing old and new and telling the story of the ages. What will be there is going to be seen as special, but what might have been would have been something quite incredible. I remember a radio producer once told me, when I was doing a piece on CBC, that only your producer knows what you didn't say. Only we know what we didn't say. But someday 20 years from now, Gregory and I are going to have a beer together and we're going to toast to the fragments that weren't, and the something else that wasn't.

TALES FROM THE TOWER MAN
Kevan Losch

Kevan Losch
Principal
H & H Custom Iron

Born and raised in the early 1960s in Vancouver, Kevan Losch enjoyed family shopping excursions to Hastings Street and the Woodward's department store. He remembers the smell of fresh baked goods, the overwhelming excitement of looking and touching every toy and of course year after year, seeing the Woodward's Christmas window displays. With every detail perfect, the miniature Christmas train, the decorations and the vibrant colours, the displays always enhanced the magic and anticipation of the season. His mind would wander while gazing through the Woodward's glass, dreaming of his wish list and wondering what would appear under the tree on Christmas day. Now he is elated to be contractor on the redevelopment of the very place that gave him so much joy and many cherished memories as a child. He anticipates walking the same sidewalks, reminiscing about the Woodward's window displays and their magic and looking up at the landmark 'W' sign illuminated and turning so majestic on its steel tower. "Thank You, Woodward's."

I WAS BORN AND RAISED IN VANCOUVER, and have lived here all my life. Like everyone it seems, I remember the old Woodward's store. My parents shopped there and Christmas was always the time of year to go down and see the display windows, which they always had, much like Toronto's Eaton's Centre. They have beautiful display windows. I don't know if they stole that concept or not but Woodward's was amazing.

I grew up in a really active household. My dad loved the outdoors. We had a cabin up at Hollyburn, and we used to go fishing and hunting up in Squamish and Whistler. So the Army & Navy was an obvious stop for us to get fishing supplies, and Woodward's was right there. So when we'd go downtown, my dad and I would go pick up our fishing goodies, and mom would take off to Woodward's. They were just a block away from each other.

I'm only 42, so I'm too young to remember but my parents first moved here in the late '50s from Ontario and they said the strip was incredibly active when they first arrived. That was where you went in the early days. What I remember is the W when the lights on the tower lit up. It was always a neat light show for us as kids.

I'm one of the partners of H & H Custom Iron. The firm has been around since 1953, and has changed hands three times. I got involved through my partner's parents. When they retired, we took over the business. We do metal fabrication, work with miscellaneous steels and some architectural things. The company has pushed towards miscellaneous steels. We've turned it around. Before, we were doing a lot of railings and miscellaneous smaller stuff, so my commitment when I came back was to take the business to the next level. Rather than doing $5,000 railings, we're now doing projects for $100,000 or $500,000.

On the Woodward's site, there is all sorts of miscellaneous steel between the floors. In between the floors, the window walls are supported in the middle by a piece of HSS attached top and bottom between the slabs. We're putting all those in. There's a lot of steel down there. Right now, I'm supplying the majority of it on demand for the rest of the site. But it's so large that they're working out contracts with some other people because obviously, I'm not large enough to take it all on myself. We've done business with ITC Construction Group for years and years and they're the general contractor for Woodward's. We have the contract for the Abbott Building, but there are five projects on the site; the W Building, the Hastings Building, which also encompasses SFU, a project in itself, the atrium and the Heritage Building.

The first construction manager for the site was David Dixon with ITC. We had done a lot of business with them already, but it was all small. One day, David comes walking down the street and I asked him if he was with ITC. He said he was, and I told him I was perturbed that we weren't getting any substantial business out of them. He looks at me, backs up a bit and says, "Nice to meet you but I've only been here for two weeks. Give me some time and I'll come and see you." About two weeks later, he comes back and says, "Remember you wanted business out of us?" I said, "Yeah," and he asks, "How much to take the W sign on the tower down?" I went, "Pardon?" And he says, "The sign has to come down, and we're going to have to look at taking it down in pieces, or in one piece, however it has to happen. How much are you going to charge me?" I looked at him and said, "I'll work it out for you." They had also started their demolition process and they needed a lot of miscellaneous brackets. That's how I got my foot in the door, because I automatically became the miscellaneous supplier of choice. I'm 10 minutes away and if it's an emergency, we can handle it, right? So it started with that chance meeting.

After that, we had a number of meetings at city hall. The heritage planner was very concerned about how much of the tower was going to stay, and how much could be kept intact. David had asked me how I wanted to handle the presentation because I was going to speak. I said, "I'm going to have to go climb the tower and take a look. I don't know how it's going to come down. I don't know how we can approach this."

I ended up climbing that tower probably 25 or 30 times, hand over hand. There's a ladder that goes up the centre of it. We ran safety lines, and I was up there non-stop taking a look at how the tower itself was put together, how the sign was attached, and deciding what remedial work was going to be needed before the sign could come down. Sitting on its original pedestal, it was quite deeply positioned in the site. There were already a lot of conversations going on between ITC and different crane companies about how it was going to come down. They had come up with a theory that the only way it could be done with the tower in one piece was if they actually drove the crane inside the building. They were going to have cut open the building, backfill it to hold up the crane, and get in close enough to actually do the lift. I went in and said, "Let's deal with the sign first, and I can do this from the street." I did all the calculations and we were close to capacity on weights. I went to the City of Vancouver Archives and dug up all the old drawings, not only for the tower, but for the sign. I had to break out all the material for the sign. That's why I climbed up and took the cover plates off, so I could see what was inside. I documented everything. Anyway, we put a program together with a price, first for taking the sign down, and for what it was going to take to work with somebody else. It's covered in lead paint, which would all have to be stripped away if we were going to keep the tower.

At that point, we had left the tower as a separate issue. The tower was decrepit; I was climbing a ladder with so many holes—it wasn't structurally sound. On the first climb, I had to take a safety line. The tower itself is just short of 90 feet and it's on top of an 85 foot pedestal. So you're 175 feet off the the main roof of the building.

What it came down to was a matter of getting the sign off first. That was our first step. I confirmed with the crane company that we could do it from the street, which was going to be far more economical than the original approach in which the building had to be opened up. It was saving the developer a whack of money so they were happy. I spent about a week up there with one of my crew gutting the sign. We had no choice, because the transformers in it weighed 1,000 to 1,500 pounds total. So all that had to come out; then be lowered off the tower and onto the rooftop of the pedestal, and from there down onto the main roof. All the wiring and the lights, for the most part, were still on it. So was the neon, which we were going to deal with after it was down. We had to get to a point where it was light enough to do the lift, and we were somewhat confined by the size of the crane we could get on to the street.

We booked the crane for a Friday, and we were there early in the morning. We climbed to the top of the tower, and the crane company sent their head safety officer up with me and one of my crew. It was a blind lift for the crane. The operator was down on the street, so he couldn't actually see where he was picking, so it was strictly off walkie-talkies. We attempted a slightly different lift than what I had planned to keep the weight as minimal as possible.

Inside, there's a main structure that supports the sign on top of its pivotal centre point. That's where we went in. We slung it off that, got everything ready and disconnected all the bolts, which took longer than what we anticipated. It wasn't something I wanted to prep ahead of time given how absolutely deteriorated that tower was. Without a crane hooked up to it, I wasn't going to spend a whole lot of time up there trying to work on this.

The bolts weren't too badly corroded because the sign had been taken down for refurbishing in 1985 and put back up. It had been lifted off with a helicopter and put back up the same way. So the bolts were only 20 years old, corroded only to the point that they were hard to get off. They had to be cut off individually and there were 15 or 20 of them.

Media was everywhere; media that wasn't even supposed to be there was there, every major TV and radio station. Plus there were between 1,500 to 2,000 people, spectators all around the neighbourhood. It was a large event, probably the largest event in the construction industry for years. The removal of this sign was symbolic. Even though demolition had already started on the site and things had happened, it was very significant that this was getting removed. It was the beginning of Woodward's being redeveloped, right. It had that public interest. I had speculated it was going to be about noon when it would come down, but unfortunately the wind kicked up; we had some issues, and we weren't in a position to lift it. We were getting very close to our maximums for the crane; I think it's 22 feet per second and wind loads up there were hitting 18 every now and again. It was bouncing back and forth, so it wasn't safe. This thing is huge, it's 19 by 15 by 3 feet, so it's a huge sail.

Finally we got to a point around 2:30 or 3:00 in the afternoon where the wind had let up. We lifted it about a foot off its pedestal, so we had it separated but we still had to wait. This was about 2:00. We were sitting there with this thing just teetering, waiting for an opportunity where we knew the wind was going to die down. We got to having just the occasional gust, so then we could attempt the lift. You have to lean the crane back quite quickly. The crowd couldn't see that it was separated. They just thought we were rigging still, or doing whatever we were doing. They weren't sure what was going on. But as soon as they saw the crane lean back, and that this thing was actually suspended in mid-air, they went absolutely crazy. Then you could see it come down to the rooftop of the main building, just to keep it safe. Then we swung it out over top, and as soon as it came out over the street—and we still had another 90 feet to go—the crowd went ballistic. You could hear them from all over. They were on rooftops, they were in windows, they were on the street. It was amazing. We got it down, we got it loaded on to the truck, we got it put into storage, and that was that.

Then there was the question of the tower. The city was asking that the tower get taken down in one piece. So I had already done my calculations about what it would cost and it wasn't a huge number. I took this as an opportunity more than a money-maker. It was historic, and it was obviously my "in" with ITC in a very solid way, and with the developer, Westbank.

The numbers were in, and it was exorbitant to pull the tower down and to have me and a remediation crew from another company working in tandem, literally, man for man. As each rivet came out, they were going to have to vacuum and collect all the lead that was coming off. It had to be done in a specialized manner because of environmental concerns. It's lead paint, and God knows what else was on it. So the amount of manpower involved in disassembling the tower was astronomical. We would have to take it down in pieces small enough to bring to a contained environment where the abatement company could actually do a full stripping.

The conversations were ongoing with the city. ITC had called and they said, "We need you to come to a meeting at city hall. You have to talk to them about what you see up there because none of us have gone up." So I said, "Okay, I'll go up and take video for you." I had already taken hundreds of pictures, not only of the sign but of the tower itself as I walked down or hanged on the actual tower. So I took the video; we went to city hall, sat down and plugged in the video for 15 people, including representatives from Westbank, ITC, and their heritage consultants. I showed them the video from top to bottom, probably about 15 minutes worth.

An interesting story came up when I was actually taking this video. The way that they were dismantling the building below me while I was up there was very safe. There were no issues with the core I was standing on, or with the tower itself. Nothing was structurally unsafe. But they were dropping the occasional large slab down one floor at a time. They would cut it out with jackhammers and when they'd torch the rebar, it would drop down a whole floor. It was probably 1,000 or maybe 2,000 pounds.

So I was up on the tower. The sign was off and the whole tower was moving in the wind twisting and doing what it was supposed to do. It was stressed and it was moving and giving. It was interesting to feel how organic it was. The sign's gone and I'm up there taking the video. I'm about a third of the way down, and I'm taking a lot of video of the impact corrosion that's going on, and of areas where it's completely rusted through. I hear this bang and it was one of these slabs, further out in the building, that had dropped. They had cut it out and it had fallen eight feet to the floor down below. All of a sudden I could feel the entire tower turn to jello and twist and torque in ways that I had never experienced. I'd been up this thing 20 times already and there had never been anything like this. I turned absolutely white. I had never been more scared in my life. Honest to God. I'm almost 170 feet off the main slab and if I'm going down, it's a long way. I immediately called the superintendent on my cell phone and said, "Get them to stop all work until I'm off this thing."

So at the city meeting, I showed them the video and how dilapidated this tower was. Following the video, the senior heritage planner looks at me and says, "What do you think?" I told him that story, looking him straight in the eye. The rest of the table was quiet and he said, "I think a soft-impact landing on taking the tower down is probably the best alternative." I had already said to them, "If you want me to go back up there and take this thing down, it's not going to happen. I'm willing to do a lot of things to move my business forward, but I'm not going back." ITC agreed, and so did Westbank. David Leung came to me afterwards and said, "I don't want you back up there." And I said, "I actually left a couple of tools up there and that's where they're staying. I'm not going back up."

So they brought down the tower with what they called a soft-impact drop. They did all their remedial work on the concrete pedestal that holds it up and dropped the unit as one piece. They tried to excavate the building so that when the tower came down, it was a soft impact and they'd have something to salvage. Are they going to be able to re-erect this? Absolutely not. It wasn't in a condition to be re-erected in the first place.

Here's what happened. They had to build a facsimile and I got the go-ahead at ITC's Christmas party. David Leung came up to me and said, "I want to let you know that it's a design-build and that tower is yours. You've gone above and beyond, and we want you to build the tower."

So I was pleased that I had pulled out every drawing I could find in the archives because now I can use the information. The original design came from the Eiffel Tower, scaled down to one-seventh or one-eighth. It was one of seven replicas that were made at the time. We're going to have a blast with this over the next year and a half or two years. I've got to get my engineers involved. We have to design it from ground up and then work with Pattison Signs on how to attach the sign to the top. What's really interesting is that there was an additional walkway, long and one-sided. The way it was designed, you actually had to exit from the inside to the outside of the tower 10 feet below the sign, and then drag yourself into this big walkway. We need an access walkway up there. Interestingly, when this was put up with its large spotlight in the '40s, it actually had a large crow's nest on it. We don't know what they'll want. So we're going to present the design to them and say, "Here's what the original was; here's what we took down; here's one with a long gangplank on one side; and here's one with a crow's nest on it. You guys pick, it's your money." At the end of the day, I'd love to see what was originally there—a large round crow's nest that gives you full access underneath.

We'll build the tower in sections and crane up the individual pieces. We'll design it, build it, get it galvanized, have it primed painted and packaged, and then fly it up in units and assemble it. There's really no other way to do it. We can't shut the street down day after day. What it's really going to come down to is, can we use one of the tower cranes on site to erect a 20 foot section at a time?

I've got one other story for you, and it touches on the crow's nest. When I first went up, the sign was still there. I was doing all my evaluations and I heard a bit of squawking above me. So I look up and perched within the tower, there's a really large crow about 15 feet above my head. He's just sitting there looking at me. So I continue climbing, and he squawks again, takes off, flies up another 10 or 15 feet, and perches on one of the cross members. He's sitting there, looking out from the corner of his eye with his head tilted. I hear him squawk and he flies off; I think, "Good, he's gone." Then I hear some faint squawking and I see two more crows at the very top, on the 'W' sign. I'm only about halfway up the tower and, all of a sudden, I feel a huge bang on my shoulder. The crow had come down into the tower, dead centre in the middle where the ladder is, and clipped my shoulder. He actually dive-bombed me. It freaked me out, but I kept going up, and he came at me again.

I decided this wasn't good and I climbed back down again. I phone the site safety officer and ask him if he's got one of those full face masks. I figure I'm okay as long as this guy doesn't hit my face. So I start climbing back up, this time with a small air horn. Sure enough, he comes after me again. I hit the air horn and he takes off. When I get up there, there are three crows. And no crow's nest; so they weren't actively nesting. I thought, "Why are these guys going so crazy?" I was lying on the large gangplank and this crow was dive-bombing me. I actually got a picture of him coming at me while I was lying flat on my back. They were not impressed that I was up there.

But here's the strange thing. I had to go back down to get something. So I climb all the way back down through the centre of the tower, and get to the rooftop where I'd left my tools. I was with a bunch of guys. As we're talking, I look up and there on the parapet wall, on top of the actual cement core that the tower stood on, is the crow. And he's sitting there looking at me. He's 90 feet in the air and I'm 100 feet horizontally away from him. I think, "He can't be looking at me, it's not possible." So we all walk away, a half dozen of us, and one of the other guys takes off in a different direction. The crow's head did not come off me. He knew exactly who I was in that group of people. His head turned and he followed me, absolutely step by step. He saw me walk into the base door. I climbed the ladders inside and when I got up through the access hole in the roof of the core building, right at the base of the tower, there he was, sitting 10 feet up, waiting for me to come back.

FOLIO VII

PHOTOGRAPHY
Eric Deis

DEVELOPMENT APPLICATION NO. DE409942
100 W. Cordova Street/101 W. Hastings Street

Henriquez Partners Architects has applied to the City of Vancouver
for permission to develop this site with a mixed-use residential, retail,
office, institutional use project which includes:

☐ retention and rehabilitation of the 1903/08 Woodward's Building, to contain retail
uses, non-profit community space and a 37-space child daycare centre (including
retention and restoration of the historic "W" sign);

☐ development of a 9-storey Hastings Building, to contain retail uses, the SFU
School for the Contemporary Arts, and 125 units of non-market housing for singles;

☐ development of a 31-storey Abbott Building, to contain retail uses, office use,
75 units of non-market housing for families and 170 units of market housing;

☐ development of a 40-storey W Building on Cordova Street, to contain retail uses
and 366 units of market housing; •

☐ provision of two levels of underground parking and loading facilities on site, and
additional secured parking at 150 West Cordova Street (parkade); and

☐ development of a large public atrium and urban park and plaza, accessible from
Cordova, Abbott and Hastings Streets.

FURTHER INFORMATION MAY BE OBTAINED AT: PROJECT FACILITATOR'S OFFICE
3RD FLOOR, EAST WING, CITY HALL, PHONE 604-871-6478

7

THE CONTEXT

Urban Design Guidelines

Developed by Larry Beasley and Hotson Bakker Boniface Haden, the Woodward's Urban Design Guidelines were presented to the four developer teams competing for the Woodward's project in March 2004 to aid them in the preparation of their proposals. Given the city of Vancouver's role as owner, investor and regulator, independent advice on appropriate urban design influences and possible built-form responses was required. The guidelines provided a baseline from which the city could evaluate and critique the different proposals and would pertain to any subsequent rezoning and development application. While certain guidelines were requirements, all other guidelines were considered to be discretionary and representative of performance goals that satisfy the public's interests and the city's preferences for the site.

The overriding intent of the guidelines was to inspire a high-quality, well-executed design response that appropriately enhanced and mediated the prevailing contextual characteristics of the adjacent Gastown, Hastings Corridor and Victory Square neighbourhoods. Further, the guidelines were meant to encourage innovation in urban form and building expression that exhibited the design expectations of the city: neighbourliness, heritage conservation, livability, safety, pedestrian amenity, public realm quality and sustainability performance. The guidelines were based on the original Woodward's site as set out in the competition, and assumed that most of the existing building would be retained and would act as the base upon which additional forms were added. The final approved project jointly developed by the Westbank team, the city of Vancouver planning staff, the Woodward's Steering Committee and the Community Advisory Committee varied significantly from these assumptions, but met and often exceeded the overall intent of the guidelines.

Public Realm

Given the long association of the original Woodward's store with community activity, the design of the Woodward's redevelopment aimed to restore the site as a neighbourhood centre with welcoming and inclusive spaces for the surrounding communities and the public. The fortress-like massing of the old Woodward's building was fractured by dividing the program into four buildings, the original 1903/08 structure and three new structures surrounding a central covered atrium, resulting in multiple pedestrian access points and routes across the site. Extending the existing Abbott lane to the atrium; creating a mid-block pedestrian street crossing, overhead pedestrian bridge and entry off Cordova Street; and locating the main entry of the complex off Hastings Street achieved ground floor permeability. The porous edges of the project site enables area residents to participate in the activities of daily life at Woodward's, such as grocery and household shopping, socializing with friends, and taking shelter from inclement weather. They also encourage connectivity between the adjacent communities of Gastown, Hastings Corridor, and Victory Square.

Inspired by the public and inclusive function of train stations, the covered steel atrium and adjoining open-air public plaza were similarly designed to accommodate different community and social activities and to be shared by all. Genuinely inclusive public spaces in the city are much needed given that many of Vancouver's public spaces are actually private lands designated for public use in return for density bonuses and are designed to be selective of users and activities. The original proposal suggested a day-and-night market opportunity; though later found to be untenable due to its direct competition with Chinatown and its internalizing effect on pedestrian traffic, the market nevertheless expressed a profound confidence in the local economy. Woodward's residents and on-site daytime users will support an estimated 70 percent of the project's commercial activities with minimal impacts on the existing commercial activity in Gastown and Chinatown. The main entries for the anchor grocery store and drugstore are off the atrium, with secondary exits to the street. While bolstering activity levels in the atrium, it is unclear how the low level of retail or activities on the street side of the project will affect the vitality of the project and the surrounding neighbourhood.

The original scheme located a public roof garden on the third floor above grade. The city questioned whether this location would make the space amenable for community use. The expansion of the Woodward's site to include the Holborn Lands after the developer competition allowed the project to create an enlarged ground-level public realm, a condition of Westbank being selected developer. With an urban park and public plaza added to the original proposed atrium, the enlarged public realm better sculpts identifiable forms for the diverse programmatic elements.

To encourage pedestrian activity around Woodward's, the ground floor consists primarily of retail units with identifiable display windows. A detailed streetscape concept integrates paving treatments, lighting, street trees and public art to improve the streetscape and expand the public realm. Original Woodward's canopies on the street facades of the 1903/08 building and new generously scaled glazed canopies for the rest of the project provide continuous rain protection and a comfortable street-level experience in Vancouver's rainy climate.

Building Height
Building heights of the development were carefully considered in the context of the overall neighbhourhood as well as the form and character of the existing building fabric. Originally 108 metres, the tower grew to 134 metres to accommodate the extra density created by the addition of an extra 100 units of non-market housing and confirmation of SFU's tenancy soon after the developer competition. The city had made reviewing the tower height a condition of Westbank being selected as project developer. It was concerned that the height of the W Building and its intrusion into a view cone from Cambie and 12th Avenue not set a precedent for other developments.

The Woodward's Community Advisory Committee, with unusual unanimity among its business, non-profit and Downtown Eastside representatives, argued the project needed the height to ensure a critical mass of people and deliver an economic pro forma that was financially viable and self-sustaining. City staff and the design team reviewed alternatives that lowered the tower height and an alternative agreement was reached with Westbank and the city planning department to decrease the W Building to 121 metres high—still firmly situating it as a new Vancouver landmark

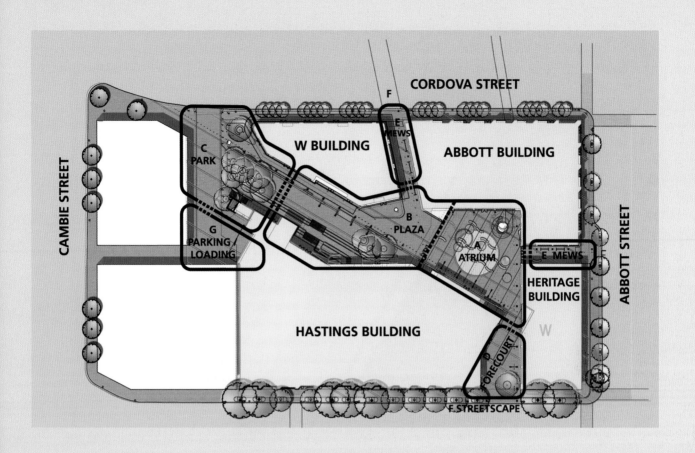

building—and to create a smaller tower on the corner of Abbott and Cordova streets to accommodate the remaining density.

Because the W Building's highest point still protrudes two metres into one of Vancouver's view cones, it required a height relaxation allowed for decorative roofs. Composed of greenery that poetically expresses the sustainable principle of water retention on the site, the roof form of the W Building is a significant design element. The W Building is only 31 metres above the century-old Sun Tower to the south and is framed in the skyline by this tower and two other towers, the 63 metre high Dominion Building, and the new 90 metre tower of the Abbott Building containing market units and 75 non-market family units. The Abbott tower is scaled to respect and acknowledge the Sun Tower while providing a graceful transition from the W Building down to the original 1903/08 building and the streetscape.

Placed on the northwest corner of the Woodward's site, the iconic stature of the W Building serves to mark the West Cordova Street "bend" where the downtown street grid changes direction. The dominance of the axial view looking east on West Cordova Street served as one of the major organizing principles for the site. The tower is distinguished from other contemporary towers in Vancouver by a tri-partite composition of base, midsection and top achieved through cut-out sky balconies, a roof-level colonnade of trees surrounding the residential

communal space, and a floor plate of 885 square metres that is proportional with the neighbouring Dominion Building and traditional flatiron buildings.

Heritage

In 1995, Fama Holdings had registered Woodward's as a heritage 'C' building on the Vancouver Heritage Register in return for a relaxation of the residential floor space regulation, severely limiting the financial viability of converting the building to social housing and non-profit uses. Identified as having particular heritage value were the original 1903/08 wood frame store, the 1925 wing, the illuminated 'W' sign, the 1927 addition that supports the W, and the 1939 block containing the auditorium/gymnasium. Considered a symbol of the Woodward's store and an icon on the Vancouver skyline a replicated neon red 'W' sign rises prominently to 75 metres, close to its original location above the 1903/08 Heritage Building and is reoriented to the terminus of the Cordova axis.

The Woodward's redevelopment project retained only the 1903/08 building for several reasons. The original Woodward's store was added to so many times and the structure had deteriorated severely over the decade-long vacancy that its historic value was questionable. SFU's School for the Contemporary Arts, moreover, had a very specific program that could not be accommodated in the existing floor heights. Retaining the 1903/08 building only and replacing the rest with three new structures express a connection with the past and a new phase in the evolution of the site. As a condition of approving Westbank as project developer for Woodward's, city council required that the project's heritage conservation be improved. A comprehensive Heritage Conservation and Interpretation Program was introduced that would see notable fragments of the historic building and interpretative displays incorporated into public areas of the new complex. This program not only preserves physical attributes of the original Woodward's store, but also presents the cultural and sentimental memories Vancouver residents have of Woodward's.

The architectural vocabulary developed for the Woodward's redevelopment is modern, yet inspired by its heritage context and the original Woodward's morphology. Rather than a "theme park" of copied historical styles, Woodward's exhibits inspiration from three specific sources: archival photographs revealing the construction

techniques of the historic Woodward's structure, the flatiron shape and construction methods of the neighbouring Dominion Building and Sun Tower, and the scale and massing of the Flatiron Building in New York constructed at the same time as the original Woodward's store. A series of elements are knitted together to resonate with the texture, scale and proportions of the original Woodward's building. Brick piers are spaced 6.7 metres apart to match the original storefront. Honest concrete frames emerge above the brick piers, recalling the actual construction techniques of the post 1908 Woodward's structures. The W Building dons vertical steel lattices that reinterpret the steel construction methods of the late 19th century.

With the addition of Woodward's four buildings edging the property line, the entire city block between Cambie and Abbott streets will have a total of nine buildings of varying heights to achieve the characteristic saw-tooth pattern. The Hastings Building façade is irregular with higher elements stepping back from a continuous street wall whose height relates to existing buildings around it. The W Building and the Abbott Building emulate the Dominion Building, Marine Building and the Flatiron Building in New York by rising steadily from the base without setbacks, but instead, with changes in the fenestration detailing and slab cut-outs to create a tri-partite façade.

Transportation

The city lane along the west property line of the original Woodward's store for parking and truck service was exchanged for a new lane outlet of similar size and use west of the consolidated Woodward's site adjacent to the Cambie Hotel. The city approved a streetcar line on West Cordova Street with the nearest stop planned for the south curb on West Cordova Street, between a mid-block crossing and the Cordova Mews entrance to the site. To preserve the heritage character of the area, 254 on-site parking stalls and service areas were located below grade concealed from view and 500 were provided in the city-owned Cordova Parkade, which is connected by an overhead pedestrian walkway to a public concourse on the Abbott Building's second level.

THE RESILIENCE OF CULTURE
Milton Wong

Dr. Milton K. Wong
Chancellor
Simon Fraser University (1999-2005)

Dr. Milton Wong was born in 1939, and grew up in Vancouver's Chinatown, the second youngest of a large immigrant family. He attended UBC and graduated with a Bachelor's degree in Political Science and Economics in 1963. He was granted a PhD (Law) from SFU in 1998. Shortly afterwards, in 1999, Dr. Wong became the first Asian-Canadian chancellor of SFU.

Dr. Wong was the driving force behind the fund-raising campaign for Science World. He is a member of the Advisory Board of the Salvation Army and of the Dean's Advisory Council and the Faculty of Commerce, UBC. For these efforts, and many others, Dr. Wong was awarded the Order of Canada in 1997.

In addition to his activities in the community, Dr. Wong is the chairman of HSBC Investments (Canada), and the founder, in 1980, of M. K. Wong and Associates, an investment firm which was sold to HSBC in 1996.

I lived in Chinatown. Woodward's is a stone's throw, and the family tailor shop is just two blocks away. So I've seen the ebb and flow of every area of the Downtown Eastside. I was brought up there, I went to school there and I delivered newspapers there. I know all those streets very well.

So you have a vested interest in what happens to the Downtown Eastside?
I may have a vested interest, but I think the whole community has a vested interest. I think the issues concern more than one person, more than one segment of society. When you're dealing with poverty and homelessness, it's a community issue. In our social policy, we have to accept the fact that homelessness is part of our everyday life, and we have to include homelessness as part of our reality. If we do that, then we have to develop social and civic policies that will be accommodating.

Haven't social policy analysts understood that by now?
No. It's only out of guilt that people are accepting it. It's public pressure. In all fairness, I think the greater community is saying, "We're responsible, I'm ashamed of it, so let's do something about it." Unfortunately, they're looking for leadership from the political side of civic society and they are unable to provide it.

Do you mean they are ill-disposed, or that it's really not their responsibility?
They're not ill-disposed. They think it's their responsibility. But they don't know how to go about doing it, so it comes down to issues of learning what constitutes a society and how did we arrive there? It gets back to some principles Jane Jacobs has written about. Those are very earthy things, their dimensions are people-oriented as opposed to having a corporate orientation.

Is the Woodward's project, as it was conceived and has developed, a significant step forward in recognizing the kind of rich and layered society that you say exists in the Downtown Eastside?
Yes and no. The original intent, when I started on this project six or seven years ago with Simon Fraser University, was to look for alternatives. I should talk about what I find so compelling in terms of revitalizing the area. That is, I believe culture builds resilience in society. If you look at cultures that have a strong identity, whether Chinese or Japanese, they have rich backgrounds. They won't disappear because they are exceptionally strong culturally. Conversely, when you destroy the identity of a culture, like we have done with Aboriginal culture, then you also destroy their dignity and respect. So if you are interested

in rebuilding and revitalizing an area, the foundation is to look at cultural development. For the last four or five years, a group of us have been putting a lot of effort into a program called the Downtown Eastside Community Arts Initiative. It's really about people who are developing cultural activities. Today there are now over 40 galleries. Every year, the Carnegie Community Centre has a cultural happening. Two years ago, they performed a one-act opera on drug addiction. Three years before, we had a play called *In the Heart of the City,* where over 100 individuals got involved, saying, "What story do we want to tell?" The members of that community are so passionate about their identity and their self-realization that there's no turning back. Yes, we have a lot of homelessness and that's what we're focusing on. The president of Simon Fraser University and I really wanted the School for the Contemporary Arts to be part of the rebuilding and we intend to contribute to that rebuilding on an ongoing basis. We have dedicated time slots for community engagements in the School for the Contemporary Arts. We're the leading school for the contemporary art in Canada, and we like to think that Simon Fraser University can and will contribute to the revitalization of a very important part of the city.

So from your perspective, it was critical that SFU move downtown?

That was my only interest. I feel very strongly that the arts are a cornerstone in any community. SFU already have lots of downtown projects but nothing in the east side of Vancouver. At Harbour Centre, they initiated the first school in Canada to have a downtown campus.

Was the model NYU?

Absolutely. NYU is a great model. Students are non-confrontational. It's a good mix; they all eat pizza and drink beer. The issue about the Woodward's site, though, is that we have 42 storeys and a lot is going to depend on the people they attract. Will they accept the milieu, or are they going to start building a fence around it? I hope not. I can tell you that the school will not allow a fence. The students will not allow it. Every day 1,100 to 1,200 students will be going in and out.

I'm interested in your sense that the arts are absolutely essential. Is that because the arts are the vehicle through which the stories you're talking about can be told, and that the stories are from people who have been marginalized and disenfranchised?

That's only one modest part, but I think it's very important. The arts are important for all parts of society. If you look at the foundation of the technology industry—iPods and computer games—intellectual stimulation begins with the arts. The vibrancy of the arts is the foundation for intellectual stimulation in all the growth industries. That's how fundamental it is. To say that we're interested in computer science is not good enough. That's just a tool. What you want is the intellectual stimulation, and that's what Vancouver has with this cross-cultural activity. We have to have a major school for the contemporary arts that will draw in the best creative minds. Those things are dynamic and iterative. Once you have one, you iterate a new level of creativity.

One of the things that is difficult for anyone from the outside to understand is that the cluster of marginalized people who live in the Downtown Eastside are a community. They don't see themselves as outsiders. In their community, they're insiders

That is the core of my volunteer work for the Downtown Eastside. We give dignity and recognition to each other. When I talk to you, I'm giving you dignity and respect, as you are to me. We don't find it from within. Going back 15 or 20 years, you can see a downward trend of social and economic status. Services were given to other parts of the community, and the people here were disenfranchised. So they began to be downtrodden. The real estate prices went down. This was a set-up for developers to come in and make money. First the population is disenfranchised, and then they're moved out, which is wrong.

It's a bit unethical too, because by moving them somewhere else you just off-load the problem.

Not only that, they don't want to move out. Adam Smith talked about an invisible hand. Unfortunately, these invisible hands don't have the money to exercise their rights.

Not many people are reading The Wealth of Nations *these days.*

That's what I'm getting at. What we are working towards down there is to develop a social compact where we will follow some principles of inclusion, which include dignity, recognition and unconditional love for humanity, for someone on the street. You don't have to invite them into your house, but we have to think in terms of that community compact. We also have to develop housing for people. We have over 2,000 street homeless, plus another 4,500 who might as well be homeless, living in leaky rooms. It's a huge problem. We should look at it from a long-term point of view and say, we'll fix this up in the next 10 years.

There are 530 market units in this complex. Is the allocation of 200 units to social housing better than none, but only half as good as 400? How do you calibrate, not just the need, but the achievement of having any amount of social housing in the first place?

Let me move my comments to a corporate model. Richard and Gregory Henriquez are fine people; Ian Gillespie is a fine person. But the corporate models we have are amoral to the point where their by-laws have nothing to do with morality. The fact is, it's people running these corporations who provide the morals. In most cases, whenever a corporation or a bank is perceived to be giving, it's really enlightened self-interest. For a 42-storey building, they'll give you the first six floors, but they still make the same amount of money. They haven't given up anything. And that goes through the whole corporate sector. The only time I see corporations really giving is when they set aside a certain sum of money in a foundation and say, "Come hell or high water, this foundation is for the betterment of the community, and it's coming out of the profits. And it's going to be adjudicated not based on what is coming in, but on the need of the community." Then I say that corporation has arrived and is contributing to a moral environment.

This question of how you engineer a society is a complex engagement here in Vancouver. There's a lot of social engineering going on.

It's because we're less structured, and we're more cosmopolitan. I can pick up the phone and talk to Jimmy Pattison, as you can to me. He recognizes me and we chat. On the other hand, you and I live a different life. This guy's a billionaire, so he has that comfort level. In the arts, we co-mingle and that's the real world here.

Why have you become the kind of thinker you are today? Although you're comfortable now, you didn't come from wealth.

I have to give a lot of credit to my sister Anna. She's 10 years older than me and she's an artist. She came back from China in 1952 and said to my father, "I want to go to art school." She had been a seamstress. She studied art in Hong Kong under a famous artist and loved it. So she took her portfolio to Emily Carr and was admitted on a conditional basis. She graduated with a book prize. Afterwards, she taught for 17 years at Pratt Graphics Centre in New York city. As a young kid of 20, I said, "I can do that." It was Boxing Day and she brought out this big canvas, already sized and she said, "Here's a brush and some paints." She gave me a few hints on how to use them. Anyway, I became her strongest patron because she taught me a whole new dimension of doing things, a new language. That's where my sensitivity to these issues comes from. For the 17 years she was in New York, I would go down there two or three times a year, and we'd walk in Soho and see the art galleries filled with Lichtensteins and Jackson Pollocks. That experience had more influence on how I look at the world than anything else.

Do you think that the Woodward's project is going to work? Is it going to do what everyone hopes it will do? It has become an emblem of this new way of thinking about the Downtown Eastside.

It can be an iconic thing that does nothing, or it can embrace the idea of a community compact. It can become a resource centre for everyone and then it will work. Buildings are buildings. It's people and their dedication in the arts and cultural side that are going to make things work. Yes, London Drugs will go in there and make money, but that's irrelevant. You can cater to the middle-class and they'll be happy. But the questions about the Downtown Eastside will only be answered with the kind of programs that Simon Fraser will be taking out to the community. It comes down to our ability to promote and to get individuals in the community at large to see a compact of inclusiveness and respect. Whether the city fathers can see that, I don't know. I've had meetings with the mayor, and the council and it seemed to go over their heads. All they can see is, "We're ashamed of what's happening. The only thing we can do is give higher density to the developer so we can get the 200 units." That's not the answer. The answer lies in the programs. I'm thinking about a simple program of just washing feet. If you go to the Downtown Eastside, the biggest issue for the homeless is dirty, infected feet. Once they're infected, you can't walk, and once you can't walk, you're finished. So why can't we have a modest thing like this? Be very biblical about it. I'm going to wash your feet, dry them, put on some disinfectant, and get you a clean pair of socks and a pair of shoes. It will work because no one else is doing it. The establishment certainly isn't. I dare them.

ONE BIG TANGLED BALL OF SPECULATION
Jon Stovell

Jon Stovell
Co-Chair
Woodward's Community
Advisory Committee

Jon Stovell has been in the real estate
investment and development industry for
over 20 years. He specializes in various
areas including finance, civic approvals,
construction and marketing. For the
past 10 years, he has served as general
manager for Reliance Holdings Ltd.,
a privately-owned Vancouver company
that has been active in the development,
ownership and management of a wide
variety of commercial and residential
real estate for over 50 years.
At Reliance, he has developed a broad base
of expertise in portfolio management
with an emphasis on urban renewal
through restoration and renovation of
heritage buildings, together with new
residential and specialty retail projects.
Mr. Stovell also volunteers his
time with the City of Vancouver
Development Permit Board Advisory
Panel (City Council Appointment),
Urban Development Institute City of
Vancouver Liaison Committee (UDI
Nominee), and as UDI Representative
for the Metropolitan Core Jobs and
Economy Land Use Plan (City Council
Appointment).

*What strikes you about the process that has led to the success of the Woodward's
project?*

What was exceptional about it was the coming together of extremely polarized
groups in a neighbourhood that had a long history of adversarial social-
economic and business politics. Five years earlier, those groups had literally
been at each other's throats, marching in the streets. And I don't just mean
the low-income community marching in the streets, I mean the business
community marching in the streets.

Who was marching against whom?

At that time, it was something called the Community Alliance and it was a loose
aggregation of business owners, long-term residents and home owners who
were apoplectic about the unrelenting injection, literally, of social service agencies, drug-enabling policies and low-income housing projects into the neighbourhood, a neighbourhood that had once been quite diverse and economically
vibrant. That had been represented by the success of Woodward's when it was
a community grocery store and shopping centre—an old style, large, multi-
department store. Woodward's dying began the descent into what many viewed
as an extremely bad year of planning, containment and social engineering,
which peaked in the protest marches, with both sides going up and down the
streets, chanting, 'You get outta our neighbourhood', 'No, you get outta our
neighbourhood'. Five or six years later, a number of intentional measures taken
by those people and the way the media was handled for the neighbourhood
resulted in the Woodward's project going ahead because it got buy-in from
these diverse groups. I was co-chair of the Woodward's Community Advisory
Committee with someone who five years earlier I would have been marching
in the streets against.

I gather you mean Lee Donahue?

Yes. That was an amazing moment. There was a point in the process where
the low-income community people and the business community people were
saying to the city, we want the development to be bigger, taller, and more
profitable, so that it can do more for the neighbourhood in terms of market
housing and non-market housing, grocery stores, and social service agencies.
The city actually had to back down. Frankly, they've had a history of using the
division in the community to do what they wanted to do. That was a high point
and, unfortunately, since then there has been a bit of a backslide. But it's still
pretty good in that the hatchet remains buried. There is some grumbling from
the Downtown Eastside community and social service groups that Woodward's

has not delivered what they want. But there is a suspicion that they need to stay in that mode because that's been the only way they've been able to accomplish anything.

What were the conditions that allowed two sides that five years earlier would have been at each other's metaphoric jugulars, to not just be talking together, but working together on the project?

I think it was a number of factors. This intense conflict had left the parties feeling exhausted. Unless we actually resorted to violence, we'd gone as far as we could, and people got back to doing what they did. I think the initiative came from the business community. The Gastown Business Improvement Association and some of the Chinatown BIAs decided to stop complaining in the media about conflict in the neighbourhood. Instead, we hired a public relations agency to tell nothing but good news stories about what was going on. We decided that the harm-reduction drug strategies and the social service strategies were out of our control and we couldn't do anything about it anyway, so we just focused on success stories. The company I worked for did several real estate projects almost as big as Woodward's, before Woodward's, and we focused on those. We also started bringing retailers into the area that were targeted to attract year-round business.

What kind of incentives did you offer that would have made it appealing?

Taking less rent to get this business instead of that business. There were also cooperation among the property owners to brand a certain type of business boutique in the neighbourhood. Our attitude was to tell a good news story and get on with business. Outside of that, the larger economic upturn made what had been marginal areas suddenly seem viable, so Woodward's, with the right incentives, became economically possible for someone like Westbank. But I think the key thing was that the province sold the property to the city. Woodward's was previously owned by a private developer who did nothing, and then it was owned by the province, who didn't have any money for social housing at the time. Selling to the city was the step that allowed the city to enter into negotiation with a developer. The city is used to working with developers, the province isn't. So from a policy and a bureaucratic point of view, it was a good thing. The low-income people were finally so desperate to get a win with Woodward's that they became more realistic and stopped the squats and the militant stuff. There was also some changes in the dynamics of the social service power groups in the neighbourhood, such as the Downtown Eastside Residents' Association, which became less influential, while Portland became more influential. Portland had a better track record doing deals. They were a little bit less puritanical and were prepared to move from waiting for government money to fall from the sky to asking how do we get something done. Certainly exhaustion can lead to cooperation.

I'm interested to hear you say there is some slippage right now. What evidence is there and what is its cause? People are no longer exhausted, and in the Woodward's project, they seem to have a winner on their collective hands.

Many people may disagree but I think it has to do with the drug situation on the street. I believe it's the same, or worse, than it was five or six years ago, but what's changed is it's been diluted. I often say that if you went out to Robson Street on a Saturday afternoon, with 30,000 people there, and you took away everybody who earned more than $30,000 a year, there would be the same number of unfortunate people on Robson as there is in Gastown or on Hastings Street. It's the dilution factor. It feels better, but all the problems and all the trouble is still there. I think what really happened is that Woodward's became a catalyst for a number of other development initiatives in that area. We're doing some, other people are doing some; we were before Woodward's and we are still. I think there is a sense that the net effect of Woodward's on the Downtown Eastside community is still threatening. Yes, they're getting a number of low-income housing units, but the flipside is that it's pushed up property values to the point where they feel that their remaining housing land and housing stock is under threat.

But the city just closed a deal on six more single room occupancy hotel buildings.
Yes. The city has a long track record of suppressing land and suppressing development in that area. They struggle with themselves. They want and don't want it, and there are factions within the city. The planning department probably wants it; the social planning department probably doesn't. Basically, taking those lands out of private ownership is a good thing because it relieves property owners of the obligation to provide low-income housing with private funding. But if the city or the province buys them and doesn't fix them up and convert them, then they're just perpetuating squalor and a horrible existence. Having to step up and admit that these SRO hotels have become a critical part of low-income housing stock is horrific. Here we are saying they're intolerable, they're unbearable, and no one should live in them, but we're buying them, putting them in amber, and saying to the occupants, "You have to stay."

Give me a sense of what Woodward's represents for revitalization of the Downtown Eastside? What can it do if it works in an optimum way?
Well, it works on two levels. One is iconic: it says "WOW!" to the broader city, it gets their attention. Something actually worked in the Downtown Eastside, there must be something going on.

So the optics are good?
The optics are fantastic. I mean compare today to five years ago. Back then, if I picked up the phone and said I was doing stuff down in Gastown, where I've worked for 15 years, people would say, "How do you get to your car? Is it safe down there? I haven't been in Gastown in 25 years." Now it's like, "How do I get in, where can I buy, do you have anything left?" So that's part of the effect Woodward's has had. On a practical level, Woodward's will do what's already been done, and what we need more of: add body heat to the area. That term is Gregory's. We just need people. People bring demand, they bring activity, vitality, support services and, more specifically, the grocery stores and the drug stores. These are things that the neighbourhood desperately needs. People need places to shop. So, it's fantastic. About five or six years ago, I was talking to Carl Weisbrod, the founding president of the Alliance for Downtown New York, the equivalent BIA neighbourhood revitalization organization in Lower Manhattan. He's famous and largely responsible for what happened there. He came here to

study what we were doing and he asked me, "What is the single most important thing for turning this neighbourhood around?" I said, "Woodward's." We said it to city councillors and we said it to everybody. I had no doubt that it would turn out to be exactly what we hoped.

There is a grocery store; London Drugs is in; the TD Bank, and SFU is obviously planning a fairly significant role?
It's all those things. But spatially, Woodward's is a huge site. Downtown is immediately to the southwest of Woodward's, which physically separated it from Gastown. So Woodward's was in a dead zone. The redeveloped Woodward's is much more than just what it brings; it has permeability in the way Gregory designed these pass-throughs, and the addition of an iconic landmark tower which, if I'm four blocks away, is identifiable as Gastown. So it works on every level: on a symbolic, macro, architectural level, and on the body heat and services level.

What about the question of tower height? Wasn't there a lot of pressure to keep things low, to avoid having something that was such a signature as the tower itself?
That was fascinating. The city was presuming this deference to the historical scale of the area, and to a "nothing could be too capitalist, nothing could be too bold" attitude. The Downtown Eastside community and the business community actually came together on that and said to the city, "No, make it big, make it tall, make it more lucrative, make it more symbolic, make it more successful, bring more people into the area." That was the key moment. When Gregory was fighting for his life on the tower issue, he consulted the Woodward's Community Advisory Committee and we sent him back to Larry Beasley with the strongest possible message: "Don't reduce the height of the tower, keep it there." They were flabbergasted. They thought they could rely on the Downtown Eastside community to resist the symbolism of the mighty economic tower.

Are you surprised at what Woodward's has become? Were you skeptical at any point?
I was only skeptical at the stage when I thought the Downtown Eastside people would force everything to fail. When your way of getting through life is to basically be at the margin, complaining about problems in order to get government funding, there is a danger in accepting success, because it means you're not needed anymore. Instead, they supported Woodward's. When we went to city council and said, "This is the first time ever that I've stood up with that guy, and that guy, and that guy and supported the same thing at the same time. So you have to say yes." Once I realized it was going to get support from the community, I didn't have any doubt that the developer and the design team would be able to deliver.

What are the measures of success and how soon before you can say, one way or another, that it has actually worked? Is one measure some kind of osmotic process where the influence of Woodward's begins to spread out to the surrounding neighbourhood?
The irony is that many people think Woodward's is the initial stage of revitalizing the neighbourhood, but it's actually the last. Every heritage building has already been redone, most of the axial streets that come into Water Street

already have boutiques on them. It's like the stock market. The stock market doesn't rise after Microsoft buys Google; it rises when everybody thinks Microsoft is going to buy Google. So this sort of speculation on the success of the neighbourhood has been going on for years, and in a sense it's already happened. Woodward's just has to be finished now. After it's completed, I don't think you're going to see this huge new wave. I think it will slowly build from there, just as the neighbourhood population and normalization of the demographics will continue to rise steadily. I think the big moves are over, largely because there's a limited amount of land. What will be ongoing are smaller developments. SFU will be a success; the condominiums have been sold and they will be a success. I think the only unproven thing centres on the large footprint retailers that are part of the project. Will the companies that support them run them long enough to establish themselves? I've noticed over the years that retail runs about five or six years behind neighbourhood densification. So those stores won't make money for a long time, and I hope that the companies that own them will understand that and see the long-term benefit of their presence. I do think Woodward's is going to be a centre for the community. It's got some infrastructure and it's going to be fantastic.

You've got people who paid a substantial amount of money for an apartment within proximate distance of people who are SRO dwellers. Are there risks involved in that mixed social dynamic?

I don't think so because that tension and polarity is already there. Most of the people who bought into Woodward's come with that understanding and that aesthetic. In how many doorways of converted lofts in Gastown do people already have to step over a guy in a cardboard box when they come out of their multi-million dollar unit? That's the great thing about Gastown and the Downtown Eastside. There's the Bentley parked on the road with the guy sitting in the cardboard box. As sad as that sounds, there's a mutual acceptance in the neighbourhood of those people. It's an amazingly diverse and tolerant area. Tolerant in both directions. The business people, the affluent people, the so-called 'normal' people are very tolerant of the panhandlers, the low-income people and the drug addicts. They're just part of the fabric. And those people are pretty tolerant of what could be a threatening socio-economic force, the scary rich people who could throw them out. Probably more than any other area of the city, there's a real mixed bag down there. And there are a lot of business people who like that edge and that tension.

One of the things that Scot Hein says is that the area has to be careful to sustain the grittiness factor. You don't want Vancouver to be all pristine glitter and glass, so pretty that it looks like a playground.

That's right. Yaletown, which is basically a warehouse district, had the physical attributes of a gritty neighbourhood but didn't have the previous built-in population, so it moved from being being a big, gritty warehouse area to a place where you get your nails done and your chihuahua washed before you put it back in your purse. That's what Yaletown turned into over 10 years. That won't happen with Gastown and the Downtown Eastside. As economically robust as it gets, it would take 30 years for it to loose it's grit. You have to remember that the starting point five years ago was an 80 percent low-income to 20 percent market housing ratio. So that's a big ship to turn around and I don't think many people down there want that to dramatically change. Another thing that the low-income people have to realise is that they have a lot there and it won't all go away in an instant.

Jim Green argues that you've got to get mothers down there. If you look at the current occupancy rate it's 85 to 95 percent single males. How do you socially engineer that demographic shift?

I think the low-income and social housing forces should stop focusing so much on singles. They've built several hundred social housing units since Woodward's and, unfortunately, a high portion of them are still targeting singles. I think that's a mistake. The area is expensive, but it is still a lot less expensive than any other area of the downtown, so by definition you should be able to create larger units for families. It is disproportionate. Even for the people that have money, it's still singles. It's a young neighbourhood, it's for young people, it's for people who are having fun and want to live in a downtown, gritty area. It's like SoHo used to be.

I don't think it will ever have a suburban family feeling with school buses and kids. It's always going to be an inner-city, gritty neighbourhood. Should there be more families and more diversity? Yes, there should and it will come slowly through natural processes related to who's coming and going from the market and non-market housing. The market housing is capable of supporting a very broad demographic mix should families choose to live there. The non-market housing is the area that needs to be diversified.

How important is SFU's presence in bringing some dynamic to the overall health of Woodward's?

It will drive retail services—restaurants and coffee bars—and it will drive street vitality and energy. We're converting the Burns Block, an old heritage building just down the street from Woodward's on Hastings, right across from Pigeon Park, into 30 self-contained rental apartments that are only 275 square feet. They have a kitchen, a bathroom, a washer and dryer—everything in that compact space. We went to Japan and figured out how to design these micro-suites. Students from SFU will probably be living in them. I did five buildings down there before Woodward's even came along, but it's all part of one big tangled ball of speculation and projection of what's going to happen in the area. Would we have done that building if Woodward's hadn't gone ahead? It's hard to say, but Woodward's was definitely a factor in our decision.

So at this stage, you don't see a downside to Woodward's?

I think the downside will only come if the city planning department, the politicians and the Downtown Eastside people conclude that Woodward's is enough, that they're going to sit back and watch it deliver. That would be a big mistake. Let's put it in context. Woodward's is about 1.1 million square feet. If I were to add up the projects by the Salient Group, with some of the other projects down there, they would easily eclipse Woodward's in terms of total square footage built in the four to five years prior to Woodward's even starting construction. Nobody thought those were going to be a panacea for the neighbourhood. But because Woodward's is such a publicity machine and because of its history in the city, there is a tendency to think it's all we need. But it represents less than half of what has already occurred down there, and it probably represents only about one-eighth of what we need to do.

I want to talk about developers and their role in the way a city gets shaped. I assume that developers are complicated creatures who need to both make money and have their egos stroked?

I think the best developers have learned to be imaginative and diverse.

The ones who do best in the city are the ones who bring goods to the table. Look at a development like Woodward's and consider what had to be brought to the table, how multifaceted it is. It brings heritage, housing, cultural facilities, public arts, and financial supports to things that are distant or nearby. It's an incredibly complex model. So the developers who thrive are the ones who have the ability to see that they can get an economic and an ego hit, as well as a contributory feeling of pride from all the different facets of the development. When developers come here from the US and from Calgary, they're flabbergasted. They're used to a system where they apply for a permit, pay their money and they get to build their building.

Vancouver seems to be conducting a rather rich experiment in urban planning. There are so many possibilities here that it's an open field for all kinds of imagination operating. Maybe you're gifted by what is also a curse.

There is a lot of overlapping and contradictory policy, and the developers who thrive are the ones who drink at the fountain of public policy. They watch what's happening and package a development that delivers on all the operating policies. In order to understand how to get change at the margin, you have to understand the policy. It takes a lot of study, but when you go up to the city, all the doors are open. The way developers make money is they buy land from property owners who are passive, uninformed or unwilling; then they go to the city and find a way to change the value of that land, to do more, or something different, than was expected.

FOLIO VIII

PHOTOGRAPHY
Lani Russwurm

8

BUILDING PROGRAM AND FUNDING

Though Woodward's draws from the Modernist goal of harnessing design for the greater common good, unlike Modernism, it does not rely solely on architectural design to achieve idealist ambitions. Rather, it is the programming accompanying the design of Woodward's that creates a microcosm of a city, where on any given day, 5,000 people from diverse social groups live, work and shop together. The mixing of programmatic elements hypothesizes that the Downtown Eastside can be rehabilitated, that the rich and poor can live inclusively together and that design can make a difference. Woodward's attempts to satisfy many community aspirations by integrating an array of day-time and night-time uses, including residential, retail, commercial and institutional. The dense, mixed-use design is intended to replace the diversity once offered by the Woodward's department store and to revitalize the site as a hub of neighbourhood activity. The unique aspect of the Woodward's mixed community is not so much the co-existence of high- and low-income housing but rather that the market units sold out in two days even with the different housing types in such close proximity and in some instances, in a shared structure, demonstrating a civic openness to living in mixed communities.

Identified as key to the economic viability of redeveloping Woodward's, 536 condominium market housing units located along West Cordova Street take advantage of the views toward Burrard Inlet and the North Shore mountains. The 43,000 square metres of market residential space is split between the W Building which has 900 square metre floor plates, and the Abbott Building, whose 650 square metre floor plates accommodate small, affordable starter units. The units have open plan concepts, geared towards first-time homebuyers, young urban professionals, seniors and investors who will create an increased market rental stock. To dispel the concept of social hierarchy as an organizing principle, the W Building penthouse levels house communal rooftop amenity spaces: a fitness room, lounge, and deck with an outdoor kitchen and 'W'-shaped whirlpool.

To ensure the financial viability of the project, Westbank entrusted Rennie Marketing Systems with successfully selling the market housing to the public. Knowing what appealed to condo buyers, Bob Rennie acted like a co-designer, enlarging the suite sizes to make them more upmarket, yet rejecting Westbank's suggestion of topping the condo tower with a multi-million dollar private club due to the public image repercussions for a project touting the '60s-style idealism of a universal society where the rich and poor live together. Having mastered the art of selling condominiums as purveyors of social identity, Rennie then launched an advertising campaign to sell Woodward's as an "intellectual property," implying that savvy people will make a smart investment based on understanding the area for what it is and what its possibilities are and wanting to live near a university. The marketing poster had a run-around frame of images contextualizing Woodward's in the surrounding gritty, mixed-bag neighbourhood of design houses and thrift shops. All the condominium units were sold in the span of two days between April 22nd and 23rd, 2006, representing over $200 million in sales. Marketers interviewed all potential buyers to gauge their commitment to living in the development, but up to 30 percent of the units may have still been bought by investors. Included in the sales were six fully accessible units on the second floor of the W Building bought by the Vancouver Resource Society, an agency providing accessible housing with support services to people with disabilities.

As the iconic tower of the Woodward's project, the W Building incorporates the majority of the market housing in a shape recalling the Flatiron Building in New York, which resulted from the intersection of two buildings set at an acute angle. Similarly, the flatiron W Building is located at the hinge point between the old historical grid and the modern city grid which are oriented at different angles. With the historic Cordova Street axis penetrating the site to define the inside edge of the W Building and the modern street grid delineating the outside street edge, the resulting triangular shape reconciles the two geometries. While some respect was paid to the immediate historical context of five storey warehouses, the W Building references the larger historical context through New York's Flatiron Building and translates it into contemporary times. As Woodward's was the big box store of its day, the exterior steel skeleton of the green screens evokes historic warehouses and train stations, giving the residential tower a recognizable aesthetic.

The non-market housing component of the Woodward's redevelopment is comprised of singles and family housing units for which the federal, provincial and city of Vancouver governments contributed $48 million and negotiated a fixed-price construction contract with Westbank. PHS Community Services operates 125 singles non-market housing units, with five of them being accessible units. This housing is intended to replace single-room occupancy units lost due to the closure of nearby low-income hotels. Located above SFU's School for the Contemporary Arts on Hastings Street, the housing has access to significant amenity space on the rooftop including a water feature and an area allocated for social services.

The inclusion of 75 family non-market housing units operated by Affordable Housing Societies in the Abbott Building increases the social diversity of the project. The Abbott Building is, from a programmatic and symbolic perspective, the project's most significant building as it so thoroughly integrates the various constituents of the community into one structure rather than ghettoizing them. The family housing units have views of the ocean and mountains and are either two or three bedrooms. The units have access to amenity space, from which Affordable Housing will operate a homeschooling program, and a large outdoor play area for children overlooking the atrium with a southern exposure to ensure use. These types of smaller, diverse spaces throughout the project allow thousands of people to co-exist in a community while avoiding ghettoizing them with economies of scale.

The retail component of Woodward's is key to the economic and social vitality of the project and the neighbourhood. Located at ground level to capture the pedestrian activity of inhabitants, workers and visitors, the approximately 5,600 square metres of retail were leased prior to the project's opening, ensuring a healthy level of activity as the community became established. Anchoring Wooodward's retail activity are a 1,700 square metre London Drugs on the Hastings Building's main floor and a 1,400 square metre Nesters Market Food Store in the base of the Abbott Building. The grocery store was named in community consultations as the most relevant use

Urban Guidelines

The city of Vancouver's Request for Proposal document outlined a series of Urban Guidelines for the expected development of the Woodward's site. As such, a number of different forms were suggested, which were based upon solid urban design principles developed to provide a baseline for the competition. The development teams were invited to bring their expertise to create a model that was positive for the community while being economically viable.

City of Vancouver Original RFP

Density 7.3 FSR

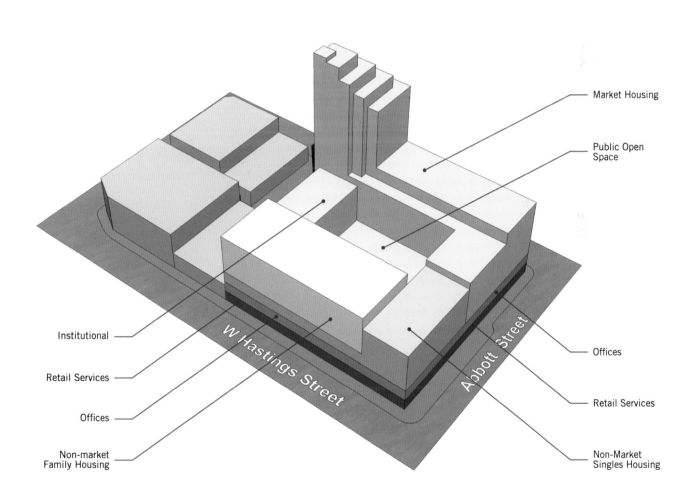

Market Housing

Public Open Space

Institutional

Retail Services

Offices

Non-market Family Housing

W Hastings Street

Abbott Street

Offices

Retail Services

Non-Market Singles Housing

for Woodward's after non-market housing. The ground floor of the 1903/08 building will include a TD Canada Trust, the first retail bank to open in the Downtown Eastside in 40 years. To replicate the function of the original Woodward's food floor, which drew in significant neighbourhood activity both in shopping and eating, the Abbott Building grocery store has been made highly accessible to the neighbourhood with two entrances, one from Abbott Street and the other off the atrium. Retail continuity on the ground level of Hastings Street, with the exception of the SFU's Visual Art Gallery, is provided, to stimulate pedestrian interest. The 1903/08 Building has smaller commercial retail units and the W Building's retail base includes a major coffeehouse.

Since SFU established its downtown campus on West Hastings Street in Harbour Centre in 1989, there had been much third party interest in incorporating SFU as an anchor institution into a new development. When Woodward's became vacant, several proposals included SFU's School for the Contemporary Arts, which is an agglomeration of various departments scattered across SFU's main Burnaby Mountain campus and Strathcona. Though SFU desired to be part of the redevelopment due to its large scale and convenient location on the transit route between the Burnaby Mountain and Surrey campuses, the funding was not secure when the city approved the final design and Westbank began construction. While the British Columbia Ministry of Advanced Education indicated that the SFU project was not a priority, SFU argued that the project was of provincial and municipal interest because of its location in the Downtown Eastside and its establishment coinciding with the Vancouver 2010 Winter Olympic Games. Finally, the advocacy of SFU, Westbank and several major supporters of SFU finally convinced the British Columbia government to create a funding model between several ministries. The combination of the $49.3 million provincial contribution and private grants raised by the University amounted to $80 million. Westbank agreed to build the space at cost and SFU negotiated a fixed-price construction contract with Westbank for the outfitted space in order to contain the risk of cost escalation. While one visual arts studio had to remain further east on Alexander Street, the remainder of the contemporary arts school's program was accommodated in the 11,150 square metre parcel at Woodward's. The school will generate significant public activity in the Woodward's complex, animating the building and streets with flows of people. All five of the school's major public venues are located above or below grade with visual connection to the public plaza and atrium. Within the school are public lobbies, teaching spaces and faculty offices to accommodate 1,200 students and several hundred staff. There are also many public performance spaces including a large "black box" experimental theatre, cinemas, music and dance performance spaces, and a visual art gallery. PHS Community Services, who is managing the singles non-market housing above SFU, is supportive of the university presence, which neutralizes gentrification by bringing a transient and generally tolerant student population to the project.

Being a less public use, the 3,700 square metres of leased office space is located on the second to fourth floors of the Abbott Building, adding a steady supply of day workers who will support local retail businesses. The federal government committed to leasing 1,400 to 3,250 square metres, or one to two floors, of office space for tenants such as the National Film Board. Because the city of Vancouver is growing and hold leases for several large spaces outside city hall that expire in 2009, it is considering relocating to between 800 to 1,400 square metres, or one floor, of the Woodward's office space.

Engaging, Empowering, Setting a Precedent

Westbank/Peterson and Henriquez Partners dissected the Urban Guidelines and performed an in depth analysis of the area and compiled a list of the program elements needed to build a viable project. PHS actively worked to identify community needs and how they could be best accommodated. The marketing team narrowed down the demographic that would likely purchase in this highly urban and edgy area and determined what amenities or features would fill in the gaps.

Westbank/Peterson Competition Entry

Density
7.57 FSR

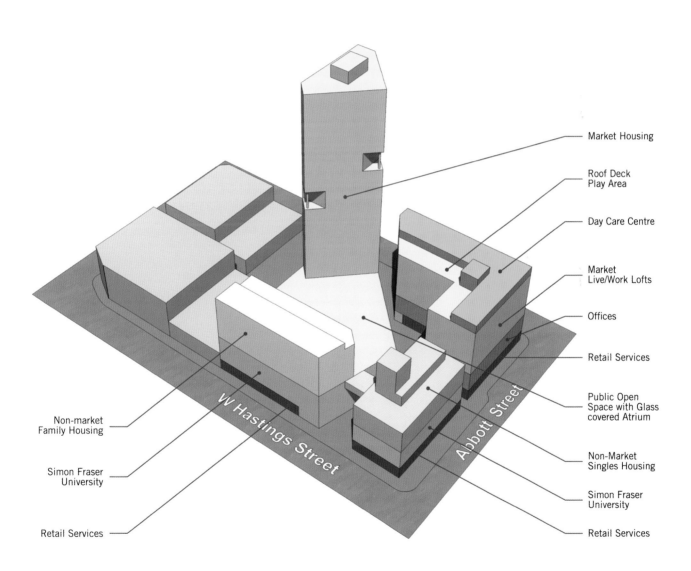

Market Housing

Roof Deck Play Area

Day Care Centre

Market Live/Work Lofts

Offices

Retail Services

Public Open Space with Glass covered Atrium

Non-Market Singles Housing

Simon Fraser University

Retail Services

Non-market Family Housing

Simon Fraser University

Retail Services

W Hastings Street

Abbott Street

The Woodward's redevelopment includes 2,900 square metres of community space for non-profit uses located in the 1903/08 heritage structure. The city of Vancouver received this outfitted parcel as compensation for the sale of the Woodward's site to Westbank. The city conducted an exhaustive review of the requests from non-profit applicants, under the categories of social services, health and culture, for use of the space. The city council approved uses that include W2, a community-based media and arts centre and AIDS Vancouver, an agency providing support services, public education and community-based research. A 37-space child development centre is located on the roof of the 1903/08 building and includes a sheltered outdoor play space beneath the relocated 'W' sign. Built with a $3 million city contribution and a fixed-price construction contract, the facility provides support for families with children and for those who may work in the Woodward's complex or in the neighbourhood.

Key to the success of amalgamating a complex mix of uses and activities onto the Woodward's site was the partnership between Westbank and all three levels of government to share the cost of the Woodward's redevelopment project, totaling $375 million, and its associated financial risks. Aside from contributing to the hard construction costs, the city contributed building permit fees, development cost levies, heritage and amenity bonus density and heritage façade grants. Westbank contributed back to the city of Vancouver a public plaza and atrium and public art while taking the financial risk for the project's residential and commercial portions and the fixed construction contracts for SFU's School for the Contemporary Arts, the non-market housing, the childcare and the shell for the non-profit community spaces.

Evolving the Design and Program

After winning the design competition the team continued to evolve the design and program to address the issues raised by the public during the selection process. There was an outcry that there were not enough social housing units therefore the city and community lobbied the provincial government to double the number to 200. Westbank/Peterson aggressively pursued a supermarket and drug store to address the needs of the tenants and families in the building as well as the neighbourhood. Negotiations were finalized with SFU to occupy 130,000 sf of the Hastings building. The original design's raised plaza was placed at grade and together with a covered atrium created the much needed interior public space for the neighbourhood.

Final Design
Under Construction

**Density
9.5 FSR**

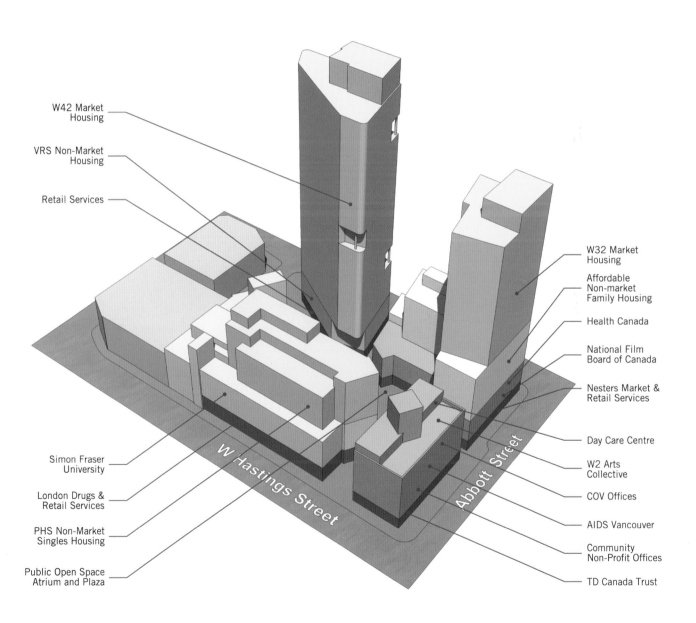

W42 Market Housing

VRS Non-Market Housing

Retail Services

W32 Market Housing

Affordable Non-market Family Housing

Health Canada

National Film Board of Canada

Nesters Market & Retail Services

Day Care Centre

W2 Arts Collective

COV Offices

AIDS Vancouver

Community Non-Profit Offices

TD Canada Trust

Simon Fraser University

London Drugs & Retail Services

PHS Non-Market Singles Housing

Public Open Space Atrium and Plaza

W Hastings Street

Abbott Street

THE IMPORTANCE OF BEING GRITTY
Scot Hein

Scot Hein
Senior Urban Designer
City of Vancouver

Scot Hein is the city of Vancouver's Senior Urban Designer. His current work is focused on the downtown core on such initiatives as Woodward's, Southeast False Creek/Olympic Village, a New Housing Plan for Chinatown, the revitalization of Gastown/Victory Square/Hastings Corridor and related public realm opportunities such as the Carrall Street Greenway, Pigeon Park, Downtown Historic Trail, CPR ROW and the Silk Road. He has been with the city of Vancouver for 12 years acting as both an urban designer and development planner on major projects. Prior to joining the city, he was in private practice where he specialized in research and development, health care, resorts and transit related developments. He is an associate member of the Architectural Institute of British Columbia and is also a registered architect in the State of Washington. He holds degrees in Environmental Design and Architecture, as well as a minor in Economics Studies. He has also established environmental awareness/built environment education programs in Canada and the United States and has served as Canada's representative for this work.

I want you to characterize what kind of city Vancouver is today. What's the environment into which the Woodward's project is being inserted?

We're clearly a schizophrenic city. There are the "haves" and the "have mores" and then the "have nots." This project is about what we might call 'setting the text' as opposed to 'reacting to context'. I have to say, I am anxious about losing the fabric of this historic core of the city. This project is a pretty significant departure. Obviously, the tower is going to be somewhat isolated, but it was rationalized because it's where the three street grids come together. It also has a certain symbolism which is pretty obvious. I am anxious that it was necessary. I think some aggressiveness had to be exercised to trump the challenges of the area and set in motion some new energy. Having said that, it is trying to be a lot of things to a lot of people and you can only do so much with even a large city block site. A lot of what Woodward's is was put on this project programmatically. It had to meet a lot of financial performance obligations and not all sites are like that, or should be like that. We need to take real care when we talk about a city on the edge of the sea that has a very rich history. Hopefully, what Woodward's sets in motion will be respectful of a part of the city which is a super-heritage precinct with a line drawn at Richards Street. Everything west of Richards Street is much more recent. How do we pull those two existences together? It's going to be a bit of a trip because the way we do urbanism, the way we think about housing typologies and mixed-use and affordability in this part of the city, will be shaped by the way we meld together those two existences.

How central is the housing question in defining how this area can be revitalized?

It's everything down here. There have been some recent efforts with the province and the city to purchase sites and to start affordable housing or social housing projects. Six more buildings were just bought. Let me put it this way: doing a tower on a podium is relatively easy. What is a more daunting challenge is insinuating respectful densification in incremental scales with a variety of development players and architects that ratchets up the fabric, but that doesn't disrupt it. We need as many people living down here as we can. We need Main Street and Hastings to come back to their former prominence. So these projects aren't going to work unless we have—and this is Gregory's term—"body heat." How much body heat can we get living in the Hastings corridor at Main Street? How can we respect the scale of Chinatown but still introduce new housing opportunities?

So body heat creates the synergies necessary to give vitality to this area. Otherwise it becomes—and your term is interesting—just a podium, an elegant, isolated island?

We need a new typology. We need new references for how to house people in liveable ways. What I am hoping is that Woodward's challenges us to rethink things and not just default to the way we've been doing towers on podiums or development in general over the last 15 or 20 years.

Why was the Westbank/Henriquez proposal the winner in the competition?

In terms of its social advocacy, Gregory's scheme was very attractive. It had the right pieces, but it needed to be reworked, particularly given the SFU program and the addition of 100 housing units. His scheme grew over the process. Just to back up a bit, we knew going into the Woodward's competition that we had to offer some specific urban design guidelines for the site. We actually treated that site as a separate sub-area of the downtown and re-zoned it with a set of guidelines prepared for us by Norm Hotson and Joost Bakker. Those guidelines studied the fabric of the area and the heights of the Sun Tower and the Dominion Building and suggested there was an opportunity to pop up a little bit, but to do it within that suggested context. We took it to council and the one clause they removed was the one that suggested a maximum height. So essentially it opened the door for very high buildings, which I have to say is still today's flavour with council. But Woodward's is a one-off with the three city grids coming together and that's how we rationalized the height of the tower. So then the question became, how do we do the absolute best with this program and with the huge aspirations of the city and the council? In a way, we reverse engineered Westbank's competition scheme, and put it back together in a slightly different format.

I gather you play a proactive role in this process. You're not passive funders?

Not at all. There were two big "uh huh" urban design moments as the process evolved. The first one came after Westbank had been awarded the project. I met Gregory and Michael Flanigan down at the Woodward's competition room, and we looked at what the next moves had to be. There were some things we had learned from the other two schemes which were relevant. I went over to Gregory's model, literally removed the tower building and said, "What if we rotate it, and put it on the Cordova axis? If we can make that happen, we have a clear sightline up Cordova Street and then the flatiron building could have a meaningful edge." We manually cranked his competition model. That was the first big move, and the height of the building certainly grew from there. The second moment came in our attempts to manage scale. Scale is an interesting thing. We knew we were going to have a 400-foot tower but a number of other things were being lobbed onto the site, including escalating construction costs and changes to the program expectations with the addition of SFU and the social housing component. It became clear that we needed to manage what was becoming a super-block project by breaking down its components into smaller pieces. The SFU piece was fairly obvious as the Hastings-fronted piece and so was the Abbott Building. But the rest wasn't so obvious. We had an interest in getting the public open space down from the third level to grade, which means we couldn't do a podium across the whole site. So the other "uh huh" moment was in Gregory's office where we were standing around the model and we said,

"We think this will work if you take the density that has to happen and shape it into a junior second tower."

The second tower wasn't part of the original proposal?

It wasn't. We had to ask ourselves, how would a second tower perform in the market place, what would those units be? So Bob Rennie needed to be convinced that we could take some of that density as a relief valve and reshape it on the Abbott-Cordova corner as the junior tower. What that did was break the project into quadrants. It almost cascaded down, transitioning from a taller tower to the Abbott Building. We asked Gregory to see if Bob could wrap his mind around that form and he did. So the second tower was born out of discussion that happened months after the competition. From there Gregory ran with it. Because he is so skilled and because we agree with his contextual approach to architecture and the social advocacy bent, how could we not be passionate about supporting him? At that point, our job was to stay out of the way and help facilitate a number of smaller design explorations, like his green wall idea and his concepts for the plaza. It will be very interesting to see what the Woodward's mix is. I think as a social incubator, it will be profoundly informative for how we can do other kinds of mixed-tenure projects. It ties into what I'm talking about in terms of the fabric of the Downtown Eastside and these new typologies. It's not only a question of responding to the new green paradigm, but also of how can you mix tenure in a way that is comfortable, respectful, liveable and safe, and in a way that won't exploit the marketplace. If I were to fly over the Downtown Eastside and look down, I want to see that its fabric would look generally intact and coherent.

What does Woodward's represent as a symbolic centre, and then what has to happen beyond the space it actually occupies?

Woodward's is the anchor.

Which is what it used to be?

Exactly, what Woodward's used to be. There is a strategy of triangulating uses so that people are moving through space, activating that space, creating identity and humanizing the environment. What Woodward's will do, through its energy and focus, is get people back out on the streets again.

Let's deal with some of the specific components. How important is the presence of SFU?

Huge. I am not sure the project would have gone ahead without SFU. It addresses the energy of the day-and-night sequence and the vitality that students bring. The fact that it is the School for the Contemporary Arts is significant. You get a real generator and you get some revenue. All of those things happen during the day and night school, and when that wanes, you've got the residential piece taking over. I think it was almost as critical to have a food store.

How responsive is the city to the concerns of gentrification on this project?

We aren't mindful of the gentrification question per se when we're looking at urban design, performance and fit. We're looking at the fabric, at the image of the city. We're looking at what happens when these projects hit the ground.

Do you and your colleagues think of yourselves as social engineers?

No. We're not. We're interested in projects that are of high quality, that work in terms of human comfort and scale, that are respectful and that have an uplifting symbolism to them. When we can, we will aggressively pack a site with density when it meets our urban design performance criteria, like 200 units of affordable housing. Woodward's is an interesting project. There are days when I feel schizophrenic. There are days that I want to default and do the opposite of what I think I should be doing. We clearly need to be doing some things differently down there. We need to be taking some risks. But I have to say, I remain very anxious about a tower going down there. In fact, when the height cap was removed I said…

It's the beginning of the end?

Well, kind of. Then I made peace with it. There are moments where you've got to look through a larger aperture, and this was a case where we had to insinuate new energy. To do that was a big move. But once you do the big move, it takes hold and starts in motion some smaller, companion moves. I was a strong advocate for this project and I am very proud of it. But I think it has a larger role to play than just performing its urbanistic function. Whether the city grows to Woodward's or not is an unanswered question; time will tell whether Woodward's has an edge, or whether it should stand in symbolic isolation, saying, "This is a big move that had to happen, did happen and was very successful." I hope it starts in motion a bunch of other things, which you won't be able to notice from this vantage point. That's where I hope it goes in the next 12 years. If the fabric continues to rejuvenate that part of the city through some tender moves, then it could be very successful.

If you were a betting man, what are the odds this thing will actually work in that fashion? And how long will it be before you can say what it has done and how well it has done it?

Good question. I would hate for us to measure it in the first five years. I would want us to understand there is going to be a little ebb and flow. There is also going to be a collision of attitudes where things play out on the ground as a kind of theatre. I almost view it as kind of machine or tool, and it's going to be awhile before we learn how to use Woodward's properly. People need to grow some confidence in risk-taking. While there has been some interest and speculation, people are probably going to hang back a bit. And the bugs will have to get worked out. We're flying by the seat of our pants. When I came here 25 years ago, my first office was in Yaletown looking over False Creek; this was before they started preloading for Expo. Pheasant and quail were running around and there was virtually nothing there. Yaletown has evolved and I sometimes think it is is too gentrified. When I think of the whole Downtown Eastside fabric, I think about the incredible promise of new energies in Gastown and in Chinatown. By the way, my measurement there will be how much neon we can get back.

How vulgar should it get?

At a certain level, vulgarity is a positive measurement of vitality. You've got the energy of Victory Square happening; you've got Gastown and, at the point where the Hastings corridor spine starts to energize, the whole thing will come together. At what point do you say, no more? There is going to be a moment where everyone recognizes that we've realized an interesting balance of gentrification, social and ethical responsibility, and a resurgence of building stock, and yet we've retained a sense of the gritty. It can become too pristine. There is a degree of grittiness that needs to remain. When Robert Stern came to town, one of his important statements was that we lacked grittiness, a kind of integrity. As a young city, it's something we have to treat almost as a gift. We tend to have a formulaic approach that says new is important. New and shiny. It's a very interesting question. Who we are? What is our image? What are our values? Should they be expressed? We have been criticized as being architecturally boring. At the same time, we have this tremendous energy, momentum and investment in design about buildings and landscape. If we want to, we can say something about who we want to be, what we want to look like, and the kind of image we want to convey to the world.

WHOLE-FILLER
Shayne Ramsay

Shayne Ramsay
CEO
BC Housing

Prior to his appointment as the chief executive officer of BC Housing, Shayne Ramsay served as chief executive officer of the Homeowner Protection Office, director of Development Services for BC Housing, and director of Housing Policy and Program Development with the former BC Ministry of Municipal Affairs and Housing. In addition to his work as the CEO of BC Housing, Mr. Ramsay is also the treasurer of the Canadian Housing and Renewal Association and president of the Crown Corporation Employers' Association. Mr. Ramsay has a graduate degree in urban planning from the University of Toronto.

What was your experience with Woodward's?

I don't have a story about Woodward's. To me, it has always been an empty, derelict building. I came to British Columbia in 1995 from Ontario and it was not a functioning store then. It had created such a big hole in the Downtown Eastside that everything seemed to collapse into it. From my perspective, it was an opportunity to regenerate the neighbourhood. Of course, I'd heard about the Downtown Eastside's reputation as the poorest neighbourhood in Canada, as a concentration of poverty, mental health and addiction issues.

How big of an operation is BC Housing?

We're one of the largest landlords in the province and we've been around for 40 years. We manage 8,000 units of housing for ourselves and we develop about 2,000 to 2,500 new housing units each year, which is more than most of the large developers, like Polygon. We're also a financial institution that manages a mortgage portfolio of more than $2.5 billion, which puts us just behind Coast Capital and VanCity. And we own more than a billion dollars in real estate assets. So we're always looking at opportunities to make investments. We've got almost 600 employees, half a billion dollar operating budget, and a capital budget of around $250 million a year. It supports 80,000 to 90,000 units of housing across the province in various forms. So we're a substantial operation.

People from outside are both captivated and bewildered by Vancouver. From your perspective, what kind of city is it and how would you characterize its problems?

On the problem side, one of the biggest issues is housing affordability. It's the least affordable city in all of Canada and is inching up there as one of the least affordable cities in the world. It's a desirable place to live but is constrained by a land base surrounded by oceans and mountains. So land cost is high and that drives up the price of housing.

It also drives up the nature of the architecture. It seems to me that the only way you can build is skyward.

Yes, and a couple of recent developments have pierced the 600 foot height level.

You've purchased somewhere in the neighbourhood of 12 buildings in the last little while. You seem to be in the process of buying up as many single-unit buildings as you can find.

It's just the single-room occupancy stock. Last April, we bought 10 buildings and we're closing on six more right now, which gives us about 1,000 rooms. It's not a great form of housing but it's housing to which we can provide some benefit, by stabilizing it, making it safer and getting some support services and good non-profit managers involved. It actually transforms the housing from drug-infested and crime-laden into something that, while not great, is at least safe and that affords an opportunity to build more permanent housing. We're doing that on another 12 city sites, 1,200 units of supportive housing, in order to stabilize the existing stock, build some new units and, hopefully, effect some significant improvements over time.

What are the yardsticks for determining whether or not this process is actually working?
We actually look at longitudinal studies of the people that are moving into supportive housing. What are their health outcomes, are they less sick? Are they able to move on to other forms of housing? Are their lives being stabilized?

What is your relationship to the Portland Hotel Society?
We partner with them, so almost all the buildings that Portland has acquired or developed in the Downtown Eastside, and in areas around Vancouver, have been in partnership with BC Housing and the city of Vancouver.

This is a strange city in lots of ways. There seems to be this ongoing dance between the market and the marginal. Is BC Housing situated somewhere along that spectrum?
I think so. When you produce new housing or acquire existing housing, you're doing it in the market, so you have to understand how those markets operate. I think Vancouver benefits from good strong councils that show leadership, and what they try to achieve is a more inclusive sense of community. So in places like False Creek and Coal Harbour, there are components of social housing along with the high-end condos. Are we winning the battle? It's tough to compete with those kinds of market forces because when you intervene in the market, or you acquire or build some housing, you're paying the same construction costs, and the same land cost, so it becomes a more and more difficult place to operate. Governments have to dig a whole lot deeper than they did even 10 years ago to produce the same number of units.

What has been BC Housing's relationship with Woodward's over the years?
We've had a history with Woodward's for quite some time. In the mid '90s, when it was under private ownership, the plan was to develop it as a mixed-market, condominium building with some social housing. We were actually negotiating contracts with a private developer for the production of the social housing. The project didn't proceed because the market wasn't ready. When the negotiations failed, we purchased the Woodward's building, just prior to the change in government.

Didn't you buy it at the time for $22 million?
That's right, and it was a difficult negotiation. It was difficult to get a value on the building and then to convince the powers that be that it was a reasonable price to pay. Then we tried to find a development partner for the building. We had discussions with the city and with a number of developers, but we weren't able to crack the nut because there weren't the non-residential uses with which you could fill up a lot of that space. And the city in those days was quite

adamant around what the building would look like: no towers on the site. It was about maintaining streetscapes. So the city wasn't taking a realistic look at the economics that were needed to make that site work.

So it wasn't a very flexible project at that point? There wasn't a lot of wiggle room for a developer or for anybody else?

No, there wasn't. And we weren't able to conclude a deal. Then with the change in government in 2001, we were asked to take another look at the building, and that's when we entered into an agreement of purchase with the city of Vancouver.

For considerably less than you paid for it. They were able to get the building for $5 million, a bargain basement price.

It was a bargain basement price. It was a rough estimate of half the market value of the site.

One of the issues that comes up whenever housing gets talked about is how you avoid creeping gentrification?

It has to be managed gentrification, but I do think it will be driven by market forces. The market has to be attractive. Government can make those initial investments, but there's not enough money to continue in the long term. You just have to insure that this managed gentrification is combined with thoughtful planning. There is a lot of social housing in the Downtown Eastside now. There are a lot of old hotels. Between us and the city, we probably own a fifth of the SRO stock in the Downtown Eastside. So there are opportunities not to displace the low-income people who are living down there.

If Woodward's works the way all the stakeholders hope it will, what effect will it have on the Downtown Eastside?

I think it will begin to attract businesses back, and other developers will begin to look at the area. That has already happened. There's been a fair amount of land speculation. Some of the largest developers in Vancouver have been buying up the older buildings downtown with the obvious hope of redeveloping them. They're not buying them to hold onto; they're going to look at redevelopment opportunities.

Can that be managed? Once the building is owned, what kinds of leverage do you have?

Not a lot. But we have a very good relationship with the city, and the city controls land use and zoning processes. So you can manage some of the growth, be respectful of the low-income community and achieve some win/wins.

When will that success start to be evident? What's the time frame?

One of the major pieces of work underway right now is development on 12 city sites. That will produce more than 1,200 new supportive housing units. It's the largest single investment in supportive housing that's ever been made in the city or the province. It's governed by a strategy of stabilizing the existing degenerating stock and replacing it over time with self-contained units and proper services. I think it can have an impact. The other thing that government is looking at stabilization units to deal with people that suffer from severe mental illness, and who are often addicted to drugs or alcohol. They're looking at opportunities to provide much better services in places like the Willingdon corrections and government facilities and the Riverview psychiatric hospital. Those are really, really difficult issues down there.

It's daunting to see the scope of the problem in the Downtown Eastside. Where do those people go? Where are they going to end up as a result of this process?

Part of the answer is that whole area of re-institutionalization. A couple of years ago, you would have never heard that phrase, but you're starting to hear it a lot more often. It's to provide a stable environment where people can get the necessary mental health and addiction services. The person's stay there could be short, or it could be much longer, depending on their particular needs.

Is Woodward's going to work? Are you optimistic about what it will be able to accomplish?

I am. We've had some good success in place like False Creek and Coal Harbour, albeit they're not the same types of population. In False Creek and Coal Harbour, you have mixed-income social developments with high-end condos and they have worked quite well. What's encouraging about the Woodward's project is that the buildings are well-designed and you have good managers for the housing, people who are connected to the kinds of services needed down there. Additionally, it begins to improve the surrounding neighbourhood. It's going to bring in a lot of people who will demand services and they'll begin to demand some changes. I think one of the things Woodward's has done is to open up the minds of the planners. I remember a meeting with the director of planning and we were looking at some of the competition models and he said, "There is no way you'll go above 10 or 12 storeys on Cordova Street." The tower on the Woodward's site will be 42 stories. So it's been an interesting turnaround.

What changed?

The cynical side of me thinks when the city became the owner, economics began to drive the project. The planners will say it was good urban design. I truly believe that you can get thoughtful density, but I think it was primarily the economics.

Is this the right time for this project?

I think it is. I'm very optimistic that it will work. I did a lot of work in Toronto and one of the things happening in Toronto now is the redevelopment of Regent Park. It's 100 percent social housing, and one of the challenges the project faces is the trepidation some of the market developers have for getting into that kind of environment. Here, it's almost completely reversed. We're in the process of redeveloping our site at Little Mountain, and the issue of mixing market and non-market housing is not even on anybody's radar screen. It has had virtually no impact on the price of the market housing.

Is Vancouver a unique city then? Are the problems that have to be dealt with here different from the problems faced by other large cities?

I think there are better partnership opportunities between the municipal and provincial governments in BC. I have observed that first hand because I worked at both the province of Ontario and the city of Toronto off and on for many years.

Why is it working here?

That's a good question. If you take a look at the housing file, you'll see that we've enjoyed a really strong partnership with the city of Vancouver. In fact, we rarely develop on any land other than on city-owned land these days. It's a well-understood partnership that has worked.

Do you look outside of Vancouver to see what other cities are doing in dealing with similar problems?

Yes. We look at the best practices around issues like homelessness. What models work best? Philip Mangano in the US has been instrumental in engaging federal and state governments around the Housing First model. We patterned our homeless outreach program around some of the work that had been done in the United Kingdom. So we do look at other places for advice. But British Columbia has done more in the area of supportive housing and assisted living than has any other jurisdiction in Canada. We're looked at as a leader and, as a result, we do tours all the time for people from across the country who want to get a sense of how we're tackling issues.

DEAL-BRAKER, DEAL-MAKER
Lee Gavel

Lee Erin Gavel
Architect
SFU

Lee Gavel received his undergraduate degree in Urban Geography from Simon Fraser University in 1974, and a Master of Architecture degree from the University of Calgary in 1978. After practicing as an architect, landscape planner and project manager in the private sector, Mr. Gavel returned to Simon Fraser University in 1987, managing the University's program for new building design and construction. Mr. Gavel has also worked as a consultant to the National Capital Commission.

As part of his present portfolio as chief facilities officer, Mr. Gavel is the university architect, a role that has made him responsible for all design and development activities for the three campuses of the University. He is responsible for real estate and property matters, operations, master planning, review of all campus design, and overseeing the capital project program. In 2008, the Architectural Institute of British Columbia bestowed upon him the Barbara Dalrymple Award for Community Service.

Mr. Gavel's involvement with the relocation of the School for the Contemporary Arts to a downtown location began in the early 1990s and has progressed through various initiatives, culminating in the present Woodward's redevelopment.

SIMON FRASER UNIVERSITY'S PRESENCE DOWNTOWN started with a little storefront operation for the non-credit post-degree program on Howe Street. Then a major effort went into establishing the original SFU downtown campus in the Harbour Centre facility, which is a story in and of itself. There were many false starts, but finally there came the right opportunity—of time, funding and real estate—to make it happen. It opened its doors in 1989. Third parties have always seen Simon Fraser as an attractive part of their development plans. Once every two months, we'd be approached by a developer to find out what we might want to do. They're interested in what we bring: a good cachet with the city, community benefits, a whole lot of things.

So it's an ongoing story of various opportunities. We knew we wanted an absolute expansion of our space, but exactly what it would be varied over time. We also had the circumstance on our main Burnaby Mountain campus, which involved our difficulty in finding provincial government funding. The arts weren't a priority in advanced education and, on our own campus, there wasn't the will to put the arts in front of a new chemistry building or a new applied science building.

Eventually, what happened was the right conjunction of interests downtown: the school finally appreciating it probably wasn't going to get anything on the Burnaby Mountain campus for a very long time, and a president who was willing to really get behind the idea of going downtown. As far back as the middle '90s there were developers who had ideas for the Woodward's block and who approached the university. The first was a gentlemen from Las Vegas who wanted to build a major casino to serve the cruise ships. He was willing to build gratis a complete school on the Woodward's site.

The firm that had really good credentials on the Downtown Eastside was Davidson Yuen Simpson and specifically Ron Yuen. They were engaged to do some schematic designs, and we got complete floor plans at that time. City politics and public reaction to the casino meant the idea didn't last very long. But from that initiative, I got a complete set of plans that cost us zero. Also, because the venture got some press, it was apparent that SFU was willing to consider moving downtown. So various initiatives kept coming back to us. The next major one was when BC Housing picked up the site and wanted to do a project through a public-private partnership.

This time around, the idea was to incorporate the school in the existing building. The casino project had proposed blowing it away and building new. BC Housing would have kept the building, carved the middle out and tried to find a way to accommodate us. It was a very tough technical problem because of the nature of the spaces we needed: double height and column-free for big theatres, dance studios, that kind of thing. It was tough to fit it into the existing building.

We had some very ingenious structural engineering work done and found a way we could have inserted it. But again, the pro forma economics weren't working, so it died a natural death as well. But we put in a considerable amount of effort. Business cases went forward to the Ministry of Advanced Education to support our being there, asking government to support our piece of the puzzle.

There were many other false starts along the way, but those are the two major ones. The final proposal came when the city of Vancouver bought the property and all the development teams in the competition engaged with Simon Fraser. The city felt it was important for us to be there. We were prepared to go with any of them. We talked to one more seriously but we knew we couldn't cast our ship with only one, so we very consciously told the city that we'll dance with the partner that brings us. So we weren't displeased when the Westbank/Henriquez partnership won. Our ability to find the funding was in question, but what was never in question was our desire to be there and our willingness to be a full participant in the design and the political decisions.

The funding is also its own story, involving relations between Simon Fraser, the Ministry of Advanced Education and the BC Government. Sometimes Advanced Education and Central Government have differences in budgets and priorities. We were consistently told by Advanced Education that this project was not on their priority list. While we understood that other things in the university system needed funding, we felt there was an argument that could be made to Central Government outside the priorities of Advanced Education. Our argument was that this project overrode the interests of Advanced Education and became a provincial and a municipal interest. We pushed that point in any discussions we had with the provincial government.

The argument prevailed, but at the cost of much pain—I use that word quite consciously. SFU found itself in a very difficult position and Westbank, to their credit, understood we were trying to get Central Government to move in a direction that it felt wasn't their responsibility. It was up to Advanced Ed and they said they had other priorities. The two of them were passing the buck back and forth and, in the meantime, the project is actively proceeding. Finally, we got to a crunch point where it took the advocacy of Westbank, along with some other major supporters of Simon Fraser in government, to overrule Central Government and to create a funding model between several different ministries.

The total project budget for Simon Fraser is $71.5 million. To get the size of the School for the Contemporary Arts as we've designed, it took some other major decision-making within SFU. We needed to house the complete school, which was scattered around various locations; they were desperate. We wanted to bring all those things together because the heart of that school is to integrate and cross the boundaries between film, dance, performance and music. So you need to have them in one place to cross those bridges, and we got to the tough place where we couldn't afford the 180,000 square feet it would have taken to bring those pieces together.

The budgeting was underway; we were having discussions with the design teams and the developer just as Vancouver was going through this huge escalation in construction costs. So it was a very bumpy road. The way we were able to make it work was to leave the visual art studios at 611 Alexander Street.

To get the size down to something that was affordable, many of our spaces had to become multi-use. At the end of the day, that will probably reinforce some of those bridges between the disciplines. There is also a teaching gallery on site.

The deal with Westbank is for 120,000 square feet because that's the program we gave them, but we ended up with 127,000. It was two-thirds of what we needed and that's why visual arts is still split off. In the future, we'll see how we begin to deal with that.

The advantage we gain in being at Woodward's isn't the mix within the project itself. While it's nice to be part of such a rich development with the condominium towers and the federal offices, the driver for us was its location within the city. This is the best opportunity to make a building of that size and of that institutional quality. You can't do it on the back of some very modest building. It takes a million square foot project to be able to subsidize the 10 percent, the 120,000 square feet, that we have.

We don't have a housing component. This was a sensitive political subject between us and the Downtown Eastside. They're very sensitive to gentrification and they saw privileged, elite students from different socio-economic backgrounds intruding into their community. So they were resistant to SFU building student housing and very early on, we had to reassure folks that we would not do that. For SFU to be part of this project we had to create a win/win for everybody. There was no point in creating enemies. In reality, the private market and the redevelopment of the Downtown Eastside will take care of that problem on its own. It's not necessary for the university to build student housing. It will occur if it's the right thing to do.

A factor that made the project sellable to the SFU community was that we're on the Hastings Street transit system, which is a regular bus today but it will become an express line in the future. It's necessary to understand Simon Fraser's three-campus model, where we have our Burnaby Mountain campus, the Surrey campus and downtown campus, all connected by Skytrain and transit. So this school really became a stop on the transit route between Burnaby Mountain and downtown Vancouver. We could make the argument that you can get off the bus, walk across the sidewalk and you're in our school. Because parents' fear of the neighbourhood is a significant issue. I'm talking about perceptions, not necessarily realities. The same issue comes up with our performances. A lot of them will attract a middle-class audience from outside the area and they're uneasy. So between transit and the bridge from the parkade directly into the Woodward's project, you can bring an audience to that location and still keep them separate from the street life, which is the perceived fear. Personally, I'm not uncomfortable or fearful in that environment. I had to take a tour of American university architects from our Harbour Centre campus out to Burnaby and as we're driving through that neighbourhood, I said, "Look, you're Americans. You're looking out at the street and you're going, 'Oh my God.' But I have to tell you, I could walk down the street at 2:00 in the morning and I may be propositioned for almost any service you could imagine, but I will not fear for my safety and I will not get shot. Whereas in an American environment that looks the same, I would fear for my life." That's the truth, but it's a hard sell, even in Canada.

My first interaction with Gregory and the team was to give him the same program we gave to everybody else in the competition. All we were doing was giving him a list of what we'd like to have, the kind of studio and its sound characteristics, that sort of thing. We didn't have a direct role. We were asked for input about which design would best satisfy our interest. So that's where it started. After the Westbank/Henriquez proposal was selected, I became fundamental to the discussions around the land, the land trade-offs and the new design that resulted from that. I'd like to think we also had some influence, not just on our building and its components, but on the overall design capacity of the public spaces and how we relate to the other pieces. Once that gelled, my job was to select and manage the architects who were going to design our piece.

Now this is where it gets complicated because at that point, we didn't know whether we were buying our piece, leasing it, or whether the government would provide it. We didn't know what our budget was, where the money was coming from, or exactly how we would be a legal entity in this project. Who gets to choose the architects, and who those architects are responsible to, depends on who's going to own the space. Towards the first part of this discussion, we said our preference was to own it, but the government was concerned about the provincial debt level and they didn't want any loan they gave us to show up on their books. So we could not cut a public-private partnership deal with Westbank that would lead to the government owning the space and leasing it to us. The problem for the government became how to fund us and still keep it off their books. A large part of the pain before we could sign on the dotted line came from all these different governmental entities trying to figure out how we could be there.

So to come back to the question about selecting architects and interaction with architects, at the start of this thing when we thought that Westbank would own the shell and we'd be leasing, Gregory was the architect for the building shell. Then we selected our own architects for the interior fit-out, partially out of concern for Gregory's capacity to deal with the whole budget and adequately represent our very detailed and atypical needs. This is a highly specialized facility and you need expertise in theatre and arts design. So we chose an architect team made of two different architectural firms, CEI and Proscenium, to do our internal fit-out. We had been pushing our team very hard to get ahead of the curve of the building shell design because we needed our technical requirements to drive the building shell, not the other way around. And they were able to do that.

So at the end of the day, all of us emotionally and intellectually supported the principle of what we were trying to do, and we just kept moving forward. It wasn't adversarial: it wasn't a case of who's trying to get an economic advantage or who's going to make a profit here. Westbank was basically willing to build it for us at cost with some risk and with faith. The three architectural firms are working for multiple clients because Westbank is paying the bills but the people they're trying to satisfy are us. They've got firm-to-firm issues of liability and design between them. It's the most terrific example I've ever experienced of everybody working to a common end without getting into a dog fight.

It's absolutely critical that Simon Fraser supports its arts as a component of a liberal arts and sciences institution. It has been a challenge doing that in the suburbs of Burnaby on top of a mountain. Where is the audience? And the facilities to do it within the campus itself have been very, very limited. They are, by official audit, the worst facilities of any kind on any campus in the province. In any case, Simon Fraser supports the idea that the arts have an important role to play, both institutionally and socially. Now, how can it best do that? There is a body of opinion within Simon Fraser that says, "Maybe Burnaby isn't the most artistic community in the world, in the sense that downtown Vancouver is, but our role might be to bring arts to the wilds of the suburbs." There is another body of opinion that says, "No, if you want to be vibrant, artistic and international, you've got to be where the artists are, where the hub and the hive and the fever is." So there are two mindsets. The School will maintain a presence on Burnaby Mountain, not in a facility sense, but it will offer programs and performances. But they needed to bring the school downtown to the artistic community in a live, visible way that both attracts money to support the programs and tells the world what it is we can do. So it's important to Simon Fraser.

As far as the Downtown Eastside goes, they don't know what Simon Fraser can do, or is doing today. As they begin to experience that, the opportunity for them to grow and be enriched by what we do is very real. By extension, from the Downtown Eastside to the rest of the city, they now have a place where they can see and be seen; SFU's presence in the Metro Vancouver artistic community gets elevated significantly. Other than Emily Carr, which occupies a different niche, there isn't any institution that has a downtown arts academic profile. UBC doesn't have anything like that, nor does anybody else.

When you move beyond the School for the Contemporary Arts, Simon Fraser's ambition is to have a full downtown campus. We now have, between our various facilities, 500,000 square feet downtown. We have our main Harbour Centre campus, the Centre for Dialogue, the School of Business, the visual arts facilities at 611 Alexander, and many other opportunities constantly coming our way. There is a market for what we do. The problem is finding the funding to be able to build the facility and mount the programs.

So it becomes a "step-by-step, you build your market, the money comes" kind of process. SFU's vision is for the School for the Contemporary Arts to be part of a campus that will look like Columbia or the City University of New York. It's not a land grant campus like Guelph. It's a building-by-building kind of campus, and most of them are in one part of town. We're very actively working towards that. My personal ambition, just to throw something in the fire, is the downtown federal post office. The federal government is trying to sell it and it's a wonderful building. A whole city block with floor-to-floor heights of 30 feet. Think of the lecture theatres and performance-based studios you could build.

FOLIO IX

ARCHITECTURAL RENDERINGS
Thomas Lee

9

The Atrium roof at Woodward's is a classic example of a complex design element for which there is no handbook. To find the solution requires years of experience and ultimately much common sense. We created a ring beam with big round seats carrying slip joints allowing the structure move independently in a seismic event. One must remember one's geometry to ensure cost-saving repetition, create a walkway around the perimeter for easy access, lift the glazing to celebrate the trusses and keep it simple wherever possible. If the engineers and the contractors do not question what you have done, you know you got it right.

Christian Schimert
HENRIQUEZ PARTNERS ARCHITECTS

PUBLIC SPACES AND EVENTS

The design of the public spaces for the Woodward's project responds to the wide array of program opportunities identified in the community visioning workshops and ideas fair held prior to the project's design. Five public open spaces—the atrium; plaza; urban park; Hastings Street entry plaza and forecourt; and the Abbott Street and Cordova Street mews entries—create a series of small, medium, and large, indoor and outdoor gathering opportunities. The public spaces have a combined area of 3,250 square metres, representing approximately one third of the site area, and are secured in the public domain as a public amenity space. The scale of the space and encumbrances to guarantee public access exceed what would normally be expected of a private development in Vancouver, embracing a fresh civic imagination of inclusive community life. Simple, robust and appropriate to the surrounding neighbourhood context, the design uses a palette of materials that harmonizes the history of the place with the new architecture emerging on the site.

The success of Woodward's as a condenser of neighbourhood activity will largely depend on the treatment, programming and management of the public space. Planning by a community-based committee will ensure that the space is meaningfully programmed, whether it is with events, exhibits, or celebrations, to draw in the community. PHS Community Services will also be on the site to ensure that the public space remains relevant to the community. If people, with all their idiosyncrasies, are allowed to inhabit the space, Woodward's will become an integral part of the city's day and night life and avoid the danger of turning into a hygienic shopping mall environment.

Atrium

As the retail and community heart of the Woodward's project and of the re-emerging historic area, the atrium is a transparent, day-lit, flexible indoor-outdoor "urban room" that invites a wide variety of activities and community programming. The space can be adapted to different events with theatrical lighting and moveable seating. Shaped like an umbilical cord, a central stair leading to a second-level public concourse emerges from a reflecting pool as a metaphorical symbol of rebirth. A large urban garden serves as an oasis for the community. The atrium is designed to be fully open to the outdoor plaza and park spaces whenever weather permits; sliding mall-front doors retract to create a large and comprehensive open space at the core of the development.

Salvaged fragments of the building, displays of Woodward's artifacts and elements of the neighbourhood's cultural landscape are incorporated in the atrium to evoke collective memories of the old Woodward's building and imbue the redevelopment with historical spirit. The architecture of Woodward's is then less a fossil and more a living, breathing interpretative place.

The central focus of the atrium is the western wall, which features an 8 metre by 15 metre photographic mural, called *Abbott & Cordova, 7 August, 1971,* of the 1971 Gastown Riot by local artist Stan Douglas. The riot began when police on horseback charged crowds who were protesting against drug laws and Operation Dustpan, a series of drug raids in the area. Because the Vancouver Police Department sees the incident as a dark moment in its history, it expressed concern about the artwork negatively impacting its present positive relationship with the public. Through the mural, Stan Douglas wanted the public to remember the riot as a moment in Vancouver history when the possibility of change was not fully realized. Controversial public art commissioned by developers is rare, but Douglas' mural suits the contentious site and narrates one important incident of public participation in the neighbourhood's history. The mural also has a democratizing function by making art, generally confined to galleries, available to the public realm, just as churches and squares integrated art with European public life prior to the invention of galleries and museums.

Urban Park and Public Plaza

The urban park and plaza act together as a multi-faceted outdoor social space to accommodate different informal and community programming events while specifically addressing the needs of on-site residents, employees, customers, students, and visitors. The plaza is large enough to host events requiring an outdoor stage, markets, and café seating. The plaza offers seating in many forms; steps, low walls, building edges, chairs and benches. The park and plaza are extensions of the Cordova Street axis, which penetrates the site, continues through the atrium and terminates at the 1903/08 heritage building, in line with the new iconic red neon 'W' sign above.

The original dilapidated sign is displayed in the public plaza as an act of collective remembrance, while the new sign serves as a fusion of heritage replication and modern-day branding. Recessed LED lights along this axis and the use of brick paving reinforce the connection through the project and organize the various landscape elements. The east and west ends of the plaza are softened by a number of tall open-canopied trees, creating a park-like treatment. Anticipating changing uses through the day and night and the occurrence of larger public events, the design achieves a strong integration of the interior atrium space and the exterior spaces of the urban park and plaza.

Hastings Street Forecourt and Entry Plaza

The Hastings Street Forecourt and Entry Plaza act as the identifiable "front porch," marking the project's formal address on Hastings Street and acknowledging the historic and future commercial importance of the Hastings Corridor. Adjacent to the 1903/08 Heritage Building, the forecourt provides welcome weather protection under a large feature canopy leading into the atrium and invites entry to the retail and non-profit community spaces. Display windows, sidewalk seating, a feature tree and paving bricks matching those in the central open space ensure the forecourt creates a smooth transition from the street to the project.

Abbott and Cordova Mews

Entries mid-block on Abbott and Cordova streets provide easy pedestrian access into and through the project and encourage retail activity at street level. The mews are six metres wide, framed by active ground level retail, partially weather-protected, and animated with lighting. Cordova Mews provides a north-south connection between the plaza and Cordova Street and joins a planned pedestrian crossing to the parkade located on the north side of the street. Abbott Mews connects the atrium and Abbott Street in an east-west direction and reinforces a strong visual connection to an existing eastern laneway.

1903/08 Roof Terrace

The roof terrace of the 1903/08 Heritage Building is programmed for childcare and community uses. A circuit for wheeled toys, play equipment, and garden plots are provided in the design. The combination of canopy trees and a partial covered area provides spatial variety and shelter from the elements.

SFU Roof Terrace

An intimate angular terrace accessible to SFU overlooks the central plaza space and is outfitted with tables, chairs and trees for students.

Singles Non-Market Roof Terrace

The singles non-market housing roof terrace on top of the Hastings Building provides a reflecting pool along the south edge of the building. The space is delineated and sheltered by a trellis with climbing plants. Trees in custom boxes with integrated seating slabs contribute to an uncluttered and visually tranquil space adaptable to a variety of activities.

Family Non-Market Roof Terrace
The family non-market housing roof terrace at the Abbott Building incorporates an outdoor children's play facility, divided and programmed for different age groups. The division is created by shade trees in concrete planters with integrated seating slabs. Several small private terraces are provided for the units on the terrace level, and are buffered from the children's play areas by residential-type plantings and small trees.

W Tower Market Housing Amenity Terrace (Club W)
Rather than penthouses, the W Building rooftop features a terrace socializing space for the market residents separated into two areas and surrounded by a cornice of raised planter with eighteen street-scale pin oak trees. The western side of the amenity terrace is focused on a W-shaped spa tub, inserted into a raised deck and surrounded by a variety of lounge seating tables and other spa-side amenities. The mezzanine space within is home to a view intensive 42nd floor fitness facility and a bouldering and climbing wall. The southern side of the terrace is composed of several groups of seating and dining furniture, a table and outdoor kitchen linking the terrace with the adjacent lounge inside. The western prow of the terrace is raised slightly to maximize sightlines over the surrounding planting and cornice.

Suggestions from the community for events at Woodward's

Grand Opening Event	Christmas Display	Wiccan Holiday
Graffiti Festival	Downtown Bike Race	Woodward's Parade
Pow-wow	Noon Hour Concerts	Heart of the City Parade
Octoberfest	Gastown Grand Prix	Earth Day Celebration
Saint Patrick's Day	Farmers Market	Community Health Fair
Community Awards Day	Craft Market	Squatters Remembrance Day
Memorial Event	Woodward's Birthday	Mother's and Father's Day
Westcoast New Year	Outdoor Theatre	Children's Day
Drumming Festival	Artropolis	$1.49 Day
Five-Pin Bowling Demo	Chinese New Year	Habitat for Sanity
Christmas Fair	Woodward's Display	Multicultural Day
Solstice Celebrations	Harvest Celebration	Free Venues for Fringe, Jazz
Canadian Awards Day	Women's March	and Folk Festivals
Tent Walk	International Conferences	City Council Events
Founding of Vancouver Parade	Spring Flower Festival	Occupation Day
Street Theatre	Canada Day	Community Plays
Block Party	Meet the Canucks Day	Fund Raising
First Nations Parade	History Events	Walking Tours
Fireworks	Christmas Celebration	Tenant Forums
Block Party	Easter Celebration	Youth Day
Community Parade	Thanksgiving Dinners	SFU Events

CENTRE MARGIN:
COMPOSING ABBOTT & CORDOVA,
7 AUGUST 1971
Reid Shier

Reid Shier
Director and Curator
Presentation House Gallery

Reid Shier is the director and curator of Presentation House Gallery (PHG) in North Vancouver, a position he has held since 2006. Previously, Mr. Shier was chief curator of The Power Plant Contemporary Art Gallery in Toronto, and from 2002 to 2004 was curator of the Contemporary Art Gallery in Vancouver. Between 1996 and 2001, Mr. Shier was the director and curator of the artist-run Or Gallery in Vancouver, and since 1996 has curated over 80 exhibitions.
In 2004, he initiated a major commission, with English artist Simon Starling, a Turner Prize winner; titled *Musselled Moore*, it is now in the collection of the Art Gallery of Ontario. He is a practicing artist and critical writer, and from 1994-98 co-edited the quarterly periodical *Boo*. In 2002, Mr. Shier edited the monograph *Stan Douglas: Every Building on 100 West Hastings*, which won the City of Vancouver Book Award. He has edited numerous publications, including monographs on Tim Lee, Anne Collier, Ron Terada and the recently published *To the Dogs* by Nanaimo poet Peter Culley, as well as the ongoing series Lynn Valley featuring projects by the world's most significant photographers.

STAN DOUGLAS' PHOTOGRAPH *Abbott & Cordova, 7 August 1971* is a complex re-creation of Vancouver's Gastown Riot, depicting an incident when Vancouver Police Department (VPD) officers attacked protestors gathered in demonstration against the enforcement of laws prohibiting marijuana possession. At 13 x 8 metres, it is monumental, and when installed as a public artwork in the atrium of the Woodward's redevelopment, it will assert itself in an ongoing and often divisive debate about Vancouver's urban space and its visual and built identity. Importantly, the invitation given to Douglas to make a permanent outdoor artwork has resulted in a challenge to some of the city's long-held assumptions about who "public art" is intended to serve. Even prior to its debut, the charged subject matter of the image resulted in the VPD's consternation regarding Douglas' choice to re-create the event. Once on view, *Abbott & Cordova, 7 August 1971* promises to provoke ongoing questions about the manner in which Vancouver histories are told and by whom.

Douglas' provocation to civic authority draws a parallel to a controversy caused by another notable public artwork and a significant formal and conceptual antecedent to his own image. Diego Rivera's mural *Man at the Crossroads,* painted in New York's Rockefeller Center in 1933, was destroyed by Rockefeller employees with sledgehammers the following year when Rivera refused to paint over a portrait of Vladimir Lenin that he had surreptitiously inserted. No one anticipates that, once installed, *Abbott & Cordova, 7 August 1971* will be similarly attacked (barring a stray shot from a service revolver), but the VPD's evident fear of Douglas' unflattering representation of their officers' conduct raises similarly vexed questions about the nature of artistic expression, particularly for those creating work in and for the public sphere. Pertinent is whether the social provocation arising from politicized images, such as those made by Rivera and Douglas, is due to what they have chosen to represent, or how they have created images with clearly unambiguous, deviant approaches to writing contemporary histories.

Abbott & Cordova, 7 August 1971 is an imaginary depiction of events in the intersection sometime before 2 am on the evening of the title. The riot had begun hours earlier, around 10 pm, when youths who had gathered for a "smoke-in" were ordered by Chief Constable Abercrombie to disburse. Abercrombie gave the protestors two minutes to move before he ordered police on horseback into their midst. Uniformed beat cops and undercover plainclothes officers, disguised as hippies but now brandishing 36 inch leather-clad hickory truncheons, followed the horses under orders to "clear the streets." What they lacked was a clear plan or any method of crowd control. Wading into the crowd, the cops were under instructions to push people onto the sidewalks where they would be forced to "move along," Shortly after 10 pm, someone in the crowd lit a firecracker (or a "cherry bomb" according to police), which spooked the police horses. They reared, panicking the crowd, and pandemonium ensued. No account concurs on what took place after this, only that the police were indiscriminantly violent.

From its beginning near the statue of Gassy Jack at Carrall and Powell streets, the riot moved progressively south and west over the course of the night. Douglas stages his photograph at the intersection of Abbott and Cordova, and locates his camera looking southwest from what would be a second-floor vantage. The photograph centres on a small number of youths sprinting toward the Woodward's department store. Mounted officers barricade other groups of youths, one in a storefront on the upper corner of the image, another against a vehicle in the lower left. Riot police block eastbound traffic on Cordova, and two undercover plainclothes cops, now with helmets on and truncheons at the ready, walk purposefully south toward Hastings Street. To the east, police manhandle two young protesters, shoving one into a paddy wagon. On the sidewalks, curious bystanders stand and gawk, apparently comfortable in their possible risk of arrest, and in the case of two young boys, sit nonchalantly on a curb enjoying the drama.

The image is constructed with meticulous attention to historical accuracy. It was shot on a set erected in a parking lot of the Pacific National Exhibition in the spring of 2008, and includes period details gathered from primary records and through interviews conducted with participants—police, bystanders and protesters—directly involved in the riot. Re-creations of the Woodward's department and Sissons Sporting Goods (now Army & Navy) stores backdrop a precisely rendered 1970s street scene. Posters glued to light standards advertise concerts going on in the city at the time: Jethro Tull, Country Joe and the Fish, Crowbar Chilliwack and Flash Cadillac. Trampled flowers, popcorn and watermelon rinds—remnants of things earlier in the demonstration given out at Maple Tree Square—litter the set's distressed concrete and patched asphalt. The clothing of the plainclothes cops reference what was worn by them on that day, sourced through an unpublished photographic souvenir in which all the VPD's undercover policemen pose as hippies before the riot, like a baseball team about to take the field for an important game.

While this visual precision lends the image extraordinary density, it may not deflect a question about whether the photograph is a picture of a riot at all. Where, we might ask, is the action? Douglas pushes everything to the periphery of the image, drawing the confrontations (there are four) toward the edges and corners, evacuating the middle of the photograph in favour of a large, empty intersection through which a few determined teens attempt to escape. The police were under instruction to keep people off the street and on the sidewalks, and throughout the night, no single confrontation ensued so much as an episodic series of skirmishes across many blocks. Douglas' mise-en-scène is largely in keeping with the historical record, but it would do no justice to the photograph's composition to ignore its tight geometry and precise articulation. What it captures—and this might reflect the experience of anyone who has actually been in or watched a riot— is a volatile mix of violence, voyeurism, fear, excitement and confusion. The action is everywhere and nowhere at the same time.

Abbott & Cordova, 7 August 1971 appears, in fact, constructed in order to upset our preconception about what a riot should look like. The action draws our gaze to the edges of the image and into an awkward confrontation with our expectation that a significant dramatic event should have centrality within an artistic image. One important question is how this troublesome and unexpected representation will function as a public installation within a semi-public, semi-private space at the heart of the Woodward's development. Here we should bear in mind that Douglas has not titled his work *The Gastown Riot,* but simply given the date and location the work recreates, a clue and cue to the work's motifs and themes. If not a riot, then what? Again, it is important to look at what the image shows, and how Douglas has arranged its space. The police control the image's perimeter, and the sidewalks are either their battlegrounds or places of spectatorship. Where the police have little control or authority is, at least in this representation, the intersection, and here the artist has rendered it as an area—however temporary—through which youths run and others see the possibility of escape.

The Gastown Riot is now frequently referred to as a 'police riot', yet Douglas has not made an image where this idea is given compositional prominence; the police are not pictured in an archetypal, anti-heroic struggle with young hippies. (Perhaps when the current police force finally sees Douglas' work, they might thank him for this). Rather *Abbott & Cordova, 7 August 1971* pictures a violent, futile attempt to orchestrate civic space, and the limits to which this was (and is) possible. Looking at the areas under police control within the spatial hierarchy of this remarkable image, one could conclude that the police are both formally and thematically peripheral. What is prominently pictured in the middle—and central to the image— is the potential of freedom in a circumscribed situation. In constructing *Abbott & Cordova, 7 August 1971* in this way, Douglas offers a counter-narrative to a polarizing civic event, opening to renewed debate a small, but significant chapter in the divisive history of Vancouver's Downtown Eastside.

PIVOTING HISTORY
Stan Douglas

Stan Douglas
Artist

Stan Douglas is a visual artist who lives and works in Vancouver. His photographs, films and videos have been seen in numerous group exhibitions nationally and internationally including three Documentas (1992, 1997, 2002) and three Venice Biennales (1990, 2000, 2005). Major solo exhibitions have been hosted by Centre Georges Pomipidou (Paris, 1993), Museo Renia Sofia (Madrid, 1993), Vancouver Art Gallery (1999), The Power Plant (Toronto, 1999), Museum of Contemporary Art (Los Angeles, 2000) and a comprehensive survey of his work, *Past Imperfect: Works 1986-2007*, was mounted by the Württembergischer Kunstverein and the Staatsgalerie, Stuttgart in 2007. In addition to making art he curated a touring exhibition of Samuel Beckett's cinematographic work, *Samuel Beckett: Teleplays* (1988), edited a book on art in Vancouver, *Vancouver Anthology* (Vancouver: Talon, 1991) and co-edited a book on the history of the projected image in art, *Art of Projection* (Ostfildern: Hatje Cantz, 2009). Between 2004 and 2006 he held the post of professor at the Universität der Künste, Berlin and currently teaches in the Graduate Department at Art Center College of Design, Pasadena.

Did you have a relationship, like it seems every Vancouverite has had, with Woodward's when the store was still open?

Absolutely. Most of us have had an encounter with that store, whether it was where you went to see Santa Claus, visited the toy department or went to the food floor for a hot dog and those great chocolate malts. It felt to me like the centre of the city, until Robson Square was built. When I was going to art school, the campus was, for the first couple of years, dispersed among various locations downtown. The first year studios were on Water Street so Woodward's became the place where I went for my art supplies, which for me at that point was hardware. But I could see it fading away even then, as the stocks slowly depleted.

How long have you been in the Downtown Eastside?

I've had a studio down there ever since I went to art school. When I graduated in 1982, my first studio was down the hall from Spartacus Books on Hastings Street, a block away from Woodward's and very close to Victory Square.

What made you gravitate towards the area in the first place?

Around 1980, I began hanging around a place called Pumps, an artists' collective that was on Cordova at Carrall Street, and I got familiar with the area. It was a nice place to be; it held a sense of the city's history and in the early '80s, it didn't feel that heavy. A lot of the old resource industry workers were still living in the single room occupancy hotels and roaming the streets in their dapper clothing. The conditions we have now, with open drug use and dealing, was not at all prevalent at the time.

When Gregory approached you, what did he want you to do?

He was doing a project in Lynn Valley and wanted to know if I would be interested in making a public artwork for it. I said, "Maybe, but I understand you've got the Woodward's commission. If you need something there, let me know."

So you're the one who suggested your involvement with the project?

We both did in a way.

You say that the place has embodied the history of where it is in the city. Is the nature of your piece historical in one sense?

We're restaging the Gastown Riot of 1971. At the time there was a long tension between city hall and the hippie element, which was getting larger and larger in Vancouver. Increasing pressure was being put upon suspected drug users and dealers. This came to a head when the hippies decided to assert what they believed to be their right to assembly with a street festival scheduled for August 7th, 1971 in Gastown, which featured free watermelon, bags of popcorn, carnations, music, and of course—a 10-foot papier-mâché joint. The police department didn't want any of this to happen. The police chief had called the fire department earlier in the week, asking if they could bring their trucks down to disperse the crowd with hoses. The fire chief told him, "We fight fires, not people." So the police assembled the mounted squad and constables in riot gear on the east side of Maple Tree Square, in order to disperse the crowd at 10 pm. They had two agendas: one was for undercover narcotics agents, who had been among the crowd all afternoon to identify and detain people who were selling, using or holding drugs, and the other was for officers to get people off the street to make it clear for traffic again. These two agendas were often in conflict as the situation became more and more violent. The riot spread throughout the neighbourhood, but the crowd couldn't go north because of the water; they couldn't go east because that was where the police were, so they started to run south and west. Meanwhile, west of Gastown around Victory Square, police had assembled and had begun to head east on Cordova, marching past Woodward's. So the people who were running away from Gastown felt trapped, which added to the atmosphere of chaos and panic. But the police were only interested in arresting what they profiled as hippie types. In the CBC footage, you see old guys from the neighbourhood calmly watching the spectacle before them without feeling threatened alongside "Straight John" couples who had been in Gastown having dinner, or at the festival itself.

Was it well documented? Because it had been going on for a number of hours, there must have been a build up?

The festival had already been going on for three or four hours when the police began to mass on the east side of the neighbourhood. Newspaper photographers were there and the CBC had a remote film crew there as well, so we had great documentation of how people looked. When we think of the '60s, we sometimes imagine a unified period in terms of style, but things were mixed up. There were '50s-style greasers and the old guys from the hotels dressed like they were in the '40s with their hats and ties.

I guess what you want to do is to somehow get all of those layers, everything from dress style to the nature of the activity going on in a single photograph?

Yes. It will be 8 metres by 13 metres.

So you're casting a mini movie for a still?

Exactly. There will be about 150 people involved.

How complicated is the reconstruction? What do you have to do to make it look like it did in 1971?

We have to lay down a light layer of asphalt and pour curbs. We have to build two building façades, age them, and put merchandise inside the shop windows. It's a very high-resolution image, so we can't really get away with too much movie magic. It's got to look real. We can't find the specific riot helmets and batons we need, so we will have to manufacture them—as well as newspapers of the day, posters and even trash. There are about 20 people portraying police, 80 hippies and three mounted officers.

What's the nature of the composition? How have you determined what it will be?
Part of it is imagination. I've planned a map of the area and have started figuring out what the angle of view is. I'll be seeing a computer rendering of the whole thing just to make sure I have imagined the height of the camera, the position of the walls and the people correctly. It'll take about three days to shoot. The whole thing will take a minimum of four pieces to make the full composition I need, but there will be numerous takes. We'll start zooming in on zones, rehearse those zones and then shoot them. We have to shoot the horses separately from the people because only stunt men can be around the horses.

What made you decide to do it as a photograph as opposed to the other media that you work in, like film for instance?
Because it's supposed to last for a long time. Moving images tend to need a lot of attention in order to keep running, whereas something static can just sit there and persist.

How does this work fit into the larger context of the work you've already done down in the Downtown Eastside?
My work often deals with pivotal moments in the history of a condition, dialectical moments that can go either one way or another. This was one of those pivotal moments; I believe this riot determined the character of Gastown later on. A lot of hippies were living illegally in industrial buildings, and zoning out the residential component of the neighbourhood was a way of punishing them. From that moment on, the neighbourhood was like a barren ghost town because no one lived there.

Where will it be installed?
At the end of the public plaza. There will be a large glass wall enclosing the atrium and the image will be imbedded inside it, floating about 10 feet off the ground. One side will have to be reversed, but the image will look equally good on both sides. The contractors didn't really want to use the process I was suggesting at first, but I asked them to give it a try and it turned out beautifully. It's got a wonderful luminescent quality. With the tiniest bit of backlighting from the sky above, or from lighting at night, the image just pops out.

A final thing. The space where the image will be installed is going to be used by everyone, from street people to university students. Is the area a matrix for the social mixing that's supposed to be going on?
That's still a question. What is this space? Is it going to be a private space, or is it public space? Is it a public space governed by civic law and patrolled by police, or is it a place that's being patrolled by privately contracted security people? My work asks the question of who controls public space.

So your image is meant to be provocative in that it raises the very questions about control and power that the event you're representing was about?
Exactly.

It is subversive then, isn't it?
A wee bit.

FOLIO X

ABBOTT & CORDOVA, 7 AUGUST 1971
Stan Douglas

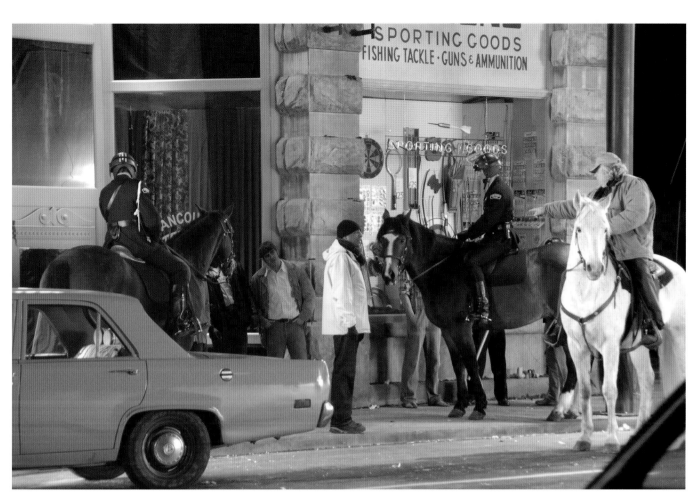

10

ETHICAL ARCHITECTURE

AGAINST A BREATH-TAKING PANORAMA of mountains and ocean, residential towers in Vancouver have risen over the last two decades to vie for a share of the view. At the street level however, visible problems of homelessness, poverty, and drugs persist. On March 11, 2008, the Metro Vancouver Homelessness Count enumerated 2,592 homeless people during a 24-hour period, an increase of 19 percent from 2005 when the count was last conducted. Of those counted, 1,547 were found during the daytime on the street and at service locations, while the remaining had stayed overnight in an emergency shelter, safe house or transition house. Two key documents summarize the city of Vancouver's affordable housing and homelessness policy in the Downtown Eastside: the *2005 Homeless Action Plan*, which prioritizes the development of 3,200 units of supportive housing, and the *2005 Downtown Eastside Housing Plan*, which encourages the development of up to 10 social housing projects, one-for-one SRO replacement and five SRO hotel purchases or renovations over five years. Vancouver's Homeless Action Plan, along with the plans of other major cities, highlights that, due to jurisdictional and revenue limitations, long-term permanent solutions to homelessness ultimately require multi-level governmental participation and funding, private sector involvement, and ongoing community consultation.

In contemporary culture, architects work either for a client, for themselves, for society, or for a mix of those interests. Working primarily for the client's benefit, the architect acts as a service-provider and the product is reflective of the client's desires. Some architects work with a strong personal vision that becomes the driving rationale for a project's design. Developers and public institutions have started engaging these "celebrity" architects to design projects with their signature style to increase a project's value, to ease it through tricky political territory, and to raise funds for it. Work by such architects is being co-opted by popular media as fashion commodities to be consumed. As architectural design increasingly becomes a tool for advancing private interest, an urgent need arises to re-examine the role of ethics, activism and critical commentary in architectural practice.

Architects whose vocation is to shape the physical environment can, and arguably should, offer creative problem-solving abilities to address the collective challenges that are enmeshed in the city's fabric. The ethical dimension underlying architectural practice is affirmed in the Architect's Oath, whereby architects "promise now that my professional conduct as it concerns the community, my work, and my fellow architects will be governed by the ethics and tradition of this honorable and learned profession." An architect's ethical obligations include giving due regard for the interests of the public who will be exposed to their work, being involved in civic activities, and rendering public interest professional services. Their vocation, then, is one of a "citizen architect," a term coined by Rural Studio founder, Samuel Mockbee, to describe those who "participate in the social, political, and environmental realities our communities are facing."

A Poetic Expression of Social Justice

The correlation between aesthetics and ethics can be observed as far back as ancient Greece in such texts as *Six Enneads* by Plontinus, a treatise which describes the aspiration of the soul towards *kalos,* a word meaning both the beautiful and the honorable. Early 20th century Modernist architects, grounded in secular utopian ideals, engaged in the political life of cities and deployed architecture as a social force for change. Unfortunately, the failure of the new, hygienic and rational communities to stimulate deep social reform triggered a backlash against the tenets of Modernism in the 1970s. A disjunction between the aesthetic and the ethical became manifest in contemporary architectural theory and practice. The chastening effect of last century's mistakes faded to collective amnesia about the architect's role in society, reducing it to a shallow fixation on self-expression, cultural commentary, and empty formalism.

While architects are often revered as aesthetic forces in setting fashion, their engagement as citizens in civic life, along with planners, property managers, and realtors, is necessary because governments alone may not have the political will, public trust or resources to effect change. In other words, architecture is both a profane, practical endeavour as well as deeply moral and social in its potential to make a difference. Architects can lead in creating environments that express humanist values of inclusion, care, and support.

With a commitment to social advocacy and a decade's worth of experience delivering social housing in the Downtown Eastside, Henriquez Partners Architects understood the significance of the Woodward's project to the economic and social welfare of the neighbourhood. As evidence of their unusual leadership, they were the only architectural design firm to handpick a developer, Westbank Projects/Peterson Investment Group, committed to design quality above financial gain. Through the development process, Henriquez Partners commandeered their extensive experience on many different kinds of projects to exercise a central role in balancing the needs of all involved constituents—the community, government, and private interests. They negotiated with the city of Vancouver on behalf of the developer to ensure the project's financial viability. They programmed uses to maximize the public benefit,

incorporating the possibility of 200 units of social housing prior to confirmation of provincial funding, including a much-needed neighbourhood grocery store and drugstore, designing an inclusive public realm, and maximizing use of the allowable on-site density to ensure critical "body heat" at the project. The city parcel for non-profit organizations in the rehabilitated 1903/08 Heritage Building was a turnkey development at financial risk to the developer. Henriquez Partners also established local community partners and proposed the involvement of a community advisory committee to engage public opinion, to encourage community ownership of the project, and to build public trust.

Henriquez Partner's continual exertion of design authority while negotiating the complex web of partnerships is evident in the optimism expressed through-out Woodward's design about the vitality of the Downtown Eastside. Enough new commercial space is included in Woodward's to meet the demands of residents and on-site users and to expand the general market for commercial goods in the Downtown Eastside, key to the revitalization of the neighbourhood. One-third of the site area is dedicated to a fully accessible and inclusive public realm. Design features such as the central atrium stairway rising as an umbilical cord from a pool of water and the vines climbing up the steel exoskeleton of the W Building poetically express the site's "rebirth" and the community's vision to live sustainably.

Authentic Expression Above Conventional Style
In the absence of belief in and awareness of a cosmological order, there are still residues of the former order and a longing for the orientation that would allow people to feel at home in the world. Architecture can give meaning by bringing together and juxtaposing physical fragments that, like the pieces of the old structure being incorpo-rated into the new Woodward's public realm, highlight the absence, recall the totality, and elicit stories of the inhabitants that will resonate with other people and genera-tions. In listening to the content of personal stories and incorporating it into a larger societal dialogue, the architect can draw people into the process of creating a built idea, of finding an authentic expression beyond style and conventional archetypes.

After 10 years of protests and sit-ins—culminating in the 2002 Woodsquat—over the future use of the Woodward's site, the city of Vancouver finally engaged the neighbourhood in an extensive process of community consultation. In a massive act of collective remembering and imagining, many stories about Woodward's shopping

experiences and the welcoming family atmosphere were recorded and translated into visions and desirable features for the new project that were distilled into project guidelines. With community ownership of the project firmly grounded and public involvement ongoing through the Woodward's Community Advisory Committee, community support for the project weathered the project's more controversial design decisions, including increasing the height of the W Building residential tower, adding a second tower, and demolishing the entire structure, except in the original 1903/08 building. Community supporters saw these decisions as necessary to incorporate all the non-market housing, provide a generous public realm, and ensure the project's financial viability, thereby increasing the public benefits of the project. Thus, in falling outside preconceived forms for the project, the Woodward's redevelopment responds to the essence of the community's desires that the project preserve the social identity and inclusive spirit of the old department store as the heart of community life while enhancing the area's economic, social and environmental health.

Because projects deal with people's stories—their relationships to each other and to a place—and the themes emerging from the stories, each project has the potential for different expressions. While drawing material inspiration from the surrounding heritage neighbourhood, Woodward's fractures the old monolithic structure, leaving building pieces in the resulting public realm, and reinterprets the local aesthetic into four related buildings of distinctly modern expression, including the modern concrete grid supporting the 1903/08 heritage façade. Played out in the public realm penetrating the heart of the project and unifying the intensely mixed-use programming, Woodward's sets the stage for the neighbourhood's larger narrative of inclusivity and potential resistance. Rather than ignore the harsh reality of Downtown Eastside street life, the public realm is, on a practical level, designed robustly to be an extension of the street and incorporate various activities while creating an oasis through trees and seating to quixotically invite inclusive inhabitation. Only time will tell if Woodward's transforms the declining Downtown Eastside into a place that reflects the vital complexities of a post-modern city.

Trusting Embodied Experience
The personal stories of inhabitants are embodied in and experienced through the fundamental relationships and activities that still give meaning, orientation, and an

ability to dwell in the absence of larger social constructs. Nevertheless, relationships with family, friends, children and communities played out in the daily activities of bathing, eating, washing and making love are slowly being eroded by mass communication and the economic ordering of our societies. Architecture can support these relationships and activities by creating spaces that focus and celebrate everyday existence. Rather than photogenic, antiseptic worlds devoid of people and communities, such architecture considers the scale of the human body and its relationship to the physical environment to richly inform the corporeal experience of space. The design of the Woodward's project was governed by universal design principles to maximize accessibility of the site by as many people as possible and includes details that encourage inhabitation such as building-integrated seating, lighting and weather-protected areas. Amenities such as water features, seating areas, children's play zones, and greenery are the finer variegations that foster community life and a humane relationship with the intensely dense and mixed environment of Woodward's.

Trusting embodied experience leads to speaking courageously from the heart about the human need for inclusion and embrace in the absence of a common cosmological order. Such critical commentary is a necessary first step for the architectural profession to overcome any lack of faith that it can make a difference. By taking more risks through a societal and community-based approach towards issues, architects can imbue the aesthetic content of architecture with social ethos to make architecture relevant and whole enough to instigate constructive changes in society.

THE PRACTICAL UTOPIAN
Gregory Henriquez

Gregory Henriquez
Architect
Henriquez Partners Architects

Gregory Henriquez is an architect best known for the design of community-based, mixed-use, institutional, and social housing projects in the Downtown Eastside of Vancouver. He is the managing partner of Henriquez Partners Architects. Past notable projects include Coal Harbour Community Centre, Bruce Eriksen Place, and Arts Umbrella.

Born in Winnipeg, Manitoba in 1963, he graduated with a Bachelor of Architecture from Carleton University in 1987 and attended the Master of Architecture Program at McGill University in 1988 where he studied under Alberto Pérez-Gómez. In his book *Towards an Ethical Architecture*, the authors discuss the urgent need to re-examine the role of ethics, activism and critical commentary in architectural practice. This discourse is founded upon the belief that meaningful architecture must be a poetic expression of social justice. He has won numerous design awards, including a 2004 Governor General's Medal in Architecture for the Lore Krill Housing Co-operative. He was elected to the Royal Canadian Academy of Arts in 2006.

Most recently, his quest to tackle Vancouver's acute homelessness crisis has led him to propose the rapid erection of temporary modular housing communities and to propose new mixed-income housing projects in the Downtown Eastside and the West End of Vancouver.

THE FOLLOWING INTERVIEW CONDUCTED BY ROBERT ENRIGHT WAS FIRST PUBLISHED IN *BORDER CROSSINGS*, ISSUE NO. 100, VOL. 25, NO. 4 IN NOVEMBER 2006.

In Towards An Ethical Architecture, *you say that at the age of 19, you thought you knew what architecture was. Was that just youthful hubris?*

A lot of arrogance and a lot of hubris. I've lost that now. I have more humility and more insight into my mortal limitations. The one thing I've learned is to not have some driving aesthetic vision that allows you to pre-ordain what architecture is. The one thing that has fed my work of late is having more questions than answers.

But while there may not be an overriding aesthetic about implementation, you've shown a consistent tendency to reconcile what you call the ethical with the aesthetic. Aesthetics and ethics have to be in some kind of harmonious relationship for you.

If you go back to the Greeks, there was no distinction between what was ethical and what was beautiful. They were intertwined. One of the things that happened with modernity was the rise of a distinction between the aesthetic and the ethical in art and architecture, and in everyone's life. We separate them and that's part of the dilemma of our shallow society. If you have an architectural practice like ours, where we deal with the profane world of developers and non-profits and cities and politics and all these things, you have to find a leadership role for the architect again. You have to circumnavigate through these things to make sure at the end of the day that the built form is in the best interests of society as a whole, that it isn't just a marketing campaign, that it isn't merely someone's solipsistic vision, and that it isn't ugly.

When you first came out of architecture school, didn't you have some surrealist tendencies?

The beautiful thing about Alberto Pérez-Gómez's way of teaching was that he pushed us to look inside ourselves to find some way of coping with the dilemmas of the modern world. Each one of us found different ways of expressing it, and Surrealism is an obvious technique for expressing the juxtapositions in the modern world which don't make sense on the surface. I did realize that it works better in theoretical architecture than it does in the real world of buildings and people's lives. What you have to do is confront the real content within the ideas and find a way to open it up so that it participates in a larger dialogue with the society as a whole. If you can do that, people are moved in a meaningful way because they become part of the creation of a built idea. They're not merely some inhabitant who's meant to be inspired by the genius of the individual who bestowed this work upon them.

You were also taken by the idea of Existentialism. I wonder how you ever imagined you would translate an existentialist disposition into the built world?

Existentialism deals with my confronting the reality of the absence of God in my family upbringing. How do you find a way of approaching divinity or some cosmological order that's meaningful in the modern world? The translation is really a multi-step process. I was first moved by the Gnostics and by a whole series of people who heralded the absence of God's once-presence in the world. It's the idea that we've lost something, yet residues still linger. There are Hassidic parables about the absence of God's presence and how that can sometimes be enough. For me, circumnavigating the presence and absence of these ideas allowed me to translate fragments of them into architecture.

Does that mean you are able to draw some aspect of that philosophical inquiry into your actual practice? I think the line from Hamlet might be an architectural dictum as well: some ideas are better realized in the breach than in the observance. Some architecture is better thought about than made. Are these ideas always circulating inside your head?

I think each project has an ability to express different ideas. There are architects, like Frank Gehry, who have a formalist tendency and you can look at his works from across the world and they're all the same, even though they are adapted to local conditions and different uses. There's a formal language that makes him similar to some painters or sculptors. I think what distinguishes our practice is that we try to deal with the ideas and the people and the place first, and then find the soft spot which resonates with the larger issues presented by the project. Because you can't deal with everything in every project. If it's Woodward's, for example, you have to find different ways of dealing with the idea of inclusivity or with the poetic dimensions of environmental or green architecture. Or, what is the larger social goal we're trying to accomplish and how do we make sure it happens in reality rather than just remaining a diagram on the page?

In your book, you quote the phrase "the hallowing of the everyday." Has that been an essential aspect of your practice?

There are two things about Martin Buber that are very special: his connection to Hassidic roots and this idea of hallowing the everyday, but also his belief in the interpersonal relationships between people. The hallowing of the everyday is an extension of the fundamental relationships in our daily lives. For Frederick Kiesler, it was the "Endless House;" it was about bathing, washing, eating, making love. Those are the things that haven't been lost. The larger societal constructs that once held this world together on some meaningful level don't exist, so how do you go about building from the ground up, how do you go about making sense of the world in the absence of some order or totality from which you could make decisions?

So when you refer to architecture's state of "current amnesia," is part of what it has forgotten those fundamentally human things?

I think society has forgotten a lot of those things. If you look at what makes us happy, or makes us feel that our lives make sense, it's the relationships with our children or our parents, our friends, our communities—all those grassroots relationships that allow us to feel safe and orientate us in the world. I think with our mass communications and our new economic world order, these things have been lost and architecture has become a tool used either by developers to build buildings or by art galleries to make money. It hasn't been seen to deal with the fundamental issues of dwelling and orientation in a very hostile world.

So when Nicolai Ouroussoff complains in the New York Times that architecture is revered as an aesthetic and not a social force, is he drawing attention to one of the tendencies you've resisted? Is his complaint an accurate one?

Architects are not engaged in the political life of cities on any active level the way they thought they were going to be in the 1960s. I think architects have become consultants. You have different types of architects for different types of use, like you have different lawyers for different types of legal practice. Some do art galleries; some do social housing; some do strip malls. It's a very sad state of affairs and I'm not really sure how we've gotten so lost. We've reached the point where Gehry is doing jewelry for Tiffany's, where less than inspired architects often do social housing, and where the best and brightest of my generation are all teaching.

Can architecture be revived?

I think it can. In episodic circumstances, there can be an architecture of resistance where we collectively try to make decisions to do the right thing. It depends if you share humanist values; if you're a hard-core, right-wing idealogue, then things are fine the way they are. But if you fundamentally believe that we have some responsibility to take care of and to nurture each other, then there's got to be a better way of existing on the planet. Architecture is an extension of those values, but it's not leading in any way, shape or form. I think if architects asked themselves whether what they were doing every time they started a job was in the best interests of the larger society, they would behave differently.

Were you surprised when you won the Woodward's competition?

Yes and no. We weren't supposed to win. But I felt good about it all the way through because we were really listening to what the city and community wanted. The city, the civic politicians and the bureaucracy set up the agenda for what they wanted. They had guiding principles, which were extremely utopian and idealistic, and we strived to meet them as best we could. I think that's what separated us from the other firms in the competition. I mean, there weren't tons of architects wanting to do this. There was a sense by the others that this neighbourhood couldn't be saved, and that there was nothing you could do except move the density somewhere else.

Is the Downtown Eastside a special place?

It was once the heart of downtown, but drug use and homelessness have grown and it's all within this 10-block radius. There was a sense that things couldn't be solved easily, and to think that architecture alone could do this was extremely naïve. That's why the program for this project became so meaningful—integrating single non-market housing with market housing, with the university and with community space. All these things became an idealistic statement about inclusivity, that somehow we could go into the poorest part of our city, make the most optimistic statement about what was possible, and let it be a catalyst for change. All the signs right now are saying it could work.

You're optimistic?

Very. You have to have blind faith. That's something my father taught me; you have to have faith in your hands, and Alberto taught me that you have to have faith in your ideas, otherwise no one's going to believe you. You have to put your heart and your soul into it.

Where is the process now?

We just demolished most of the old building. We saved the original 1903/08 building which is three bays on Hastings and six on Abbott Street. We had what's called a roll-over implosion and it all came tumbling down. It was quite exciting. It looks a bit like Lebanon right now, and they're just taking away all the debris.

But when your building went down it wasn't like what happened in St. Louis with Pruitt-Igoe in 1972. That building complex must haunt architects who are working on large-scale housing projects.

There was a real arrogance in early and mid-Modernism that housing people was enough, that ghettos were okay and that economies of scale were acceptable. I think there's an understanding here in Canada that community can't be thousands of people and if it is, they have to have spaces that are smaller and more diverse. Even though Woodward's is a larger scale than Pruitt-Igoe, it's not all social housing. We have 536 market housing units as well, we have a school for the contemporary arts, we have non-profit spaces, we have public spaces for the whole city and we have an atrium and plaza and mews. The aesthetic I link them to is closer to a train station than a shopping mall, so they become part of the city. I think it has to be 24/7, day in, day out. There have to be people working, living and shopping there.

Are the problems ongoing?

Sure. Homelessness is growing in Vancouver. Because of the success of the condo market, the rising cost of land makes even renting extremely high. There's a huge issue in affordability now. There are drug issues that are not going away. It's a complex problem that isn't only about architecture; it's also about politics and societal values. We have the first safe injection site in Canada in the Downtown Eastside. Their licence was just renewed for a year and a half and it's run by the Portland Hotel Society. We feel very connected to those issues, and as citizens, not even as architects, we have a moral obligation to deal with these problems. We send troops all over the world to solve other people's problems, but we can't confront the reality of homelessness, poverty and addiction in our own society. I think that's where it begins.

One of the things you say an architect must do is to give meaning by eliciting a story where no script exists. I love the idea, but I have trouble imagining a place where there isn't a story.

But the story isn't always apparent, and it isn't something which people carry around in their hands like a little bible. So the idea is to elicit the real story. What is it that the people who are going to inhabit this space want to say about their lives, or their existence, or their time on this planet? How can that story resonate with other people and hopefully for other generations?

So what is the narrative of the Woodward's project?

The narrative is about inclusivity and humanity's ability to co-exist on all social and economic planes, to not ghettoize ourselves by living behind walls. Woodward's has single-room occupancy housing—which is the poorest of the poor in our society—right across from $1.5 million, sky-balcony, three-level apartments. These people are going to share a common ground plane.

So this will also be a narrative of difficulty. Won't there will be resistance built into this narrative on the part of some people?

I think so, and that's normal and probably healthy. I think at the same time, all families don't always get along. Their trying and showing up is half of it. The next half is hard work.

We talked earlier about the ethical and the aesthetic but I want to push further and talk about the ethical and the poetic. How will this idea of the poetic manifest itself in this project?

I'll give you a very simple example. Our tower, which is 400 feet high, is a hot-water radiant-heated highrise and uses an existing steam plant that's been around since the turn of the century. So environmentally that's very good. At the same time, it has plants growing 400 feet up the side which, because there's no air-conditioning in the building, will act as sun shades in the summer. They'll also act as windbreaks for the plaza down below, and they're going to be beautiful objects unto themselves. We're recalling both Flatiron buildings and Vienna-esque steel train station metalwork. Along with the vine growing on the actual steel structure itself, it's a sort of Jackson Pollock expression. It's only one element of the design, but it deals with the poetic expression of sustainability at the same time that it tries to tread a little more carefully on this planet. That's one example. Another is, how do you deal with the central stair in the atrium which links all of the retail and the parking? Our current design is a giant umbilical cord, which emerges from this pool as a metaphoric symbol of rebirth. So you find poetic expressions for things that are obviously functional and that also have an ethical message about the possible rebirth of this place on earth.

You've used that birth metaphor before in an earlier project at the time your wife was pregnant? Are you interested in working the human body into the spaces you design?

Everyone measures the world against their body. We're upright, that's who we are. Maurice Merleau-Ponty talks about the relationship between our body and the world. It's also part of the phenomenological roots from which Alberto comes.

So does the Winnipeg poet Robert Kroetsch, who includes in Seed Catalogue, "the gopher is the model. Stand up straight," a line which explains the grain elevator in the prairies.

I like that. I thought they built them that way so the trains wouldn't get lost. For me, part of the connection between Surrealism and Frederick Kiesler is that the fragment has the ability to recall the totality, so fragments of things can somehow inform and send messages about the presence and absence of an idea. I think we carry around a lot of subconscious stuff about our bodies, and most buildings don't consciously deal with a relationship to the human figure as well as they should.

So is one aspect of architecture a sort of Frankensteinism, where you piece these fragmented ideas together into a new and benign monster?

If I could get to Frankenstein, I'd be happy. I think we're closer to just recalling the absence and trying to send a very strong message that something is missing. I don't know what it is, but everyone comes with their own personal story about the absence of order or the absence of cosmological awareness which will allow us to feel at home in the world. These fragments, or these parts of the body, are projections of this healthy reproductive state that I long for. It seems pretty basic.

Is architecture a practice in which it's easy to lose sight of those connections? One of the problems architects have is they often build things that take up a lot of space and cost a lot of money.

There is unquestionably a whole economic and political dimension to what we do. A lot of money is required to build these things, so Ian and Ben had to sell 536 condos, which they did. Apartments worth hundreds of millions of dollars were sold to the public in a single day. At the same time, the architect's role is to imbue this with some kind of poetic content and social mission; otherwise we're just draftsmen. And it's not so hard. This is also something my father taught me: if you have the courage of your convictions, very few people will disagree with you. If you really believe and speak from your heart, the world listens and generally follows suit. I've had very good experiences that way. Maybe Vancouver is a special place, but I think this is a landscape where anything is possible. I really believe that. The biggest failing of my profession is its inability to have sufficient faith in itself and in humanity to believe that it can make a difference.

One of the things Pérez-Gómez says is that architecture is the poetic expression of social justice. He's emphasizing that architecture is both practical and deeply moral and social. Is that taught in school? Do young architects graduate as idealists, and before long they become practical, greedy realists?

I think the type of person who goes into architecture goes in like that. Unfortunately, most of our universities are bent on giving people skills, which are almost useless by the time they get to my office. It should be more reflective, which is the beauty of what Alberto did at Carleton. He inspired hundreds of us to look inside ourselves and to believe that we could make a difference, that the state we were in was really the sum total of people's decisions in the past, and that our decisions, projected into the future, could affect history. The idea that the individual architect has that ability is a beautiful one. He believes that ultimately, our responsibility is to take a leadership role in all of this.

You're hopeful about the role that architecture can play in the world?
I have to be. Otherwise, we should pack up our tools and go away. Otherwise, I'd become an artist. But let's talk about the art world for a minute: I'm dealing with Stan Douglas on this piece of public art for Woodward's. He's brilliant and he's going to do a 30 x 50 foot image on glass in the centre of the atrium which will be a commentary on the history of the Gastown Riot. The problem with most art is that it's in art galleries and not integrated into society, it's not in the public realm, in churches and in piazzas. What we're trying to do with Woodward's is to bring art back into that public realm. So Stan will be doing this huge piece which will be part of this neighbourhood. I can't say enough good things about him. His rigour is unbelievable and his images move me.

Why is there a quotation of the Flatiron Building in your project?
The Flatiron came out of the intersection of two buildings in New York that sit at very tight, acute angles. The interesting thing about the Woodward's site is that it is actually a hinge between the old historical grid and the modern city grid coming at a different angle. The resulting flatiron building exists at the point where these two geometries coincide and reconciles them: the Cordova axis comes sliding through into the centre of the site, becomes the atrium and constructs the edge of the flatiron building.

So you use a previous model from architecture to create a conversation about the space you're in. Does a humanist architecture also pay attention to achievements from the past?
It is an historical context, so there has to be respect paid to your ancestors on some level, even though this building is way out of scale with its neigbours. Most of Gastown is five-storey high warehouse buildings. We searched for some sort of workable archetype. The Flatiron Building was built at exactly the same time as Gastown and is only 100 feet shorter than the one we're building, so it was something that allowed us to say to people in the heritage community, "Listen, we're not raping and pillaging; we're learning from the past and trying to find a way to re-appropriate and translate that past into the 21st century."

Tell me about the Abbott Building.
From a programmatic and symbolic perspective, the Abbott Building is the most significant one on the site. Within one vertical tower, you have a food store in the basement, which the neighbourhood doesn't yet have; you have one

level of federal offices and one level of civic offices; you've got seven levels of family non-market housing with a sky playground, which are owned by the city and run by a non-profit group, and on top of that is market housing. All this is within one vertical structure. To my knowledge, nothing like it exists in North America.

Is the function of this building to so thoroughly integrate the various constituents of the community that you won't have anything like the ghettoizing that happened in St. Louis in 1956 where blacks and whites refused to live together?

The units sold out in five hours and there were thousands of people left wanting units afterwards. So our societal values have evolved here to the point where no one worried about it. Let's put it this way: there's enough wealth here that we can be generous. The beauty of this project is that somehow all of the amenities of our city can be shared by everyone, and we've gone a long way to see that everyone is living in equally beautiful housing. The social housing still has a view of the water and the argument could be made that it has better outdoor space for the kids than the market housing.

It will be interesting to to see what dynamic then emerges out of this hot-house culture that the Abbott Building will create.

It's a microcosm of a city. It's a big enough building to think of in that way. There are neighbourhoods in Vancouver that have market and non-market housing right next door to each other, these happen to be on top of one another. The thing that makes it unique is not that they're co-existing, but that they're being planned together and sold together, and they're being integrated. SFU will occupy most of the Hastings Building. There's a drugstore in the base and then Simon Fraser has five floors with five performance venues, a big black box theatre, a cinema, a dance theatre, two visual arts galleries and practice studios above. It's 130,000 square feet of art school. The whole project is 1 million square feet.

Are you going to be able to sustain this humanist aesthetic from which you've been operating?

The success we've had with the Woodward's project has taken off some of the stress of running a business and, in that sense, it has allowed us to dream more. Sometimes when you're caught in the day-to-day subsistence of an architectural practice, you take work to feed yourself and to employ your staff. You have to keep the machine moving. It's called "bread and butter work" in the business. If one is lucky enough, you get to the point where you have more choices, it actually allows you the opportunity to step back and reflect upon what you're doing and ask more meaningful questions. I find that I take more risks. There are things in *Towards An Ethical Architecture* that are very critical of the profession and the way in which buildings are produced. But at the same time, it's more in line with the values I cherished in my youth. I think one of the things our profession has lost is the ability to believe we can dream and we can take risks and, bit by bit, day by day, we can change the world.

AFTERWORD
ARCHITECTURE AS THE POETIC EXPRESSION OF SOCIAL JUSTICE
Alberto Pérez-Gómez

Alberto Pérez-Gómez
Architectural Theorist

Alberto Pérez-Gómez is the Saidye Rosner Bronfman Professor at McGill University School of Architecture, chair of the History and Theory of Architecture Program and director of Post-Professional Programs.

Born in Mexico City, he obtained his undergraduate degree in architecture and engineering at the National Polytechnic Institute in Mexico City, did postgraduate work at Cornell University and received a Master of Arts and PhD from the University of Essex in England.
For his book, *Architecture and the Crisis of Modern Science* (MIT Press, 1983), Dr. Pérez-Gómez was awarded the Alice Davis Hitchcock Award, an annual prize recognizing the most distinguished work of scholarship in architectural history published by a North American scholar. Other books include *Polyphilo or the Dark Forest Revisited* (MIT, 1992), *Architectural Representation and the Perspective Hinge* (MIT Press, 1997), co-authored with Louise Pelletier.
His most recent book is *Built upon Love: Architectural Longing and Aesthetics* (MIT Press, 2006), which uncovers the relationship between poetics and ethics in architecture. Currently, Dr. Pérez-Gómez is engaged in a project to redefine the nature of architectural education by revisiting its historical sources during the Enlightenment and the early 19th century, an imperative task in light of the failures of globalization revealed in the events of September 2001.

I. The Architect as Navigator

Often at night along the mountain tops,
when gods are revelling by torch light,
you came carrying a great jar
(like one shepherd's use) but of heavy gold.
You filled the jar with milk
drawn from a lioness, and made a great cheese
unbroken and gleaming white.

Alcman of Sart
(Sardis, Asia Minor, writing in Sparta, 7th.C. BCE, tr. by W. Barnstone)

Tekton was the father of Pherecles, who built a majestic ship for Paris. This *daidalon* was the most important of all wooden artifacts in the Trojan War—besides the Horse itself, of course, a deceptive kind of vessel whose parts were also fitted together admirably, with perfectly "harmonic" joints, capable of magically reproducing life. Tekton associates the knowledge of making the ship with the wisdom necessary for its practical use, *the art of navigation,* and thus represents a particular architectural expertise, one that has surprisingly little to do with the fashionable notion of the "tectonic" as a legitimizing expressive power in modern buildings.

In *The Republic,* Plato describes the problematic state of affairs aboard a seaworthy vessel that seems nevertheless in imminent danger. "The captain is larger and stronger than any of the crew, but a bit deaf and short-sighted, and doesn't know much about navigation. The crew are all quarreling with each other about how to navigate the ship, each thinking he ought to be at the helm; they know no navigation and cannot say that anyone ever taught it them, or that they spent any time studying it; indeed they say it can't be taught and are ready to murder anyone who says it can." The real navigator is always in a precarious position, for the sailors would rather praise a strong deceitful man capable of controlling and manipulating the captain, pretending that he knows what he is doing, while being incapable of setting the ship on a true course. The sailors on the ship are bound to regard the true navigator as a gossip and star-gazer, while in fact he must be a keen student of his crew's temperaments and potentially divisive mixtures, and of natural "temperaments" as well: knowledgeable of the seasons of the year, the sky, the planets, and the wind, all indispensable for successful navigation, including the many stories about his ancestors who acted appropriately in diverse particular, and often dangerous situations.

The talent and intellectual capacity of the navigator is not very different from the *radio studiorum* that Vitruvius evokes in his *Book I* and which he calls *raciocinatio,* the body of knowledge or discourse, originally *theoria* or *contemplatio.* The possession of such "theory" is of the utmost importance for any architect, having truly "practical" consequences. In spite of the fact that, as Vitruvius points out, this is a discourse that is common to many other disciplines, all diverse from architecture, and which depend on the apprehension of *mathemata* for their disclosure of order and on rhetoric for their articulation; disciplines such as music, allowing humanity to take measure of temporality; optics, which show the geometrical properties of light and the proportional weakness of the human sight; medicine revealing the humoral proportions for the healthy human body, and even law, legislating the order of the political body. This common theoretical *corpus,* mediated at the time of Vitruvius by a stoic comprehension of the practical repercussions of thought and historical precedents, has its ultimate origin in the gazing of the stars, the ancient *bios theoreticos* which, despite its aloofness from the concerns of making and the productive arts, prompts a sense of wonder that lies at the origin of reflective thought, science and philosophy, as it reveals to our immediate perception the unquestionable reality of order in the natural world, a sense of harmony that would be otherwise perennially absent from human affairs.

Indeed, it could be argued that despite the well-known Greek suspicion concerning the epistemological status of the products of human making, the hybrid qualifier *techné-poiesis* was deliberately applied to architecture, already pairing the autonomy of *techné* as a purely human activity that depended on manual dexterity, with *poiesis,* a making/uttering that was always conceived as related to divine creation. *Poiesis* was of course closer to our spiritual faculties, however suspicious it may have appeared to Plato for being the product of "inspiration" or "erotic mania," kindred to intellectual pursuits, yet distinct—and paradoxically "sometimes" superior in its status as truth—from *episteme,* which denoted clear thought with a universal claim to "truth as correspondence." Indeed, *Timaeus* himself states: "... the sight of day and night, the months and returning years, the equinoxes and the solstices, has caused the invention of number, given the notion of time, and made us inquire into the nature of the universe; thence we have derived philosophy... all audible musical sound is given us for the sake of harmony, which has motions akin to the orbits of our soul and which, as anyone who makes intelligent use of the arts [and crafts] knows, is not to be used, as is commonly thought, to give irrational pleasure, but as a heaven-sent ally in reducing to order and harmony any disharmony in the revolutions within us."

If there is a true reason for wishing to be born, writes Aristophanes, it is only to contemplate the dancing stars. This, we must emphasize, is not merely a poetic metaphor for our capacity to experience a sense of purpose in human existence. Human culture and its architecture might simply not have developed had we been born upright, but under a perpetually overcast sky (like the atmosphere of the planet Venus, for example). The dance of heavenly luminaries is the original experience of order, disclosed in human affairs through the cathartic effect of ritual and tragedy, art and architecture. Without this capacity to contemplate, disclose through speech, and emulate through making "sense" of the given order, the gloom of Theognis, who wrote in the mid-6th century BCE, "best of all things—is never to be born," might have resulted in an unbearable nihilism of despair well before Nietzsche, coinciding not with the "end of the classical," but with the waning of the pre-classical mythical age.

Vitruvius's remarks in *Book I* on the education of the architect also include the recognition that there is a technical knowledge specific to the discipline, one which to be effective, must be of the hands, and learnt through apprenticeship. You will not call an architect if you fall ill; there is a technical knowledge particular to medicine, as there is one specific to buildings, gnomons, and the construction of machinery (the artifacts that Vitruvius identifies as proper to the discipline of architecture). *But without the wisdom of navigation, one that allows for orientation in the cultural world, the discipline is meaningless.*

The architect as navigator is a philosopher and storyteller, a politician and social activist. His material is discourse, yet he is one in which the vocation of the contemplative life is decidedly participatory and practical, cast forward by the breath of Metis, the mother of Daedalus, whose cunning intelligence was crucial for Zeus to succeed in his political affairs. If architecture is to be capable of revealing a sense of purpose for our troubled culture, the architect as navigator might facilitate the mimetic possibilities of architecture by keeping an eye on the heavenly star-dance. In our times of excessive mist and technological glare, however, these possibilities must be often disclosed indirectly through a critical appreciation and articulation of the brightness, luminosity and significant depth of the most eloquent artifacts of our architectural tradition. It is in the shield of Achilles that:

> *Shines the image of the master mind:*
> *There earth, there heaven, there ocean he designed;*
> *The unwaried sun, the moon completely round;*
> *The starry lights that heaven's high convex crowned[...]*
> *A figured dance succeeds: such once was seen*
> *In lofty Gnossus, for the Cretan queen,*
> *Formed by Daedalean art; a comely band*
> *Of youths and maidens, bounding hand in hand[...]*
> *Now all at once they rise, at once descend,*
> *With well-taught feet: now shape, in oblique ways,*
> *Confusedly regular, the moving maze[...]*

In the labyrinth that is both a symbol of our human condition and the archetypal architectural "idea," the navigator may disclose the coincidence of order and disorder, clarity and mystery. The time of poetry/the space of architecture, is that incandescent instant/clearing in which life and death are no longer contradictory, but appear as truly one.

These intentions may be stated philosophically as universal truths, but they must be expressed architecturally through culturally specific projects. Indeed, the conditions for a genuine architectural practice have changed in accordance to particular cultural and historic situations. In our world of plurality and skepticism, the role of the architect as navigator demands close involvement with the community and proactive invention of programs that may enable social participation. This concern transcends mere aesthetic pursuits to attain the common good, and involves the ability to convincingly argue the case for a project in a democratic dialogue, guiding others away from the shortsightedness of self-interest.

II. Orientation

The navigator's sense of orientation is one that has its roots in deeply-felt experience, in an experience that presupposes nothing and attempts to grasp nascent being. Whether interpreting natural or topographic signs, or reading the cultural world, the navigator's truth is *aletheia,* a "truth in becoming," never permanent or absolute, but one that might do justice to both the experience of value in the primacy of perception, in which all works of humanity are *not equal,* and the need to remain vigilant of repressive or fallacious constructions. This is difficult work among skeptic sailors interested only in pleasure-cruising. How are the sailors to be made aware that such an order is indeed manifest, and that it is a human prerogative to grasp it, engage in it, and care for its preservation? This is of course wisdom itself, often mistaken for a mere technique. For, as Plato reminds us, also in *The Republic,* the eyes and the mind may be unsighted in two ways: "by a transition either from light to darkness or from darkness to light." If this is true, we must reject the conception of education professed by those who say that they can put in the mind knowledge that was not there before—"rather as if they could put sight into blind eyes." Real knowledge takes place as a recognition by the crew of something they already knew, an insight of the individuals' potential completion through participation in a higher truth driven by compassion. The navigator educates, but this activity, both in schools and in the practice of architecture, "should not be concerned to impart sight, but to ensure that some who had it already should be turned in the right direction and looking the right way."

Architecture has its own universe of discourse. The meanings that appear as it frames cultural situations cannot be merely transcribed to texts or other universes of discourse. It allows us to partake, through human action, from a sense of direction. The navigator is well aware of this. He knows that his words and promises will not preempt the autonomy of practice; the process of making is also a process of discovery. His wish to share ideas and orient the community, thereby enabling a project, never becomes a deterministic, prescriptive discourse. His words are not merely critical but generative, pregnant with the breath of ethical concern and true compassion; they are never merely "deconstructive," but truly a political position, activated through wondrous storytelling, his rhetorical skill.

Once in the public sphere, the architect does not determine or control the meanings of the buildings that are the outcome of projects. It is for "others" to decide. And yet, the issue of responsibility—truly a response-ability—remains pressing for the architect. Education and discourse, the navigational dimension of architecture, has therefore a dual role. It allows for an appropriate practice, an ethical and compassionate practice, enabling the practitioner to speak properly, bringing to presence memory (the past) and hope (the future) in order to act appropriately. It also enhances the reception of the work, demonstrating the cultural relevance of the poetic, showing the way in which fiction—the utterance and construction of emplotted narratives—may be superior to factual information in its capacity to reveal relevant truths for humanity.

III. Common Ground: Woodward's

The extraordinary proliferation of incongruous formal expression in the international architecture scene has, in recent years, brought to critical attention the need to better understand the ethical imperatives of architecture. While so-called brand architecture may be more or less aesthetically successful, its response to ethical and social questions often leaves much to be desired. It has also become increasingly self-evident that merely "sustainable" architecture that establishes a better relation to the natural environment through technical devices is not sufficient. Rather the issue seems to be one of "cultural sustainability:" an architecture capable of addressing, through poetic and innovative narratives, the new realities of our increasingly complex and heterogeneous social fabric.

Proclaiming the Woodward's redevelopment, marketing billboards across Vancouver boldly promised 'Community' under a lustrous red 'W', the old department store's iconic neon sign. Woodward's 1993 closure had intensified the sense of dispossession in the Downtown Eastside, a neighbourhood long-affected by poverty, homelessness and drug addiction. The redevelopment of Woodward's into a complex of multi-use buildings, offering significant urban spaces and integrating market and social housing makes an optimistic claim for inclusion, one that may be seen as a Canadian model in its quest to become home for an heterogeneous array of cultures.

The Vancouver architectural firm of Henriquez Partners Architects has, over the years, developed into a veritable laboratory, testing formal strategies to engage social issues, in quest of an architecture of social justice. Their concern has been *meaning* rather than aesthetics, driven by the conviction that beauty and social justice are inseparable, that the best architecture, a truly poetic architecture, is one that demonstrates their conjunction. The Woodward's project, under the inspired direction of Gregory Henriquez, epitomizes this basic position.

Throughout the planning of the Woodward's project, 'community' was invoked by local residents, developers, architects, bureaucrats and politicians to convey often competing interests, needs and aspirations. At the heart of these discussions was the question of what comprises community in a world absent of larger social narratives that once held people together. Such a dialogue reflects the spirit of Canadian democracy, which has historically flowed from an ethic of accommodating differences over segregation and led to our current politics of inclusion. To take a leading role in contemporary issues, the architect of the 21st century must be a social activist, a realist, a poet, a political technician and a utopian. It is crucial to point out that a program such as Woodward's does not magically appear out of "consensus." The role of the architect here is "interpretative" (rather than naïvely "creative," seeking novelty for its own sake), bringing to the table a depth of cultural and historical experience to propose a better future for all.

FOLIO XI

BLESSING THE SITE

Woodward's:
The Hastings Street Store Chronology
From Establishment to Reconstruction

Prepared by Commonwealth
Historic Resource Management Limited

12 December 2008

1892   Charles Woodward, aged 40 and recently arrived from Ontario, establishes Vancouver's first department store (a store with separate 'departments' that sell different kinds of merchandise) at Main and Georgia streets. The store caters to working people.

1895   Woodward's opens its Drug Department and irritates the industry for refusing to mark up prices. John (Jack) Woodward, Charles' eldest son, is the pharmacist. He will die within five years of tuberculosis, the same disease that killed his mother and two siblings.

1897   The mail order department is established. The first catalogue is sent out, and this continues until 1953.

1902   Charles decides to move to Hastings and Abbott streets, where he purchased a building lot at a good price. This location was available to the middle-class as well as to workers, and was also accessible to the docks. A consortium of six partners joined Woodward and incorporated on September 12th as Woodward Department Stores Limited.

1903   The new Woodward's store opens on November 4. Hastings Street is decorated with lights and a four-piece orchestra plays inside. White signs painted on the brick exterior advertise the departments within.

1904   Charles Woodward buys out the other directors by selling the Main Street store.

1908   The store is expanded from four to six floors.

1908   Charles' sons, William Culham (Billy) Woodward and Percival Archibald (Puggy) Woodward, join the store as bookkeeper and salesman respectively. Both sons attend their first Woodward's board meeting.

1910   First 25-cent Day, in which selected items are sold at a fixed price. With inflation, the price climbs over the years to 45 cents, 88 cents, 95 cents, and finally (in 1951) to the famous $1.49 Day.

1910   Woodward's installs a peanut butter machine as an attraction.

1912	Charles Woodward retires as a millionaire. He hands control over to John Little, manager of the Drug Department, and moves to California. Billy and Puggy Woodward take up management roles.
1913	Charles comes out of retirement and is once again listed as president.
1915	Puggy Woodward is named vice-president; less than a year later, he leaves because of the challenges of working with his family. Billy Woodward retains seniority, but keeps his title of secretary-treasurer.
1916	Billy Woodward enlists with the 1st Canadian Heavy Artillery and sees action in France for three years. Puggy Woodward is denied active service because of poor eyesight.
1918	Puggy returns to management at Woodward's.
1919	Puggy transforms the 2,500-square-foot 'food floor' into a self-service groceteria, the first of its kind in North America. Although criticized for its lack of service, it saves customers 10 to 15 percent.
1924	Charles Woodward is elected as a Member of the Legislative Assembly and holds his seat until 1928.
1925	A new wing extends the store north along Abbott Street to Cordova Street.
1926	Charles Woodward opens a store in Edmonton, Alberta. He and his wife are the sole owners.
1927	An 80-foot high steel tower, resembling the Eiffel Tower, is built and topped with a revolving searchlight. The brick base of the tower becomes home to the peanut butter machine, which operates until 1985.
1927-29	A large seven-storey addition is built along Cordova Street, reflecting the economic boom.
1930-31	Woodward's builds the largest parking garage in Canada, accommodating 500 cars. A pedestrian tunnel beneath Cordova Street links the garage to the Food Floor.
1930	Woodward's introduces its intricate Christmas window displays with mechanized Santa, bears, dolls, and reindeer.
1937	Charles Woodward dies. Billy, a superb leader, becomes president. Puggy, a marketing genius, becomes vice-president.
1938	On June 19th, the RCMP forcibly evict unemployed protestors from a sit-in in the post office. The protestors march through the area and shatter the windows at Woodward's. The windows are quickly repaired, and it is business as usual the next work day.
1938-39	An addition along the west side of the store extends from Hastings to Cordova. It includes a gymasium for staff; however, the gym is soon converted to the 1,000-seat Woodward's auditorium.
1939-45	Billy Woodward serves as a member of the War Supply Board, volunteering his business expertise to the Canadian government. Puggy Woodward becomes general manager during his brother's absence. Woodward's promotes Victory Loans and makes donations to the War Chest. The store twice wins the War Finance Victory Award. Servicemen enjoy dances in the auditorium.
1940	The searchlight atop the tower is ordered removed as a precaution against the possibility of enemy air raids.
1941	Billy Woodward is named lieutenant-governor of British Columbia and serves for five years.
1942	The Woodward's Staff Advisory Council is formed to give employees a voice with management. Staff benefits include shopping discounts, life insurance, scholarship funds for children, a subsidized meal service, and frequent social events.
1942	Billy's son Charles Namby (Chunky) Woodward joins the military and serves with the 12th Manitoba Dragoons.

1945	*The Beacon*, a bimonthly staff newsletter, begins production.
1946-47	Major additions and renovations add 132,000 square feet along Hastings Street. The store gains a more simplified and modern character. The bakery adds ovens that can produce 25,000 loaves of bread a day. A new coffee roaster can produce 500 lbs of coffee per hour. New freight elevators with a 2-ton capacity rise up the 8 floors and 2 basements at 100 feet per minute.
1947	Chunky Woodward joins the sales force as a buyer.
1948	Woodward's opens a store in Port Alberni, its first branch. Another 23 stores will open over the next 40 years.
1949	Woodward's expands its purchasing to the worldwide market.
1950	Park Royal, Western Canada's first shopping centre, opens with Woodward's as an anchor tenant.
1952	Woodward's offers customers its first credit card.
1953	Woodward's introduces profit-sharing to staff, based on their number of years in service.
1954	Puggy Woodward retires.
1954	BC Electric discontinues the interurban tram, which terminated a block from Woodward's at Hastings and Carrall. This makes the store less accessible to the region's shoppers. The theatres along Hastings Street are moving to Granville Street. These and other factors, along with the growth of regional shopping centres, mark the beginning of the decline of Hastings Street.
1955	Puggy Woodward and his wife devote themselves to philanthropy, funding the UBC Health Sciences Centre and other causes.
1956	The 15-foot-high revolving 'W' sign, illuminated with 652 light bulbs, is placed on top of the steel tower.
1957	Billy Woodward dies suddenly. His son Chunky succeeds him as president.
1957	A new parking garage is built. It is the largest in the Commonwealth, accommodating 800 cars. An enclosed bridge over Cordova Street links the garage with the store.
1959	The Woodward's store at the new Oakridge Shopping Centre opens as the chain's flagship store, taking the honour away from the Hastings Street store after 56 years.
1963	Mona Brun becomes the face of Woodward's with her cooking show, *Culinary Capers*, on CBC television. Woodward's maintains various cooking shows over the next 23 years.
1965	Hastings Street business and property owners organize the Improvement of the Downtown East Area Society (IDEAS) to help stop the decline of the area. Tax assessment values have dropped by half.
1968	Puggy Woodward dies.
1971	The Hastings Street store continues to be modernized, with a three-storey addition along Cordova Street adding nearly 10,000 square feet.
1971	On August 7, the Gastown Riot takes place. Youth converge in the area to protest drug laws and raids. Police order the crowd of 2,000 to disperse, then charge on horseback, close to the Woodward's store.
1972	A Woodward's Staff Advisory Council member, representing more than 6,000 store employees, is appointed to the board of directors.

1973	The Downtown Eastside Residents Association (DERA) is formed in an effort to improve the area's living conditions.
1987	The company reports its first annual loss since becoming a public company in the 1950s.
1983	The food floor operations are sold to Canada Safeway.
1985	Chunky Woodward relinquishes family control of the business by selling shares to Cambridge Shopping Centres Ltd.
1988	Housing advocate and DERA member Jim Green sees the decline of Woodward's and puts together an adaptive reuse plan for the building with the intention of using it for social and non-market housing. The plan is met with little interest by government officials.
1989	The Woodward family passes management responsibilities to the new company president, Hani Zayadi, with hopes of financial improvements.
1990	Chunky Woodward dies. The chain loses $59 million this year.
1992	Woodward's celebrates 100 years of operation in Vancouver. The company runs 26 stores in British Columbia and Alberta. Much of the Hastings Street store has been converted to factory-outlet shops offering discounted merchandise.
1993	The Woodward's chain ceases business and is sold to the Hudson's Bay Company. The Hastings Street store is abandoned and sits empty.
1995	Fama Holdings, owned by Kassem Aghtai, purchases the Hastings Street store for $17 million. Fama immediately sells the parking garage to the city of Vancouver for $11 million. Fama announces plans to build 400 market condominiums on the site, with no plans for social housing.
1995	The Woodward's Cooperative Housing Society, formed by local residents, lobby the city of Vancouver to block the Fama development until a social housing component is added.
1995	The city of Vancouver approves a preliminary application for mixed-use of the building, to comprise 200 market condominiums, 200 co-operative housing units, and retail space. Conditions set by the city are not met by Fama, who denies the viability of including non-market housing. The lack of affordable housing in the plan leads to community protests.
1996	The province of British Columbia announces a partnership with Fama and the city of Vancouver to include more than 200 units of co-operative housing in Woodward's.
1996	The city's Development Permit Board amends earlier approval to include a 197-unit co-op development in Woodward's.
1996	The building is listed on the Vancouver Heritage Register as a 'C' building (the lowest category).
1997	Fama announces its withdrawal from the Woodward's project after the city of Vancouver and the province of British Columbia determine that the terms for a partnership between the two governments and Fama are impossible to meet.
1997	Supporters of the Downtown Eastside community hold a sit-in at Fama's office in West Vancouver.
1997	Fama is granted a demolition permit to begin removal of inner walls, old mechanical systems, and other internal components. The building is subsequently stripped of most of its features. No new construction is authorized.

1997 The city grants Fama a development permit for all market housing. The project does not proceed, as Fama concludes that the condo market for the area is 'no good.'

2000 Markley Stearns announces his intention to buy Woodward's and develop it into a high-tech computer 'hub'. The deal falls through as the high-tech bubble bursts across North America.

2001 After three years of negotiation, the province of British Columbia purchases the Woodward's building from Fama for $21.9 million, with the intention of developing the building for commercial use, to house SFU's School for the Contemporary Arts, and to provide social housing. No partner is found to help the province with the commercial component. The project is sidelined as the provincial government changes from the NDP to the Liberal Party and the new government freezes 1,700 planned social and co-op units, eventually cancelling 1,000 of them.

2002 The 200 co-op units promised for Woodward's are built by the Lore Krill Housing Cooperative at two locations, one of which is a block away from Woodward's.

2002 Madison Bellevue Apartments Corporation optioned the Woodward's building from the province for $18 million. It plans to provide retail and residential space, including rentals and assisted rentals; however, the company cannot secure funding for the project. Their option expires in late November.

2002 Woodward's becomes a rallying point for Vancouver's social housing movement.

2002 Members of the Downtown Eastside community, including many homeless people, occupy the Woodward's store in a three-month-long 'Squat' (called the 'Woodsquat'). Protesters set up tents on the sidewalk and reside inside the building. The event raises broad awareness for the need for additional social housing in the neighbourhood. In response, the province places some 54 of the squatters in local shelters and hotels.

2002 Artist Stan Douglas exhibits his large photographic composition, *Every Building on 100 West Hastings*, which shows the blockface across from Woodward's. The accompanying book, edited by Reid Shier, describes this as 'the worst block in Vancouver.'

2003 The city of Vancouver purchases the Woodward's store from the province for about $5 million. The city plans to redevelop the building and include at least 100 units of non-market housing.

2003 The 'W' sign is relit as a symbol of revitalization. The city rents the building to the film industry as a set.

2003 The city begins a public consultation process, including community visioning workshops and an ideas fair, to give the public an opportunity to voice ideas for the redevelopment of the Woodward's store. The community expresses its desire to see the revitalization of the building and the neighbourhood, rather than their gentrification. The City uses the outcomes of the workshops as guiding principles for redevelopment and planning. The public calls for a development that will be socially, environmentally and economically sustainable, including community and commercial elements, with both market and non-market housing.

2003 Vancouver is awarded the 2010 Winter Olympic Games. Mayor Larry Campbell vows that the world will see a different and improved Downtown Eastside by 2010, with the Woodward's redevelopment being a central component.

2004 The city of Vancouver invites developers to submit proposals for the redevelopment of the Woodward's site, based on the guiding principles mentioned above.

2004 Westbank Projects Corporation and Petersen Investment Group, with Henriquez Partners Architects, are selected from a field of eleven applicants. The selection is based partially on public input at a series of open houses. The plans call for leaving only the 1903/08 portion of the building standing, with salvaged fragments of the demolished buildings incorporated into the new construction.

2005	On March 2nd, SFU and the city of Vancouver announce that the SFU School for the Contemporary Arts will relocate to the site, pending budget approval. Plans include 200 social housing units, 536 market condominiums, retail stores, federal government offices, and a large drug store and grocery store. Other elements of the project include a centre for non-profit organizations and a children's day care in the historic portion of the building.
2005	On July 25th, Mayor Larry Campbell is joined by the Woodward's Steering Committee co-chairs Jim Green and Judy Rogers, Westbank developer Ian Gillespie, his partner Ben Yeung of Peterson Investment Group, and Gregory Henriquez of Henriquez Partners Architects to mark the beginning of preparatory site work at a groundbreaking ceremony.
2006	Westbank puts the market housing units on sale. They sell out on the first day of public sales with units starting at $239,000 for a one-bedroom suite and as high as $1.1 million for a three-level sky balcony suite, generating more than $200 million in total sales.
2006	All but the original heritage portion of the building (1903/08) is demolished by 'implosion' to make way for the new construction.
2007	The city of Vancouver issues a Development Permit for the Woodward's project. Excavation, shoring and foundations are completed. The province will contribute $49.3 million towards the building of SFU's School for the Contemporary Arts and the university will raise the remaining $22 million.
2009	Occupancy permits are issued and the first residents of Woodward's. People in the W42 and W32 towers and family non-market housing take possession of their units and begin to move-in.
2010	Construction is projected to finish in early 2010. With the Woodward's Redevelopment complete, the "Woodward's Experiment" begins.

FOLIO XII

ARCHITECTURAL DRAWINGS
Dallas Hong

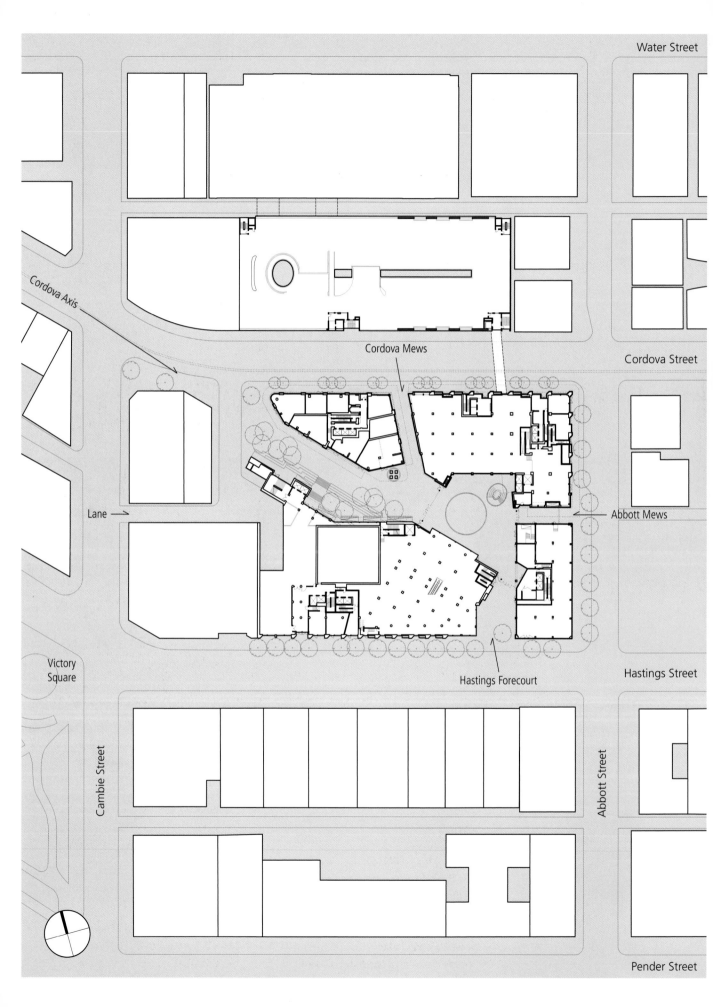

Water Street

Cordova Axis

Cordova Street

Cordova Mews

Lane

Abbott Mews

Victory
Square

Cambie Street

Hastings Forecourt

Hastings Street

Abbott Street

Pender Street

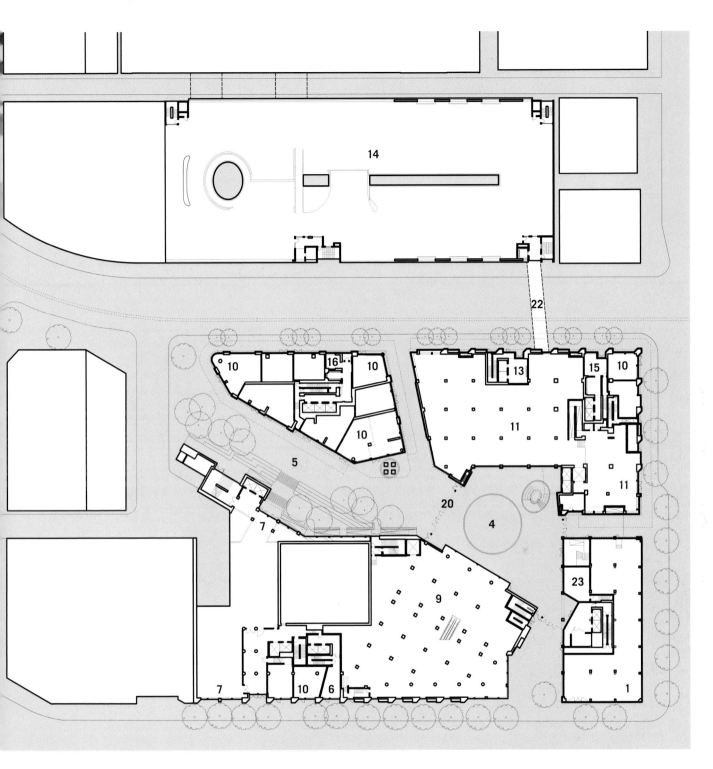

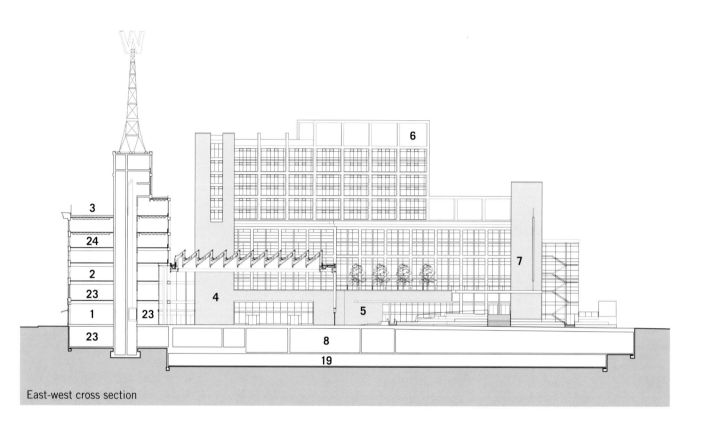

East-west cross section

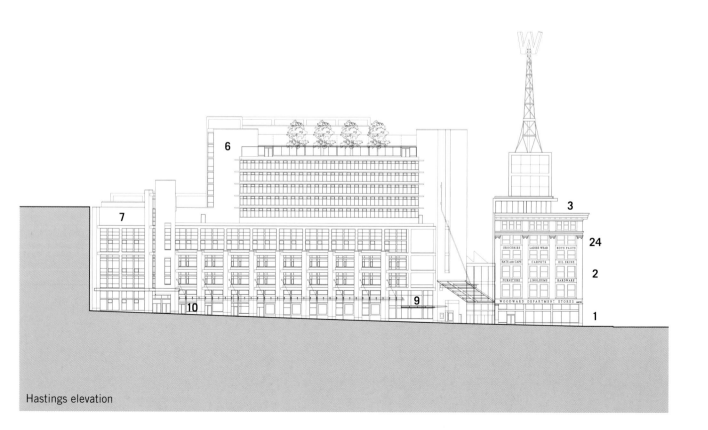

Hastings elevation

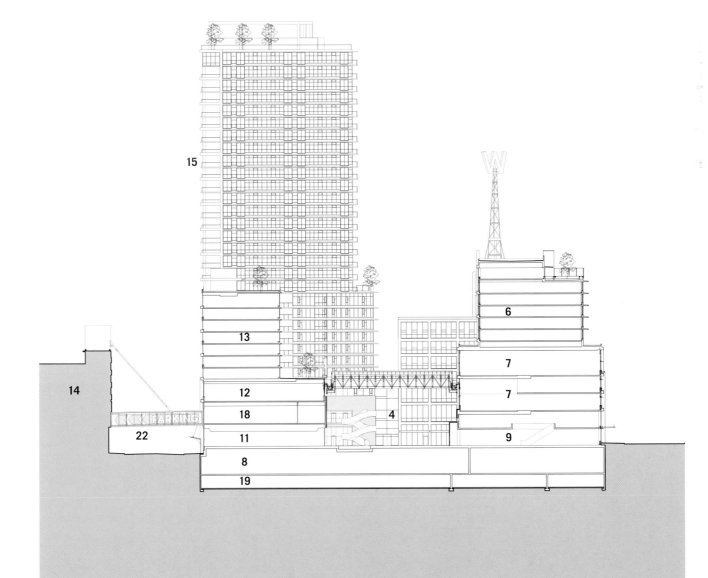

North-south cross section

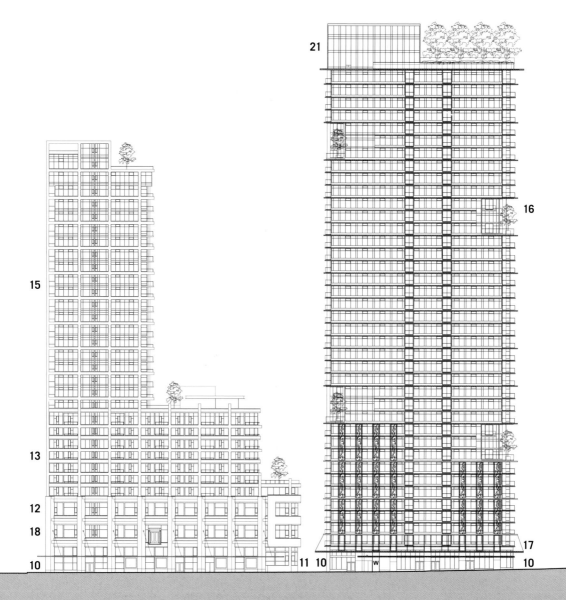

15

13

12

18

10

11

21

16

17

10

10

10

w

Cordova elevation

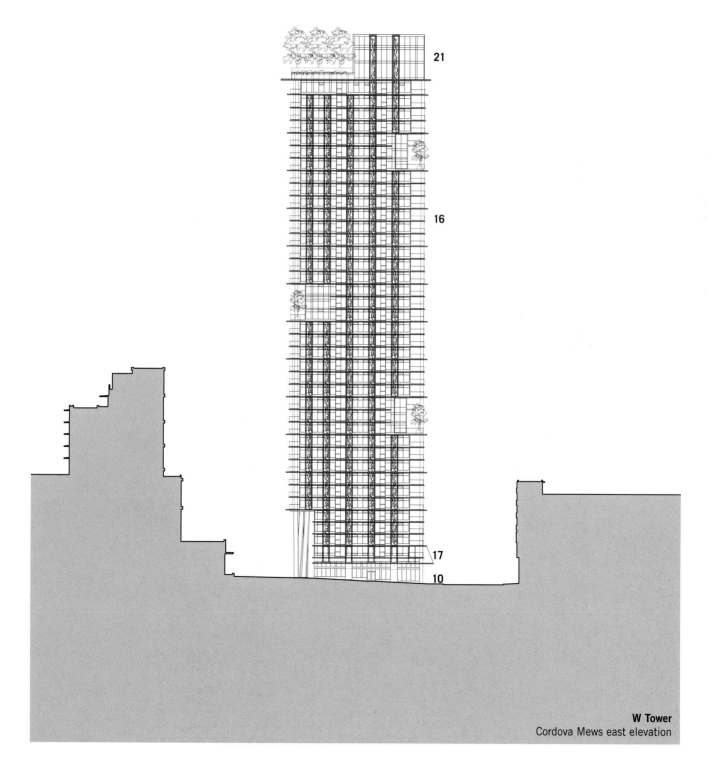

21

16

17

10

W Tower
Cordova Mews east elevation

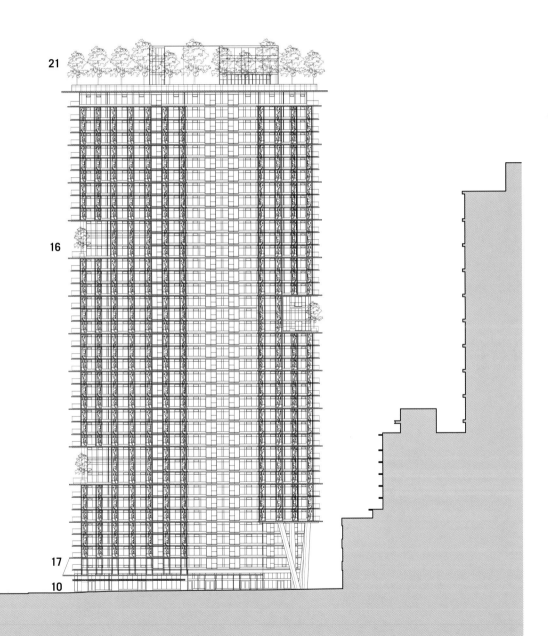

21

16

17

10

W Tower
South elevation

W Tower
Typical floor plan
Typical one bedroom (643 sf)

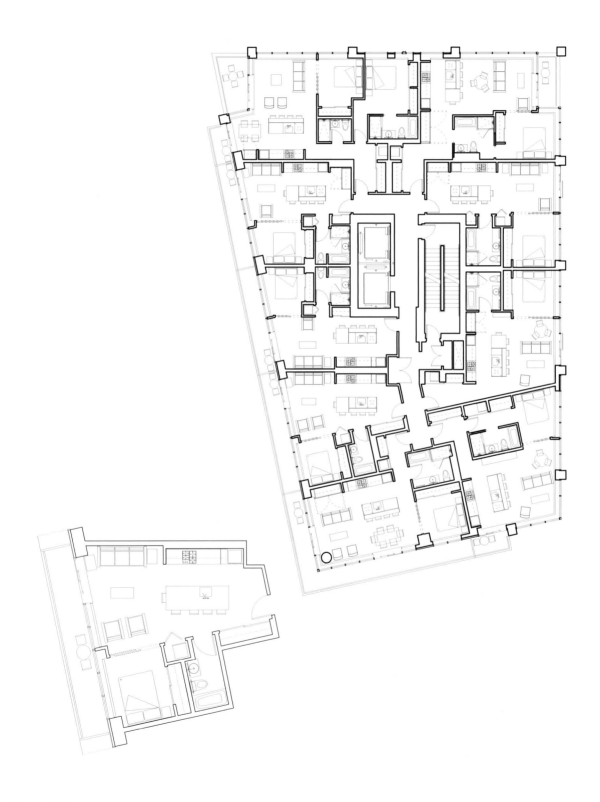

Abbott Building
Market housing typical floor plan
Typical one bedroom 558 sf

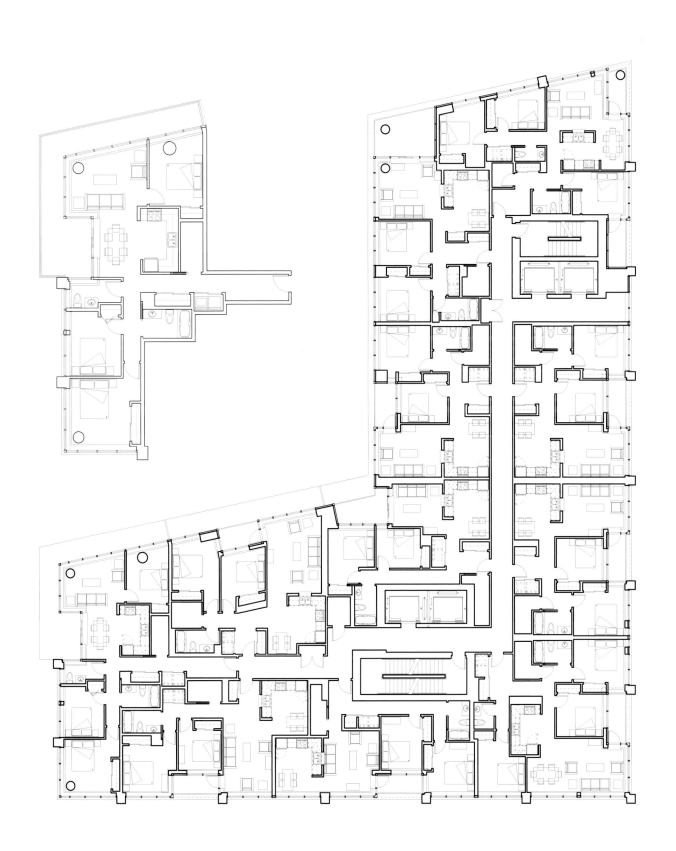

Abbott Building
Family non-market typical floor plan
Typical three bedroom 1150 sf

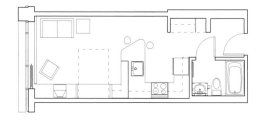

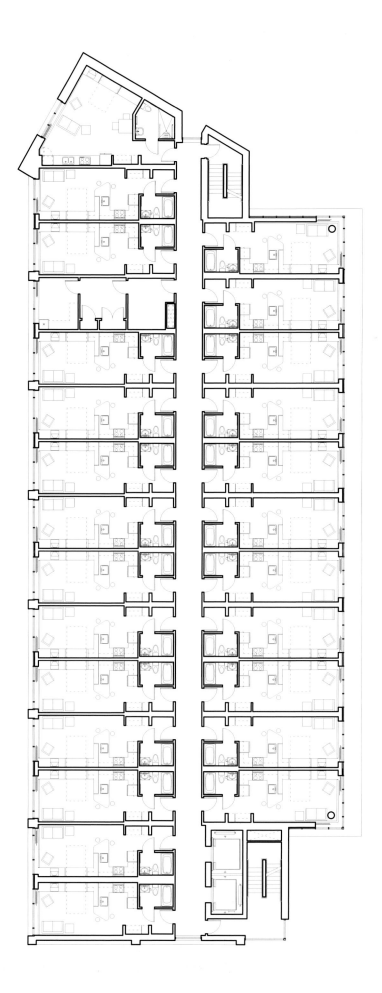

PHS Singles
Non-market housing typical floor plan
Typical studio 357 sf

City Councillor, Jim Green

Bibliography

Baker, Linda. "Amid Gentrification, Vancouver Seeks Balance." *Architectural Record,* January 2008: 34.

—. "A Gentler Gentrification: Retaining Cultures Within a Revitalization." *AIA Seattle Forum,* Winter 2008/2009: 18-21.

—. "Redevelopment Project Doubles as Social Experiment." *The New York Times,* 25 November 2009: B6.

Blomley, Nicholas. *Unsettling the City: Urban Land and the Politics of Property.* New York: Routledge, 2004.

Boddy, Trevor. "Canada's Poorest Postal Code." *The Globe and Mail* (Toronto), 11 January 2006.

—. "Design Is the Mortar in Social Housing That Works." *The Globe and Mail* (Toronto), 1 December 2006.

Bula, Frances. "Can Woodward's Be All Things to All People?" *The Vancouver Sun,* 14 November 2005: B2-3.

—. "Common Vision." *The Vancouver Sun,* 3 May 2008: B1, B3.

—. "Design Panel OKs Woodward's Project." *The Vancouver Sun,* 8 December 2005: B1, B5.

—. "When East Meets West: Future of the Downtown Eastside up for Grabs." *The Vancouver Sun,* 13 May 2006: C1.

Carmichael, Amy. "Urban Redevelopment with an Edge." *The Globe and Mail* (Toronto), 8 August 2005: S1-2.

Chodikoff, Ian. "An Ethical Plan: Vancouver Architect Gregory Henriquez Discusses His Approach and Attitudes Towards the Importance of the Architect's Ability to Engage and Empower a Community." *Canadian Architect,* February 2007: cover, 38-41.

—. "Henriquez Partners Architects Proposes Scheme to End Vancouver's Homelessness." *Canadian Architect,* February 2009: 11.

Deck, Kelly. "Woodward's Tests an Architect's Passion: Gregory Henriquez Juggles Diversity, Density and Drama as Major Project Nears Completion." *The Globe and Mail* (Vancouver), 20 March 2009: S6.

Enright, Robert. "The Practical Utopian: The Architecture of Gregory Henriquez." *Border Crossings,* November 2006: 55-65.

Fenlon, Brodie. "Gregory Henriquez: The Architecture Solution." *The Globe and Mail,* Online Discussion. 18 February 2009. <http://www.theglobeandmail.com/archives/article971237.ece>.

Frey, Warren. "Vancouver Landmark About to Become a Social Experiment." *Journal of Commerce* (Vancouver), 13 September 2006.

Glave, James. "Under One Roof." *Canadian Geographic,* October 2009: 48-60.

Grdadolnik, Helena. "Crosstown Examined: An Ambitious but Necessary Mixed-Use Development Proposal for the Old Woodward's Department Store Site Is Poised to Stitch Together the Loose Fabric of Vancouver's Downtown Eastside." *Canadian Architect,* January 2006: 20-25.

—. "Putting Housing into Context: Two Housing Projects in Vancouver Break with Convention to Create Strong Contextual Responses" *Canadian Architect,* April 2003: 20-23.

—. "Woodward's Takes Shape: Nothing Like it in North America." *The Tyee* (Vancouver), 30 March 2006. <http://thetyee.ca/Views/2006/03/30/WoodwardsTakesShape/>.

Harker, Douglas E. *The Woodwards: A Family Story of Ventures and Traditions.* Vancouver: Mitchell Press Limited, 1976.

Harris, Michael. "The Woodward's Experiment." *Vancouver Magazine,* 1 September 2009.

Hill, Mary Frances. "Beyond The Stark Lens." *The Vancouver Sun,* 1 November 2008: F1.

Hot Issue: *Woodward's Occupation.* Vancouver: 2002.

Howell, Mike. "'W' Well on Its Way to Completion: Woodward's Project Includes 'Significant' Arts Space." *The Vancouver Courier,* 8 April 2009.

Kamping-Carder, Leigh. "At the Gastown Riot." *The Walrus,* July/August 2009.

Kirby, J. "Developer's Dreams Go Far Beyond Vancouver: Gillespie Unknown In Much of Country." *National Post,* 25 April 2006.

LaPointe, Michael. "A City, A Hole, A Dream: Woodward's." *Tooth & Dagger,* 12 April 2007: 6-8.

Lazaruk, Susan. "Woodward's Almost Finished: A Place Where All People, Rich and Poor Can Live." *The Province* (Vancouver), 3 April 2009: A17.

Lorinc, John. *The New City: How the Crisis in Canada's Urban Centres Is Reshaping the Nation.* Toronto: Penguin Canada, 2006: 161-63.

Macdonald, Nancy. "Hitting Gold on Skid Row: The Most Notorious Slum in Canada Gets a Makeover." *Maclean's,* 18 August 2008: 18-19.

Mackie, John. "Woodward's Project Shows WOW Factor." *The Vancouver Sun,* 3 April 2009: A4.

—. "Renovations Reveal Reminder's of City's Past." *The Vancouver Sun,* 24 November 2007: F10-11.

—. "The Last Days of a Vancouver Icon." *The Vancouver Sun* 16 Sept. 2006.

—. "'W' Removal Marks Start of Woodward's Project." *The Vancouver Sun,* 24 June 2006: B8.

Matas, Robert. "Woodward's Gets Its Welcome Mat Ready." *The Globe and Mail,* 3 April 2009: S2.

McMartin, Pete. "Clearly a Community Endorsement." *The Vancouver Sun,* 25 April 2006: .

Montgomery, Charles. "Sad City: Ours Is One of the Most Beautiful, Vibrant, and Livable Cities in the World. Why Aren't We Happy?" *Vancouver Magazine,* September 2008: 88-90, 92, 94, 96.

Morrow, Fiona. "A Night to Remember (or Forget): A Controversial Photograph Depicting Vancouver's Gastown Riot Goes on Display in New York Before Settling into Its Downtown Eastside Home." *The Globe and Mail* (Toronto), 30 October 2008: F1-2.

Paulsen, Monte. "'Stop Gap Housing' Idea Could Make a Big Dent in Homelessness." *The Tyee,* 19 December 2008. <http://thetyee.ca/News/2008/12/19/StopGapHousing/>.

Pemberton, Kim. "Marrying Architectural Vision to Values: Gregory Henriquez and Buildings That Serve the Public Good." *The Vancouver Sun,* 27 November 2004: I4-5.

Pérez-Gómez, Alberto, Christopher Grabowski, Helena Grdadolnik, Jim Green and May So. *Towards an Ethical Architecture: Issues Within the Work of Gregory Henriquez.* Vancouver: BlueImprint, 2006.

Rochon, Lisa. "How Do You Build Hope? Start with Plywood and Guts." *The Globe and Mail* (Toronto), 2 May 2009.

—. "From Five Star Glam to Eastside Grim: Developer Ian Gillespie is Building Both Luxury Hotels and a Bold Project for Vancouver's Downtown Eastside." *The Globe and Mail* (Toronto), 28 April 2007.

Seccia, Stefania. "Woodward's: What Will the Building's Legacy Be?" *Megaphone,* 24 July 2009.

Shier, Reid, ed. *Stan Douglas: Every Building on 100 West Hastings.* Vancouver: Contemporary Art Gallery and Arsenal Pulp Press, 2002: 62-92.

Stueck, Wendy. "BC Architect Building Toward a Solution for Everyone: An Interview with Gregory Henriquez." *The Globe and Mail,* 15 February 2009.

Vidaver, Aaron, ed. "Woodsquat." *West Coast Line,* Fall/Winter 2003/2004: 33.

Watson, Heather. "Top Model: Westbank Wins the Woodward's War." *Terminal City* (Vancouver), 16 July 2004.

—. "The Woodward's Phoenix Rises." *Terminal City* (Vancouver), 14 October 2004.

Weder, Adele. "It Makes a Village." *Azure,* March/Apr. 2006: 94-98.

Woodward Stores Limited. *So Much to Celebrate: Woodward's 100th Anniversary.* Vancouver: Woodward Stores Ltd., 1992.

Woodward Stores Limited with Robert D. Watt, ed. *The Shopping Guide to the West: The Woodward's Catalogue 1898-1953.* Vancouver: Douglas and McIntyre, 1978.

Documentary Television and Video

"Canada's Slum: The Fix." Webcast. CTV and The Globe and Mail (Vancouver). 24 March 2009. <http://v1.theglobeandmail.com/thefix/>.

"W Stories: Building a Community Legacy at Woodward's." VHS. W2 Community Media Arts. 11 March 2009. <http://www.creativetechnology.org/video/w-stories-building-a-community>.

"Woodward's: the Competition." Dir. and Prod. Robert Duncan and Carolyn Schmidt. International Documentary Television Corporation and CBC Newsworld, 2005.

"Woodward's Construction Site Tour." *GVTV.* Shaw Cable Network (Vancouver). 25 November 2008.

"Woodward's Design Competition." *GVTV.* Shaw Cable Network (Vancouver). 17 February 2005.

"Woodward's Developer/Architect Profile." *GVTV.* Shaw Cable Network (Vancouver). 3 March 2005.

"Woodward's Mayor and Council Site Tour." *GVTV.* Shaw Cable Network (Vancouver). 28 April 2009.

Woodward's Redevelopment Team

Developer	W Redevelopment Group (Westbank Projects/Peterson Investment Group)
Architect	Henriquez Partners Architects
Community Partner	PHS Community Services Society
Residential Marketing	Rennie Marketing Systems
Construction Management	Intertech Construction Group Managers (2005) Ltd.
Residential Interior Design	McFarlane Green Biggar Architecture + Design
SFU Interior Architects	Proscenium Architecture/CEI Architecture
Heritage Consultant	Commonwealth Historic Management
Heritage Architect	Jonathan Yardley Architect
Landscape Architect	Phillips Farevaag Smallenberg
Structural Engineer	Glotman Simpson
Mechanical, Sustainability, Materials Handling	Stantec Consulting
Electrical	Nemetz (S/A) & Associates Ltd.
Building Code	LMDG Building Code Consultants Ltd.
Building Envelope	RDH Building Engineering Ltd.
Civil Engineering	Citiwest Consulting Ltd.
Quantity Surveyor	BTY Group
Surveyor	Matson Peck & Topliss
Geotechnical	Trow Associates Inc.
Enviromental (Site)	EBA Engineering Consultants Ltd.
Elevator	John W. Gunn Consultants Inc.
Traffic Engineering	Bunt & Associates
Wind Tunnel Testing	Daley Ferraro Associates
Acoustical Engineering	Brown Strachan Associates
Environmental (Building)	SFE Global
Graphics	Letterbox Design Group
Insurance	Jardine Lloyd Thompson
Legal	Kornfeld Mackoff Silber Koffman Kalef
Specialized Engineering	Ted Newel Engineering Ltd. / J.D. Johnson Engineering Ltd.
Specifications	J. Findlay & Associates
Water Feature	Vincent Helton
Signage	Gallop/Varley

Project Financing:

Financing by	BNP Paribas (Canada)
Insured by	Canada Mortgage and Housing Corporation
Arranged by	Citifund Capital Corp.

Henriquez Partners Project Team

Artour Adamovitch
Mathew Bulford
Zhong Yan Chen
John Cheng
Beth Davies
Jaime Dejo
Dallas Hong
Shawn Lapointe
Thomas Lee
Babak Manavi
Fred Markowsky
Allan Moorey
Betty Quon
Erik Roth

Christian Schimert
Ellen Scobie
May So
Frank Stebner
Ivo Taller
Noreen Taylor
James Tod
Michael Toolan
Terry Tremayne
Fredy Urrego
David Weir
Peter Wood
Phoebe Wong

Words cannot express the level of rigor required to build a project of such enormous complexity. These talented individuals led the design, approvals and site field reviews for an intense "fast-tracked" period of six years. The stamina and dedication of each person was integral to the success of the project. I remain humbled and very grateful that such a gifted team chose to dedicate their professional skills and sacrifice personal time to allow the Woodward's redevelopment to become a reality.

Gregory Henriquez

Book Design, Photography, and Image Credits

Pablo Mandel *CircularStudio.com*—Book design
Jen Eby—Cover design
Christian Dahlberg—Cover artwork

Bush, Murray—Woodsquat 2002: *119, 180-185.*
Calhoun, Barry (barrycalhounphotography.com)—Woodsquat 2002: *24-31.*
City of Vancouver, Archives—Bu P704: *35,* M-11-51: *60,* Van Sc P114: *62,*
     CVA809_18: *101.*
City of Vancouver, Staff—*143, 153.*
Cruz, Jonathan (jonathancruz.com)—*111, 130-133, 359.*
C.Y. Loh & Associates—W Tower shop drawings: *233.*
Deis, Eric (ericdeis.com)—Photographs: *188, 222-225.*
Dobson, Susan—Portrait photo: cover flap.
Douglas, Stan—Abbott & Cordova, 7 August 1971: *308-309.*
DYS Architecture—Competition Model: *20.*
GBL Architects—Competition Model: *20.*
Goldie, Colin—Woodward's model: *262, 263.*
Grabowski, Christopher (mediumlight.com)—Photographs: *43, 187, 313-317, 367.*
Hudson's Bay Company—I-282: *61,* I-1704: *63,* I1711: *64,* I-285: *65.*
King, Celia, Co-Design Group—Visioning workshop: *68-71.*
LaPointe, Shawn—Demolition time lapse: *146-149.*
Lee, Thomas—Renderings: *284-287, 289, 290, 293.*
Lepper, Derek (dereklepper.com)—Construction photographs: *10, 14, 18, 46, 52, 72,*
     80, 85, 104, 112, 120, 156, 164, 168, 173, 174, 177, 189-192, 196, 201, 202,
     212, 219, 227, 234, 239, 240, 264, 270, 276, 294, 298, 318, 327, 328.
Letterbox Design Group—W Marketing Brochure: *88-99.*
Li, Yun Lam—Woodward's Mural: *151-155.*
Manavi, Babak—PHS Community Services Society building: *102.*
Matheson, Bob—Shangri-La: *103.*
Nigel Baldwin Architects—VanCity Place for Youth: *18.*
Norbury, Rosamond—*304-307, 310-311.*
Phillips Farevaag Smallenberg—Site plan: *229.*
Radvenis, Eugene—Renderings: *21, 137-142.*
Royal BC Museum, BC Archives—Portrait A_01889: *34.*
Russwurm, Lani—Construction photographs: *250-253.*
Vancouver Public Library, Special Collections—VPL27900: *36,* VPL25804: *37,*
     VPL28097: *38,* VPL29280: *38,* VPL27803: *40.*
Westbank Staff—Blessing the Site: *336-339.*

Select Photograph and Image Notes

Acknowledgements

Books of this kind are inescapably collaborative and this one is the rule that proves exceptional. From the time I was approached to be involved in the story of the Woodward's redevelopment, the work has been rewardingly shared by a group of gifted individuals, all of whom had in mind the same goal: to flesh out the complexities of this remarkable project.

First of all, my sincere thanks go to the more than two dozen interviewees who gave their time and thoughts to articulate those complexities. The candour and intelligence of this wide-ranging group is everywhere apparent in the various texts that explain their contribution to the realization of the new Woodward's. Equally important were the essays supplied by a trio of writers—Reid Shier, Alberto Pérez-Gómez and Chris Macdonald—who took specific areas of the Woodward's project and richly elaborated them. In this regard, I owe special thanks to May So who provided the interchapters that act as an armature around which the rest of us could build the book. I am also indebted to the various photographers whose documentation of the building and the various transformations and developments it has undergone has made this book a richer visual experience.

There are five other individuals who have been instrumental in making *Body Heat* a reality. Dimiter Savoff has been a dream publisher, having the trust and patience to leave well enough alone, even when it wasn't going so well. James Tod at Henriquez Partners has been exemplary in performing any and every task that was set before him. James has been utterly indispensable to this book project. Jen Eby, the book's initial designer, has the soul of an artist and the organizational skills of a general. Babak Manavi and Pablo Mandel, the designers who inherited the book from Jen, did an especially sensitive job in fine-tuning it to its final form. Whatever visual focus and strength this story has is a product of their collective ordered intelligence.

Finally, Gregory Henriquez, the project architect, has been the book's generator and sustainer. Without his vision, enthusiasm and example, there would be no Woodward's project to be written about. It has been a great privilege to collaborate with him. When you work with someone, you often find out too much about what they're like, and that knowledge is loss. With Gregory, it was all gain.

Robert Enright

In our practice, we talk about cultural sustainability, which deals with concepts like social justice, inclusivity, accessibility and getting beyond the fundamental problem of greed and materialism. These issues need to be addressed in order to reverse our current aggressive assault upon nature.

Gregory Henriquez

For more information on Woodward's visit

www.archimemo.ca

www.henriquezpartners.com